Worlds of Women

Susan M. Socolow, Samuel Candler Dobbs Professor of
Latin American History, Emory University
Series Editor

The insights offered by women's studies scholarship are invaluable for exploring society, and issues of gender have therefore become a central concern in the social sciences and humanities. The Worlds of Women series addresses in detail the unique experiences of women from the vantage points of such diverse fields as history, political science, literature, law, religion, and gender theory, among others. Historical and contemporary perspectives are given, often with a cross-cultural emphasis. A selected bibliography and, when appropriate, a list of video material relating to the subject matter are included in each volume. Taken together, the series serves as a varied library of resources for the scholar as well as for the lay reader.

Controlling Reproduction

Controlling Reproduction

An American History

Edited by
Andrea Tone

Worlds of Women

Number 2

A Scholarly Resources Inc. Imprint
Wilmington, Delaware

Scholarly Resources Inc.
104 Greenhill Avenue
Wilmington, DE 19805-1897

Library of Congress Cataloging-in-Publication Data

Controlling reproduction : an American history / Andrea Tone, editor.
      p.   cm. — (Worlds of Women ; no. 2)
    ISBN 0-8420-2574-X (cloth : alk. paper). — ISBN 0-8420-2575-8
(paper : alk. paper)
    1. Birth control—United States—History. 2. Birth control—United
States—History—Sources. 3. Abortion—United States—History. 4.
Abortion—United States—History—Sources.
I. Tone, Andrea, 1964–   . II. Series.
HQ766.5.U5C65   1997
363.9'6'0973—dc20   96-20020
                                                          CIP

⊗The paper used in this publication meets the minimum requirements of
the American National Standard for permanence of paper for printed library materials, Z39.48, 1984.

Acknowledgments

This volume originated in a parking lot conversation with Susan Socolow. My deepest thanks to her and to Richard Hopper and Linda Pote Musumeci at Scholarly Resources for seeing it through to completion. The staffs at Simon Fraser University Library, the Health Sciences Library at the University of Washington at Seattle, particularly Colleen M. Weum, the Special Collections Department at the Library of Congress, and the Health Sciences and Law Libraries at Emory University offered invaluable support; I gratefully acknowledge their assistance. Thanks also to Michael Bellesiles for sharing his expertise in legal history, to Cornelia Hughes Dayton for last-minute editorial help, to Scott Perchall for research assistance, and to Joan Sokolovsky and especially John Tone for being there for me.

About the Editor

Andrea Tone is assistant professor of history at the Georgia Institute of Technology in Atlanta. She is the author of *The Business of Benevolence: Welfare Work in Progressive America* (1997) and is currently writing a social history of the female contraceptive industry in twentieth-century America.

Contents

Introduction

Historians of American women emerged with incandescent drive and determination in the 1960s. Energized by the rise of second-wave feminism, they sought to restore the experiences of women to the established record of the nation's past. The project of women's history challenged the validity of how American history had previously been structured and taught. Historians began with the assumption that an unnecessarily narrow definition of the "legitimate" field of study had marginalized women's roles. By giving pride of place to male elites and legislative politics, scholars had claimed as normative the history of a few. Along the way, they had overlooked the experiences of the majority, including women, who had led their lives outside a privileged, political realm.

Women's history demanded a radical overhaul of how the past was unmasked, assessed, and interpreted. It redefined value and worth in a way that made room for a serious discussion of women as historical actors. It insisted that women were missing from the pages of history books not because they were historically insignificant but because scholars had devalued their contributions and failed to excavate their experiences from the right places. If the locus of discovery shifted, women's past would be unearthed and restored. In its attempt to locate the "female world" hitherto hidden from the historian's gaze, women's history claimed as its starting point the centrality of a domestic woman's sphere isolated from the public, political world—a feminized realm bounded by church, home, friends, and kin that had produced a remarkable and uniquely female historical experience.

Since the mid-1980s the turn toward gender history has challenged some of the basic assumptions and tenets of women's history. Whereas the first generation of women's historians unhesitatingly asserted the existence of a "female experience" (or at least a female experience fragmented along the predictable fault lines of race, region, and class), gender historians have questioned the essentialism embedded in the very category "woman." They often have preferred to think of women as composites of multiple identities, insisting, for example, that a female textile worker, mother of three, Baptist, and Southerner be viewed as simultaneously all, but never simply one, of these identities. To bracket and classify a single variable—woman—as the most encompassing signifier of human experience belies the heterogeneity, simultaneity, and mutability of the human condition. Thus, rather than refer to any type of universal "female experience," gender historians have explored how masculine and feminine roles are defined, articulated, reshaped, and interpreted in particular settings and instances. Instead of posing the question "How did women experience X?," which presupposes a common female response, they asked "How is womanhood cast at moment X and why?"[1]

Controlling Reproduction: An American History tries to bridge the gap between these camps by finding common ground in a debate that has animated and at times sharply divided the discipline. Conceding (as do most historians of women today) that there has never been a universal women's history, it suggests that empirical realities—from the availability of safe contraceptives to the legality of abortion—have circumscribed the experiential boundaries in which women have lived. In short, as multiple and pliable as gender constructions are, interpretations of what women should, can, and cannot do have been woven into structures and institutions such as public policy, the law, and the marketplace in ways that have restricted opportunities for them *because they are women.*

When discussing the history of reproduction, the validity of a woman's history anchored in the commonalities of female experience becomes especially apparent: it is women who get pregnant, have abortions, and bear children. This is not to say that all women want or will do any or all of these things, or that men play no role in making them happen. Nor is it to suggest that women experience these events identically. It is merely to contend that until tomorrow's technological wonders dictate otherwise—a theme toyed with in the 1994 film *Junior*—biological packaging has mapped a path of possibilities that is women's to walk on alone.

It is precisely because biology is not destiny, however, that gender must assume a central place in the history of reproduction generally and of reproductive control specifically. As soon as we reject the conceptualization of maternal sexuality (women as biologically destined mothers) as normal, natural, and fixed, we begin the long task of trying to explain how and why this view came to enjoy rhetorical hegemony. Gender analysis helps us to understand the construction and longevity of the concept of maternal sexuality. Historical interpretations of biological difference ("because women have ovaries they are particularly prone to hysteria," for example) and the ease with which these interpretations have been parlayed into policies and practices ("the best way to cure female hysteria, then, must be to remove the ovaries") speak volumes about how gender creates and cements political and social relationships. We cannot fully comprehend the American Medical Association's (AMA) campaign against abortions in the midnineteenth century, for instance, without first understanding how declining fertility rates in the same time period, achieved through a higher abortion rate and the increased use of birth control, challenged gender and sexual norms. The AMA's avowal that the fulfillment of a woman's reproductive role was a necessary stage in her psychosocial development was in good measure a response to women's escalating sexual autonomy. At precisely the same time that women uncoupled reproduction and sexuality through family limitation, the medical profession, claiming "science" as its ally, reasserted their inseparability. Like other important episodes in reproduction history, the AMA's campaign took place against a gendered backdrop.

The AMA story illustrates a larger point: controlling reproduction has never been exclusively a private matter between a woman and her partner. Legislation, court decisions, medical practices, cultural norms, and technological innovations have restricted and expanded reproductive options at varying moments in American history. The intervention of external agencies has made personal choices and private acts matters of public policy and national debate. In short, the regulation of bedroom behavior has never been left to those in the bedroom. Complex and changing, the history of controlling reproduction in the United States has involved multiple actors and arenas from the very beginning.

Controlling Reproduction seeks to illuminate this historical multiplicity. It defines reproductive control broadly to include not only fertility restriction (abortion, birth control) but also women's ability to direct what happens to them during pregnancy and childbirth. Furthermore, it combines previously published articles on the history of American reproduction with a wide array of primary sources, including excerpts from court cases, statutes, medical journals, popular manuals, advertisements, and congressional hearings. The selections explore reproductive control at different times and

places: from abortion in colonial New England to sexual sterilization in early twentieth-century Virginia to the Dalkon Shield tragedy of the 1970s. While relating the history of reproduction to
women and gender, the reader also places it within a larger history
of politics, law, medicine, sexuality, business, and social change.
On the way, *Controlling Reproduction* introduces readers to some
of the most significant debates and controversies currently guiding
the study of reproduction.

Chapter I focuses on the techniques as well as on the cultural
and legal acceptance of birth control and abortion during the colonial era and early Republic. Selections address and shatter two re-
silient myths: first, that birth control is a modern invention; and
second, that abortions have been legal in America only since 1973,
the year of the Supreme Court's famous *Roe v. Wade* decision. As
Linda Gordon's pioneering study of birth control, *Woman's Body,
Woman's Right*, and Angus McLaren's more recent *Reproductive
Rituals* have demonstrated, birth control has existed since ancient
times. To claim that women were passive victims of physiological
ignorance or technological underdevelopment ignores the degree
to which they have successfully prevented pregnancy for centuries. Gordon notes, for example, that Egyptian women in 1850 B.C.
frequently used vaginal suppositories made of crocodile dung or
honey to impede sperm motility. Prostitutes in preindustrial Japan
used vaginal sponges made of bamboo tissue paper. When women
in early America depended on suppositories and sponges to prevent pregnancy, they were relying on techniques and a tradition of
birth control that had existed for centuries. Similarly, the decriminalization of abortion in 1973 reinstated a policy of toleration that
had dominated colonial and early national life. For most of American history, abortion in the initial stage of pregnancy has been
legal. Women in early America could restrict fertility in myriad
ways without fear of cultural, religious, or legal censure.[2]

Such acceptability gave women considerable control over reproduction. It is important, however, that we not romanticize this
control as indicative of a golden era in the history of reproductive
health or female power. Having abortions in colonial America usually entailed ingesting abortifacients, potions that so poisoned or
irritated the body that miscarriages occurred as a side effect. The
few mechanical abortions that were done were painful and dangerous and were performed without the benefit of anesthesia or antibiotics. Significantly, Cornelia Hughes Dayton's gripping account of

the cultural handling of sexuality, deviance, and abortion in a colonial village centers on the community's response to an abortion *fatality*. The need to weigh the advantages of legal liberty against the larger social, technological, and political orbit in which those liberties existed must remain at the forefront of investigations of the history of control over reproduction.

The question of female power and control is again raised in Chapter II, which explores the impact of professionalized medicine on perceptions of reproduction and women. The expanding involvement of male physicians in female reproduction affected women in several ways. As the medical profession acquired greater stature in antebellum America, it reified and inflated the social significance of biological differences. In medical books, but also in the marketplace, before the law, and in everyday social parlance, women were increasingly depicted as captives of their reproductive organs. The displacement of female midwifery and female-centered "social" childbirth was another important by-product of male medicalization. Feminist scholars such as Barbara Ehrenreich, Deirdre English, and Barbara Rothman have described the declining stature of female healers and the rise of female patient passivity as part of a long process by which the predominantly male medical profession marginalized women. The rising popularity since the 1960s of female midwifery, the home-birth movement, and feminist health collectives and centers operated by and for women suggest that many women agree with this assessment enough to strive to reclaim female control over reproductive health.

Not every historian has subscribed to this apparent demonization of medicine. In her 1990 Pulitzer Prize-winning biography of midwife Martha Ballard, Laurel Thatcher Ulrich urges historians to approach the midwife's world "on its own terms . . . ; to consider midwifery in the broadest possible context, as one specialty in a larger neighborhood economy, as the most visible feature of a comprehensive and little-known system of early health care, as a mechanism of social control, a strategy for family support, and a deeply personal calling."[3] Judith Walzer Leavitt's article on the decline of social childbirth, reprinted here, applies this approach to look at how middle-class women themselves understood the growing involvement of male medical experts in the birthing process. By exploring the medicalization of reproduction through contemporaries' eyes, Leavitt enables us to understand why so many women wanted and welcomed male practitioners in the birthing room.

From 1800 to 1900 the fertility rate of American women dropped from 7.04 children per mother to 3.56. Chapter III examines the reasons for this change, highlighting the widespread availability of birth control and abortion in the nineteenth century and the heightened importance of family limitation for middle-class men and women. Daniel Scott Smith's now-classic analysis of *coitus interruptus* (male withdrawal before ejaculation), the most common birth control method in nineteenth-century America, opens the chapter. Smith argues that the increasing popularity of *coitus interruptus* reflected women's growing power to influence male sexual behavior, a power he labels "domestic feminism." His interpretation raises important questions about the social meanings attached to the use of particular methods of fertility control, while his provocative discussion of domestic feminism revisits the question of how female power, as a historical construct, is best defined and measured.

In the closing decades of the nineteenth century, federal and state governments abandoned their earlier laissez-faire attitudes toward reproduction. Through law they classified as deviant a whole complex of behaviors and practices. For the first time in American society, abortion and birth control became illegal; their supporters and practitioners, in turn, were branded criminals. Public concern over the dropping birth rate and the high incidence of abortion (estimated to terminate one in five pregnancies by the 1850s), combined with the AMA's lobbying, fueled the legislative response to birth control and abortion. By 1900 every state had adopted abortion restrictions, forcing women who wanted the procedure to rely on the black market. Significantly, the new laws frequently contained "therapeutic clauses" that permitted doctors to perform abortions if they believed that a woman's life was in danger. On balance, then, late nineteenth-century laws did not end abortions so much as they made legal access to them a physician's rather than a woman's right. Chapter IV examines this process of criminalization and the regulation of new laws. Leslie Reagan's article unveils a partnership between doctors and the state that was crucial to the regulation of Illinois's 1867 and 1871 antiabortion statutes.

Twentieth-century campaigns for reproductive rights represented, among other things, a concerted attempt to dismantle the legal and medical obstacles to reproductive control constructed in the previous century. Chapter V begins an exploration of the history of the struggle for safe, effective birth control and legal, affordable abortions. As Linda Gordon's article shows, the notion of a single birth control movement is misleading. Historically, there have been many birth control movements, each advocating a different set of ideas and goals, each tailoring its program to fit the priorities of its constituency and the exigencies of the day.

Undergirding Gordon's article and her larger study, *Woman's Body, Woman's Right,* is her contention that women were central actors in the battle for birth control. At one level, the struggle was about legalizing birth control; at another, she insists, it encompassed much more. Women's demands for safe and legal birth control were part of their feminist critique of American society, a critique that tied maternal sexuality to continuing social, political, and economic subordination. Women were active agents in the long struggle for birth control because they framed that struggle in feminist terms. Rooted in the desire to give women control over both their bodies and their destinies, the battle for birth control was logically women's fight to fight. According to Gordon, the history of birth control in America is one of a social movement; "it is about birth control, sexuality, and women. But it is [also] about women as subjects, women trying to create the conditions of their lives in their own interest."[4]

Enthusiasm for fertility control has not always supported a feminist, leftist, or liberal agenda. Chapter V continues by exploring the rhetoric of "race suicide," the fear advocated by individuals such as Theodore Roosevelt that the dropping fertility rate of native-born, middle-class whites was imperiling the moral, physical, and intellectual vitality of the country. It also examines the conservative, racist goals of many fertility control advocates who sought to restrict the growth of "undesirable" groups through birth control and coerced female sterilization. Touting the social, sexual, economic, and political benefits of sterilization, eugenicists succeeded in passing mandatory laws in most states by the early 1930s. This tragic chapter in American history has relevance today. Current discussions of the suitability of reversible sterilization contraceptives such as Depo-Provera and Norplant for women of color and poor women often resurrect the racist, reactionary arguments of the 1920s and 1930s.

Chapter VI turns to legal rights and the decriminalization of abortion and birth control in the 1960s and 1970s. It reviews the most important Supreme Court cases up to and including *Roe v.*

Wade and *Doe v. Bolton* in 1973. It also looks at the 1970s pro-life movement that gained momentum in the aftermath of *Roe* and the concerns that this movement championed.

Legal rights alone, however, do not guarantee women access to reproductive services. In 1977, Congress passed the Hyde Amendment, restricting poor women's access to abortions by curbing the use of Medicaid funds for abortion care. In doing so, Congress impeded the possibility of a universal application of *Roe* by ensuring that the right to have an abortion was one that only middle-class women could afford to exercise. State measures have echoed the restrictive spirit of Congress. Laws requiring parental notification and consent for minors, for instance, have reasserted the family unit as the most appropriate authority for regulating juvenile behavior. In addition, the orchestrated harassment of physicians who perform abortions and the escalating violence at clinics have jeopardized the access that legal rights were designed to provide. The legality of abortions will become a moot point if there are no longer any doctors willing to perform them.

Moreover, while many feminists have worked hard to protect abortion rights from further onslaughts, others such as Elizabeth Fox-Genovese and Mary Poovey have cautioned that the insistence on individual legal rights that brought victory in 1973 may, in the long term, work against the larger interests of women.[5] In tying the demand for safe, legal abortion rights so directly to the rhetoric of individualism and privacy, abortion activists have endorsed what some believe to be a libertarian platform that may backfire when it comes time to fight for other feminist goals. By demanding in the name of privacy that the government keep its "laws off our bodies" (as popular bumper stickers proclaim), pro-choice feminists may have forfeited, or at least undercut, their "right" to demand simultaneously that the government sponsor day care centers and national health care in the name of social justice. The debate raises a disturbing question about the relationship between law and reproductive concerns. At what point do individual rights and social justice collide? An excerpt from Rosalind Petchesky's *Abortion and Woman's Choice* deftly illuminates the multiple and at times conflicting ideologies framing the reproductive rights argument.

Industrial and technological changes also have had an impact on reproductive options. Chapter VII looks at how the industrial world and women's demands for reliable birth control have intersected and collided. Although technological innovations affecting contraceptives were negligible before the mass marketing of oral contraceptive pills in 1960, the birth control industry already had become a multimillion-dollar enterprise by the time of the Depression. Andrea Tone's article looks at the construction of the 1930s market and examines how its functioning affected contracepting women. Along with its mushrooming profits, the birth control industry's gendered designation of women as "contraceptive consumers," in which female sexual liberty is tied to market dependence, continues to be of critical importance today. Women, told that reproduction is their problem and promised by glossy magazine ads that the latest birth control technology guarantees safe and carefree sex, continue to be the primary consumers of contraceptives in the United States. Technological innovations since the 1960s, of course, have dramatically expanded women's contraceptive choices. Unfortunately, however, this expansion has exacted at times a social cost. The physical and psychological problems created by the use of oral contraceptives, intrauterine devices, Norplant, and, most recently, Depo-Provera dramatically attest to the void between the "freedom to choose" and the certainty, after one does, of reproductive health. Notwithstanding the 1990s rhetoric of unfettered sexual independence, contracepting women now more than ever are forced to entrust their health and welfare to the expertise of the Food and Drug Administration, the pharmaceutical "trust," and the medical profession.

This is not to suggest that women today are simply the victims of contraceptive and reproductive technology. Millions have found their interests and health well served by the wide array of new contraceptive choices. Millions more have profited from—indeed, have demanded access to—the latest reproductive technologies. Infertility, callously labeled the "career woman's disease" by antifeminists, has been minimized by new medical procedures such as in vitro fertilization. Tests such as amniocentesis have reassured women and forewarned them about potential fetal problems. At the same time, however, by allowing technology to be central to the "management" of female reproduction, women have turned over knowledge of what is happening to their bodies to machines and to the physicians who monitor them.

A close examination of the impact of contraceptive and reproductive technology supplies a methodological model with which to explore the larger history of reproductive control in America. One of the fastest growing fields in biomedical engineering today, reproductive technology has not developed in a chronological vacuum: new procedures and machines have incorporated centuries of gendered thinking about women and their role as potential and actual childbearers in society. With technology, as with other important components of the history of reproduction, we must unravel the threads of this story carefully in order to observe and evaluate critical moments of change, instances of female power, and glaring discrepancies between rhetoric and reality. Only then can we separate the old from the new in the rich and complex history of American reproduction.

Notes

1. See Joy Parr, "Gender History and Historical Practice," *Canadian Historical Review* 76, no. 3 (September 1995): 354–76.

2. Linda Gordon, *Woman's Body, Woman's Right: A Social History of Birth Control in America*, rev. ed. (New York: Penguin Books, 1990), 42–44; Angus McLaren, *Reproductive Rituals: The Perception of Fertility in England from the Sixteenth Century to the Nineteenth Century* (London: Methuen, 1984).

3. Laurel Thatcher Ulrich, *A Midwife's Tale: The Life of Martha Ballard, Based on Her Diary, 1785–1812* (New York: Alfred A. Knopf, 1990), 32–33.

4. Gordon, *Woman's Body, Woman's Right*, xiv.

5. Elizabeth Fox-Genovese, *Feminism without Illusions: A Critique of Individualism* (Chapel Hill: University of North Carolina Press, 1991), chap. 3; Mary Poovey, "The Abortion Question and the Death of Man," in *Feminists Theorize the Political*, ed. Judith Butler and Joan W. Scott (New York: Routledge, 1992), 239–56.

I

Birth Control and Abortion
in Early America

1 "Taking the Trade": Abortion and Gender Relations in an Eighteenth-Century New England Village

Cornelia Hughes Dayton

Abortions in the first stages of pregnancy were not only common in colonial America, but they also were culturally sanctioned and completely legal. The most widespread abortion technique was the ingestion of an abortifacient, a potion that induced miscarriage by irritating or poisoning the body or digestive tract; recipes for abortifacient brews of aloes, pennyroyal, and especially savin (extracted from juniper bushes that grew wild in North America) occupied an important place in traditional American folk medicine. Less frequently practiced were mechanical abortions that attempted direct fetal expulsion through the insertion of an instrument. Here, Cornelia Hughes Dayton, a historian at the University of California at Irvine, shows how the experiences of a small community with one woman's failed abortion illuminate broader gendered understandings of sexuality, criminality, and reproduction in early New England.

IN 1742 IN THE VILLAGE of Pomfret, perched in the hills of northeastern Connecticut, nineteen-year-old Sarah Grosvenor and twenty-seven-year-old Amasa Sessions became involved in a liaison that led to pregnancy, abortion, and death. Both were from prominent yeoman families, and neither a marriage between them nor an arrangement for the support of their illegitimate child would have been an unusual event for mid-eighteenth-century New England. Amasa Sessions chose a different course; in consultation with John Hallowell, a self-proclaimed "practitioner of physick," he coerced his lover into taking an abortifacient. Within two months, Sarah fell ill. Unbeknownst to all but Amasa, Sarah, Sarah's sister Zerviah, and her cousin Hannah, Hallowell made an attempt to "Remove her Conseption" by a "manual opperation." Two days later

From Cornelia Hughes Dayton, "Taking the Trade: Abortion and Gender Relations in an Eighteenth-Century New England Village," *William and Mary Quarterly*, 3d Ser., 48, no. 1 (1991): 19–28, 40–49. Reprinted by permission of the *William and Mary Quarterly* and the author.

Sarah miscarried, and her two young relatives secretly buried the fetus in the woods. Over the next month, Sarah struggled against a "Malignant fever" and was attended by several physicians, but on September 14, 1742, she died.[1]

Most accounts of induced abortions among seventeenth- and eighteenth-century whites in the Old and New Worlds consist of only a few lines in a private letter or court record book; these typically refer to the taking of savin or pennyroyal—two common herbal abortifacients. While men and women in diverse cultures have known how to perform abortions by inserting an instrument into the uterus, actual descriptions of such operations are extremely rare for any time period. Few accounts of abortions by instrument have yet been uncovered for early modern England, and I know of no other for colonial North America.[2] Thus, the historical fragments recording events in a small New England town in 1742 take on an unusual power to illustrate how an abortion was conducted, how it was talked about, and how it was punished.

We know about the Grosvenor-Sessions case because in 1745 two prominent Windham County magistrates opened an investigation into Sarah's death. Why there was a three-year gap between that event and legal proceedings, and why justices from outside Pomfret initiated the legal process, remain a mystery. In November 1745 the investigating magistrates offered their preliminary opinion that Hallowell, Amasa Sessions, Zerviah Grosvenor, and Hannah Grosvenor were guilty of Sarah's murder, the last three as accessories. From the outset, Connecticut legal officials concentrated not on the act of abortion per se, but on the fact that an abortion attempt had led to a young woman's death.

The case went next to Joseph Fowler, king's attorney for Windham County. He dropped charges against the two Grosvenor women, probably because he needed them as key witnesses and because they had played cover-up roles rather than originating the scheme. A year and a half passed as Fowler's first attempts to get convictions against Hallowell and Sessions failed either before grand juries or before the Superior Court on technical grounds. Finally, in March 1747, Fowler presented Hallowell and Sessions separately for the "highhanded Misdemeanour" of attempting to destroy both Sarah Grosvenor's health and "the fruit of her womb."[3] A grand jury endorsed the bill against Hallowell but rejected a similarly worded presentment against Sessions. At Hallowell's trial before the Superior Court in Windham, the jury brought in a guilty verdict and the chief judge sentenced the physician to twenty-nine lashes and two hours of public humiliation standing at the town gallows. Before the sentence could be executed, Hallowell managed to break jail. He fled to Rhode Island; as far as records indicate, he never returned to Connecticut. Thus, in the end, both Amasa Sessions and John Hallowell escaped legal punishment for their actions, whereas Sarah Grosvenor paid for her sexual transgression with her life. . . .

The Grosvenor-Sessions case dramatically highlights key changes in gender relations that reverberated through New England society in the eighteenth century. One of these changes involved the emergence of a marked sexual double standard. In the mid-seventeenth century, a young man like Amasa Sessions would have been pressured by parents, friends, or the courts to marry his lover. Had he resisted, he would most likely have been whipped or fined for the crime of fornication. By the late seventeenth century, New England judges gave up on enjoining sexually active couples to marry. In the 1740s, amid shifting standards of sexual behavior and growing concern over the evidentiary impossibility of establishing paternity, prosecutions of young men for premarital sex ceased. Thus, fornication was decriminalized for men, but not for women. Many of Sarah Grosvenor's female peers continued to be prosecuted and fined for bearing illegitimate children. Through private arrangements, and occasionally through civil lawsuits, their male partners were sometimes cajoled or coerced into contributing to the child's upkeep.[4]

What is most striking about the Grosvenor-Sessions case is that an entire community apparently forgave Sessions for the extreme measures he took to avoid accountability for his bastard child. Although he initiated the actions that led to his lover's death, all charges against him were dropped. Moreover, the tragedy did not spur Sessions to leave town; instead, he spent the rest of his life in Pomfret as a respected citizen. Even more dramatically than excusing young men from the crime of fornication, the treatment of Amasa Sessions confirmed that the sexually irresponsible activities of men in their youth would not be held against them as they reached for repute and prosperity in their prime.

The documents allow us to listen in on the quite different responses of young men and women to the drama unfolding in Pomfret. Sarah Grosvenor's female kin and friends, as we shall see, became preoccupied with their guilt and with the inevitability of

God's vengeance. Her male kin, on the other hand, reacted cautiously and legalistically, ferreting out information in order to assess how best to protect the Grosvenor family name. . . .

Finally, the Grosvenor case raises more questions than it answers about New Englanders' access to and attitudes toward abortion. If Sarah had not died after miscarriage, it is doubtful that any word of Sessions's providing her with an abortifacient or Hallowell's operation would have survived into the twentieth century. Because it nearly went unrecorded and because it reveals that many Pomfret residents were familiar with the idea of abortion, the case supports historians' assumptions that abortion attempts were far from rare in colonial America. We can also infer from the case that the most dangerous abortions before 1800 may have been those instigated by men and performed by surgeons with instruments.[5] But both abortion's frequency and the lineaments of its social context remain obscure. Did cases in which older women helped younger women to abort unwanted pregnancies far outnumber cases such as this one in which men initiated the process? Under what circumstances did family members and neighbors help married and unmarried women to hide abortion attempts?

Perhaps the most intriguing question centers on why women and men in early America acted *covertly* to effect abortions when abortion before quickening was legal. The Grosvenor case highlights the answer that applies to most known incidents from the period: abortion was understood as blameworthy because it was an extreme action designed to hide a prior sin, sex outside of marriage.[6] Reading the depositions, it is nearly impossible to disentangle the players' attitudes toward abortion itself from their expressions of censure or anxiety over failed courtship, illegitimacy, and the dangers posed for a young woman by a secret abortion. Strikingly absent from these eighteenth-century documents, however, is either outrage over the destruction of a fetus or denunciations of those who would arrest "nature's proper course." Those absences are a telling measure of how the discourse about abortion would change dramatically in later centuries.

The Narrative

The chronicle opens in late July 1742 when Zerviah Grosvenor, aged twenty-one, finally prevailed upon her younger sister to admit that she was pregnant. In tears, Sarah explained that she had not told Zerviah sooner because "she had been taking [the] trade to remove it."[7] "Trade" was used in this period to signify stuff or goods, often in the deprecatory sense of rubbish and trash. The *Oxford English Dictionary* confirms that in some parts of England and New England the word was used to refer to medicine. In Pomfret, trade meant a particular type of medicine, an abortifacient, thus a substance that might be regarded as "bad" medicine, as rubbish, unsafe and associated with destruction. What is notable is that Sarah and Zerviah, and neighboring young people who also used the word, had no need to explain to one another the meaning of "taking the trade." Perhaps only a few New Englanders knew how to prepare an abortifacient or knew of books that would give them recipes, but many more, especially young women who lived with the fear of becoming pregnant before marriage, were familiar with at least the *idea* of taking an abortifacient.

Sarah probably began taking the trade in mid-May when she was already three-and-a-half-months pregnant.[8] It was brought to her in the form of a powder by Amasa.[9] Sarah understood clearly that her lover had obtained the concoction "from docter hollowel," who conveyed "directions" for her doses through Amasa. Zerviah deposed later that Sarah had been "loath to Take" the drug and "Tho't it an Evil," probably because at three and a half months she anticipated quickening, the time from which she knew the law counted abortion an "unlawful measure."[10] At the outset, Sarah argued in vain with Amasa against his proposed "Method." Later, during June and July, she sometimes "neglected" to take the doses he left for her, but, with mounting urgency, Amasa and the doctor pressed her to comply. "It was necessary," Amasa explained in late July, that she take "more, or [else] they were afraid She would be greatly hurt by what was already done." To calm her worries, he assured her that "there was no life [left] in the Child" and that the potion "would not hurt her."[11] Apparently, the men hoped that a few more doses would provoke a miscarriage, thereby expelling the dead fetus and restoring Sarah's body to its natural balance of humors.

Presumably, Hallowell decided to operate in early August because Sarah's pregnancy was increasingly visible, and he guessed that she was not going to miscarry. An operation in which the fetus would be removed or punctured was now the only certain way to terminate the pregnancy secretly.[12] To avoid the scrutiny of Sarah's parents, Hallowell resorted to a plan he had used once before in arranging a private examination of Sarah. Early one afternoon he arrived at the house of John Grosvenor and begged for a room as "he was weary and wanted Rest."[13] John, Sarah's thirty-one-year-old first cousin, lived with his wife, Hannah, and their young children in a homestead only a short walk down the hill but out of sight of Sarah's father's house. While John and Hannah were busy, the physician sent one of the little children to fetch Sarah.[14]

The narrative of Sarah's fateful meeting with Hallowell that August afternoon is best told in the words of one of the deponents. Abigail Nightingale had married and moved to Pomfret two years earlier, and by 1742 she had become Sarah's close friend.[15]. . .

This is how Abigail recollected Sarah's deathbed story:

> On [Sarah's] going down [to her cousin John's], [Hallowell] said he wanted to Speake with her alone; and then they two went into a Room together; and then sd. [*sic*] Hallowell told her it was necessary that something more should be done or else she would Certainly die; to which she replyed that she was afraid they had done too much already, and then he told her that there was one thing more that could easily be done, and she asking him what it was; he said he could easily deliver her; but she said she was afraid there was life in the Child, then he asked her how long she had felt it; and she replyed about a fortnight; then he said that was impossible or could not be or ever would; for that the trade she had taken had or would prevent it: and that the alteration she felt Was owing to what she had taken. And he farther told her that he verily thought that the Child grew to her body to the Bigness of his hand, or else it would have Come away before that time; and that it would never Come away, but Certainly Kill her, unless other Means were used.[16] On which she yielded to his making an Attempt to take it away; charging him that if he could perceive that there was life in it he would not proceed on any Account. And then the Doctor openning his portmantua took an Instrument[17] out of it and Laid it on the Bed, and she asking him what it was for, he replyed that it was to make way; and that then he tryed to remove the Child for Some time in vain putting her to the Utmost Distress, and that at Last she observed he trembled and immediately perceived a Strange alteration in her body and thought a bone of the Child was broken; on which she desired him (as she said) to Call in some body, for that she feared she was adying, and instantly swooned away.[18]

With Sarah's faint, Abigail's account broke off, but within minutes others, who would testify later, stepped into the room. Hallowell reacted to Sarah's swoon by unfastening the door and calling in

Hannah, the young mistress of the house, and Zerviah, who had followed her sister there. Cold water and "a bottle of drops" were brought to keep Sarah from fainting again, while Hallowell explained to the "much Surprized" women that "he had been making an Attempt" to deliver Sarah. Despite their protests, he then "used a further force upon her" but did not succeed in "Tak[ing] the Child . . . away."[19]. . . At the time of the attempt, Hallowell explained to the women that he "had done so much to her, as would Cause the Birth of the Child in a Little time." Just before sunset, he packed up his portmanteau and went to a nearby tavern, where Amasa was waiting "to hear [the outcome of] the event."[20] Meanwhile, Sarah, weak-kneed and in pain, leaned on the arm of her sister as the young women managed to make their way home in the twilight.

After his attempted "force," Hallowell fades from the scene, while Zerviah and Hannah Grosvenor become the key figures. About two days after enduring the operation, Sarah began to experience contractions. Zerviah ran to get Hannah, telling her "she Tho't . . . Sarah would be quickly delivered." They returned to find Sarah, who was alone "in her Father's Chamber," just delivered and rising from the chamber pot. In the pot was "an Untimely birth"—a "Child [that] did not Appear to have any Life In it." To Hannah, it "Seemed by The Scent . . . That it had been hurt and was decaying," while Zerviah later remembered it as "a perfect Child," even "a pritty child."[21] Determined to keep the event "as private as they Could," the two women helped Sarah back to bed, and then "wr[app]ed . . . up" the fetus, carried it to the woods on the edge of the farmstead, and there "Buried it in the Bushes."[22]

On learning that Sarah had finally miscarried and that the event had evidently been kept hidden from Sarah's parents, Amasa and Hallowell may have congratulated themselves on the success of their operation. However, about ten days after the miscarriage, Sarah grew feverish and weak. Her parents consulted two college-educated physicians who hailed from outside the Pomfret area. Their visits did little good, nor were Sarah's symptoms—fever, delirium, convulsions—relieved by a visit from Hallowell, whom Amasa "fetcht" to Sarah's bedside.[23] In the end, Hallowell, who had decided to move from nearby Killingly to more distant Providence, washed his hands of the case. A few days before Sarah died, her cousin John "went after" Hallowell, whether to bring him back or to express his rage, we do not know. Hallowell predicted "that She woul[d] not live."[24]

Silence seems to have settled on the Grosvenor house and its neighborhood after Sarah's death on September 14. It was two and a half years later that rumors about a murderous abortion spread through and beyond Pomfret village, prompting legal investigation. . . .

Women's Talk and Men's Talk

Gender affected how the conspiring young adults responded to Sarah's impending death and how they weighed the issue of blame. . . . An inward gaze, a strong consciousness of sin and guilt, a desire to avoid conflict and achieve reconciliation, a need to confess—these are the impulses expressed in women's intimate talk in the weeks before Sarah died. The central female characters in the plot, Sarah and Zerviah Grosvenor, lived for six weeks with the daily fear that their parents or aunts might detect Sarah's condition or their covert comings and goings. Deposing three years later, Zerviah represented the sisters as suffering under an intensifying sense of complicity as they had passed through two stages of involvement in the concealment plan. At first, they were passive players, submitting to the hands of men. But once Hallowell declared that he had done all he could, they were left to salvage the conspiracy by enduring the terrors of a first delivery alone, knowing that their failure to call in the older women of the family resembled the decision made by women who committed infanticide.[25] While the pain and shock of miscarrying a five-and-one-half-month fetus through a possibly lacerated vagina may have been the experience that later most grieved Sarah, Zerviah would be haunted particularly by her stealthy venture into the woods with Hannah to bury the shrouded evidence of miscarriage.[26]

The Grosvenor sisters later recalled that they had regarded the first stage of the scheme—taking the trade—as "a Sin" and "an Evil" not so much because it was intended to end the life of a fetus as because it entailed a protracted set of actions, worse than a single lie, to cover up an initial transgression: fornication.[27] According to their religion and the traditions of their New England culture, Sarah and Zerviah knew that the proper response to the sin of "uncleanness" (especially when it led to its visible manifestation, pregnancy) was to confess, seeking to allay God's wrath and cleanse oneself and one's community. Dire were the consequences of hiding a grave sin, so the logic and folklore of religion warned.[28] Having piled one covert act upon another, all in defiance of her parents, each sister wondered if she had not ventured beyond the pale, forsaking God and in turn being forsaken.

Within hours after the burial, Zerviah ran in a frenzy to Alexander Sessions's house and blurted out an account of her sister's "Untimely birth" and the burying of the fetus. While Alexander and Silence Sessions wondered if Zerviah was "in her right mind" and supposed she was having "a very bad fit," we might judge that she was in shock—horrified and confused by what she had done, fearful of retribution, and torn between the pragmatic strategy of silence and an intense spiritual longing to confess. Silence took her aside and demanded, "How could you do it?—I could not!" Zerviah, in despair, replied, "I don't Know; the Devil was in us." Hers was the characteristic refuge of the defiant sinner: Satan made her do it.[29]

Sarah's descent into despondency, according to the portrait drawn in the women's depositions, was not so immediate. In the week following the miscarriage she recovered enough to be up and about the house. Then the fever came on. Bedridden for weeks, yet still lucid, she exhibited such "great Concern of mind" that Abigail, alone with her, felt compelled to ask her "what was the Matter." "Full of Sorrow" and "in a very affectionate Manner," Sarah replied by asking her friend "whether [she] thought her Sins would ever be pardoned." Abigail's answer blended a reassuringly familiar exhortation to repent with an awareness that Sarah might have stepped beyond the possibility of salvation. "I answered that I hoped she had not Sinned the unpardonable Sin [that of renouncing Christ], but with true and hearty repentance hoped she would find forgiveness." On this occasion, and at least once more, Sarah responded to the call for repentance by pouring out her troubled heart to Abigail—as we have seen—confessing her version of the story in a torrent of words.[30]

Thus, visions of judgment and of their personal accountability to God haunted Sarah and Zerviah during the waning days of summer—or so their female friends later contended. Caught between the traditional religious ethic of confession, recently renewed in revivals across New England, and the newer, status-driven cultural pressure to keep moral missteps private, the Grosvenor women declined to take up roles as accusers. By focusing on their own actions, they rejected a portrait of themselves as helpless victims, yet they also ceded to their male kin responsibility for assessing blame and mediating between the public interest in seeing justice done and the private interests of the Grosvenor family. Finally, by trying to keep the conspiracy of silence intact and by allowing Amasa frequent visits to her bedside to lament his role and his delusion by Hallowell, Sarah at once endorsed a policy of private repentance and forgiveness *and* indicated that she wished her lover to be spared eventual public retribution for her death.

Talk among the men of Pomfret in the weeks preceding and following Sarah's death centered on more secular concerns than the preoccupation with sin and God's anger that ran through the women's conversations. Neither Hallowell nor Sessions expressed any guilt or sense of sin, as far as the record shows, *until* Sarah was diagnosed as mortally ill.[31] Indeed, their initial accounts of the plot took the form of braggadocio, with Amasa (according to Hallowell) casting himself as the rake who could "gitt Red" of his child and look elsewhere for female companionship, and Hallowell boasting of his abortionist's surgical technique to Sarah's cousin Ebenezer. Later, anticipating popular censure and possible prosecution, each man "Tried to Cast it" on the other. The physician insisted that "He did not do any thing but What Sessions Importuned him to Do," while Amasa exclaimed "That he could freely be Strip[p]ed naked provided he could bring Sarah . . . To life again . . . , but Doct Hollowell had Deluded him, and Destroyed her."[32] While this sort of denial and buck-passing seems very human, it was the antithesis of the New England way—a religious way of life that made confession its central motif. The Grosvenor-Sessions case is one illustration among many of how New England women continued to measure themselves by "the moral allegory of repentance and confession" while men, at least when presenting themselves before legal authorities, adopted secular voices and learned self-interested strategies.[33]

For the Grosvenor men—at least the cluster of Sarah's cousins living near her—the key issue was not exposing sin but protecting the family's reputation. In the weeks before Sarah died, her cousins John and Ebenezer each attempted to investigate and sort out the roles and motives of Amasa Sessions and John Hallowell in the scheme to conceal Sarah's pregnancy. Grilled in August by Ebenezer about Sarah's condition, Hallowell revealed that "Sessions had bin Interseeding with him to Remove her Conseption." On another occasion, when John Grosvenor demanded that he justify his actions, Hallowell was more specific. He "[did] with her [Sarah] as he did

. . . because Sessions Came to him and was So very earnest . . . and offered him five pounds if he would do it." "But," Hallowell boasted, "he would have twenty of[f] of him before he had done." John persisted: did Amasa know that Hallowell was attempting a manual abortion at John's house on that day in early August? Hallowell replied that Amasa "knew before he did anything and was at Mr. Waldo's [a Pomfret tavernkeeper] to hear the event."[34]

John and Ebenezer, deposing three or four years after these events, did not mention having thrown questions at Amasa Sessions at the time, nor did they explain why they did not act immediately to have charges brought against the two conspirators. Perhaps these young householders were loath to move against a male peer and childhood friend. More likely, they kept their information to themselves to protect John's wife, Hannah, and their cousin Zerviah from prosecution as accessories. They may also have acted, in league with their uncle Leicester, out of a larger concern for keeping the family name out of the courts. Finally, it is probable that the male cousins, partly because of their own complicity and partly because they may have believed that Sarah had consented to the abortion, simply did not think that Amasa's and Hallowell's actions added up to the murder of their relative.

Three years later, yet another Grosvenor cousin intervened, expressing himself much more vehemently than John or Ebenezer ever had. In 1742, John Shaw at age thirty-eight may have been perceived by the younger Grosvenors as too old—too close to the age when men took public office and served as grand jurors—to be trusted with their secret. Shaw seems to have known nothing of Sarah's taking the trade or having a miscarriage until 1745, when "the Storys" suddenly surfaced. Then Hannah and Zerviah gave him a truncated account. Shaw reacted with rage, realizing that Sarah had died not of natural causes but from "what Hollowell had done," and he set out to wring the truth from the doctor. Several times he sought out Hallowell in Rhode Island to tell him that "I could not look upon him otherwise Than [as] a Bad man Since he had Destroyed my Kinswoman." When Hallowell countered that "Amasa Sessions . . . was the Occasion of it," Shaw's fury grew. "I Told him he was like old Mother Eve When She said The Serpent beguil'd her; . . . [and] I Told him in my Mind he Deserved to dye for it."[35]

Questioning Amasa, Shaw was quick to accept his protestations of sincere regret and his insistence that Hallowell had "Deluded" him.[36] Shaw concluded that Amasa had never "Importuned

[Hallowell] . . . to lay hands on her" (that is, to perform the manual abortion). Forged in the men's talk about the Grosvenor-Sessions case in 1745 and 1746 appears to have been a consensus that, while Amasa Sessions was somewhat blameworthy "as concerned in it," it was only Hallowell—the outsider, the man easily labeled a quack—who deserved to be branded "a Man of Death." Nevertheless, it was the stories of *both* men and women that ensured the fulfillment of a doctor's warning to Hallowell in the Leicester Grosvenor house just before Sarah died: "The Hand of Justice [will] Take hold of [you] sooner or Later."[37]. . .

The Law

The Pomfret meetinghouse was the site of the first public legal hearing into the facts behind Sarah Grosvenor's death. We can imagine that townsfolk crowded the pews over the course of two November [1745] days to watch two prominent county magistrates examine a string of witnesses before pronouncing their preliminary judgment.[38] The evidence, they concluded, was sufficient to bind four people over for trial at the Superior Court: Hallowell, who in their opinion was "Guilty of murdering Sarah," along with Amasa Sessions, Zerviah Grosvenor, and Hannah Grosvenor as accessories to that murder.[39] The inclusion of Zerviah and Hannah may have been a ploy to pressure these crucial, possibly still reluctant, witnesses to testify for the crown. When Joseph Fowler, the king's attorney, prepared a formal indictment in the case eleven months later, he dropped all charges against Zerviah and Hannah. Rather than stand trial, the two women traveled frequently during 1746 and 1747 to the county seat to give evidence against Sessions and Hallowell.

The criminal process recommenced in September 1746. A grand jury empaneled by the Superior Court at its Windham session first rejected a presentment against Hallowell for murdering Sarah "by his Wicked and Diabolical practice." Fowler, recognizing that the capital charges of murder and accessory to murder against Hallowell and Sessions were going to fail before jurors, changed his tack. He presented the grand jury with a joint indictment against the two men not for outright murder but for endangering Sarah's health by trying to "procure an Abortion" with medicines and "a violent manual opperation"; this time the jurors endorsed the bill. When the Superior Court trial opened in November, two attorneys for the defendants managed to persuade the judges that the indictment was faulty on technical grounds. However, upon the advice of the king's attorney that there "appear reasons vehemently to suspect" the two men "Guilty of Sundry Heinous Offenses" at Pomfret four years earlier, the justices agreed to bind them over to answer charges in March 1747.[40]

Fowler next moved to bring separate indictments against Hallowell and Sessions for the "highhanded misdemeanour" of endeavoring to destroy Sarah's health "and the fruit of her womb." This wording echoed the English common law designation of abortion as a misdemeanor, not a felony or capital crime. A newly empaneled grand jury of eighteen county yeomen made what turned out to be the pivotal decision in getting a conviction: they returned a true bill against Hallowell and rejected a similarly worded bill against Sessions.[41] Only Hallowell, "the notorious physician," would go to trial.[42]

On March 20, 1747, John Hallowell stepped before the bar for the final time to answer for the death of Sarah Grosvenor. He maintained his innocence, the case went to a trial jury of twelve men, and they returned with a guilty verdict. The Superior Court judges, who had discretion to choose any penalty less than death, pronounced a severe sentence of public shaming and corporal punishment. Hallowell was to be paraded to the town gallows, made to stand there before the public for two hours "with a rope visibly hanging about his neck," and then endure a public whipping of twenty-nine lashes "on the naked back."[43]. . .

In the series of indictments against Hallowell and Sessions, the central legal question became who had directly caused Sarah's death. To the farmers in their forties and fifties who sat as jurors, Hallowell clearly deserved punishment. By recklessly endangering Sarah's life, he had abused the trust that heads of household placed in him as a physician.[44] Moreover, he had conspired with the younger generation to keep their dangerous activities secret from their parents and elders.

Several rationales could have been behind the Windham jurors' conclusion that Amasa Sessions ought to be spared the lash. Legally, they could distinguish him from Hallowell as not being *directly* responsible for Sarah's death. Along with Sarah's male kin, they dismissed the evidence that Amasa had instigated the scheme, employed Hallowell, and monitored all of his activities. Perhaps they saw him as a native son who deserved the chance to prove himself mature and responsible. They may have excused his actions as nothing more than a misguided effort to cast off an unwanted lover. Rather than acknowledge that a culture that excused male sexual irresponsibility was responsible for Sarah's death, the Grosvenor family, the Pomfret community, and the jury men of the county persuaded themselves that Sessions had been ignorant of the potentially deadly consequences of his actions. . . .

If Sarah Grosvenor's life is a cautionary tale in any sense for us in the late twentieth century, it is as a reminder of the historically distinctive ways in which socialized gender roles, community and class solidarity, and legal culture combine in each set of generations to excuse or make invisible certain abuses and crimes against women.

Notes

1. The documentation is found in the record books and file papers of the Superior Court of Connecticut: *Rex v. John Hallowell et al.*, Superior Court Records, Book 9, 113, 173, 175, and Windham County Superior Court Files, box 172, Connecticut State Library, Hartford. Hereafter all loose court papers cited are from *Rex v. Hallowell*, Windham County Superior Court Files, box 172, unless otherwise indicated. For the quotations see Security Bond for John Hallowell, undated; Deposition of Ebenezer Grosvenor, probably April 1746; Indictment against John Hallowell and Amasa Sessions, September 20, 1746; Deposition of Parker Morse.

2. One such abortion was reported in *Gentleman's Magazine* (London), II, No. 20 (August 1732), 933–34; see Audrey Eccles, *Obstetrics and Gynaecology in Tudor and Stuart England* (London, 1982), 70.

3. Indictment against John Hallowell, March 1746/47.

4. The story of the decriminalization of fornication for men in colonial New England is told most succinctly by Carol F. Karlsen, *The Devil in the Shape of a Woman: Witchcraft in Colonial New England* (New York, 1987), 194–96, 198–202, 255.

5. If abortions directed by male physicians in the colonial period were more hazardous than those managed by midwives and lay women, then, in an inversion of the mid-twentieth-century situation, women from wealthy families with access to, and preferences for, male doctors were those most in jeopardy. For a general comparison of male and female medical practitioners see Laurel Thatcher Ulrich, *A Midwife's Tale: The Life of Martha Ballard, Based on Her Diary, 1785–1812* (New York, 1990), 48–66, esp. 54.

6. Married women may have hidden their abortion attempts because the activity was associated with lewd or dissident women.

7. Deposition of Zerviah Grosvenor. In a second deposition Zerviah used the word "Medicines" instead of "trade"; Testimony of Zerviah Grosvenor in Multiple Deposition of Hannah Grosvenor et al.: hereafter cited as Testimony of Zerviah Grosvenor. Five times out of eight, deponents referred to "the trade," instead of simply "trade" or "some trade."

8. So her sister Zerviah later estimated. Testimony of Rebecca Sharp in Multiple Deposition of Hannah Grosvenor et al.

9. After she was let into the plot, Zerviah more than once watched Amasa take "a paper or powder out of his pockett" and insist that Sarah "take Some of it." Deposition of Zerviah Grosvenor.

10. Deposition of John Grosvenor; Deposition of Zerviah Grosvenor; Testimony of Zerviah Grosvenor in Multiple Deposition of Hannah Grosvenor et al. "Unlawful measure" was Zerviah's phrase for Amasa's "Method." Concerned for Sarah's well-being, she pleaded with Hallowell not to give her sister "any thing that should harm her"; Deposition of Zerviah Grosvenor. At the same time, Sarah was thinking about the quickening issue. She confided to a friend that when Amasa first insisted she take the trade, "she [had] feared it was too late"; Deposition of Abigail Nightingale.

11. Deposition of Zerviah Grosvenor; Testimony of Zerviah Grosvenor.

12. Hallowell claimed that he proceeded with the abortion in order to save Sarah's life. If the powder had had little effect and he knew it, then this claim was a deliberate deception. On the other hand, he may have sincerely believed that the potion had poisoned the fetus and that infection of the uterine cavity had followed fetal death. Since healthy babies were thought at that time to help with their own deliveries, Hallowell may also have anticipated a complicated delivery if Sarah were allowed to go to full term—a delivery that might kill her.

13. Testimony of Hannah Grosvenor in Multiple Deposition of Hannah Grosvenor et al. Hannah may have fabricated the account of Hallowell's deception to cover her own knowledge of and collusion in Hallowell and Session's scheme to conceal Sarah's pregnancy.

14. Deposition of Zerviah Grosvenor. Hallowell attended Sarah overnight at John Grosvenor's house once in July; Multiple Deposition of Sarah and Silence Sessions.

15. On Abigail's husband, Samuel, and his family see Clifford K. Shipton, *Biographical Sketches of Those Who Attended Harvard College in the Classes 1731–1735* (Boston, 1956), IX, 425–28; Pomfret Vital Records, Barbour Collection, Connecticut State Library. All vital and land records cited hereafter are found in the Barbour Collection.

16. Twentieth-century obstetrical studies show an average of 6 weeks between fetal death and spontaneous abortion; J. Robert Willson and Elsie Reid Carrington, eds., *Obstetrics and Gynecology*, 8th ed. (St. Louis, MO, 1987), 212. Hallowell evidently grasped the link between the two events but felt he could not wait 6 weeks, either out of concern for Sarah's health or for fear their plot would be discovered.

17. A 1746 indictment offered the only other point at which the "instrument" was mentioned in the documents. It claimed that Hallowell "with his own hands

as [well as] with a certain Instrument of Iron [did] violently Lacerate and . . .
wound the body of Sarah"; Indictment against John Hallowell, endorsed "Igno-
ramus," September 4, 1746.

18. Deposition of Abigail Nightingale.

19. Joint Testimony of Hannah and Zerviah Grosvenor in Multiple Deposition
of Hannah Grosvenor et al.; Deposition of Hannah Grosvenor; Deposition of
Zerviah Grosvenor.

20. Deposition of John Grosvenor; Deposition of Hannah Grosvenor; Deposition of Ebenezer Grosvenor.

21. Testimony of Hannah Grosvenor, Alexander Sessions, and Rebecca Sharp
in Multiple Deposition of Hannah Grosvenor et al. In a second statement Hannah
said that "the head Seemed to be brused"; Deposition of Hannah Grosvenor.

22. Testimony of Rebecca Sharp, Hannah Grosvenor, and Alexander Sessions
in Multiple Deposition of Hannah Grosvenor et al.; Testimony of Silence Sessions in Multiple Deposition of Sarah and Silence Sessions.

23. Joint Testimony of Hannah and Zerviah Grosvenor in Multiple Deposition
of Hannah Grosvenor et al.; Deposition of Parker Morse of Woodstock, April
1746.

24. Deposition of John Grosvenor.

25. See Laurel Thatcher Ulrich, *Good Wives: Image and Reality in the Lives of
Women in Northern New England, 1650–1750* (New York, 1982), 195–201; and
Cornelia Hughes Dayton, "Infanticide in Early New England," unpublished paper presented to the Organization of American Historians, Reno, Nevada, March
1988.

26. Burying the child was one of the key dramatic acts in infanticide episodes
and tales, and popular beliefs in the inevitability that "murder will out" centered
on the buried corpse. For two eighteenth-century Connecticut cases illustrating
these themes see Dayton, "Infanticide in Early New England," n. 31. For more
on "murder will out" in New England culture see David D. Hall, *Worlds of Wonder, Days of Judgment: Popular Religious Beliefs in Early New England* (New
York, 1989), 176–78; and George Lyman Kittredge, *The Old Farmer and His
Almanack* (New York, 1920), 71–77.

27. Testimony of Zerviah Grosvenor.

28. Hall, *Worlds of Wonder*, 172–78.

29. Testimony of Silence Sessions in Multiple Deposition of Sarah and Silence
Sessions; Testimony of Alexander Sessions in Multiple Deposition of Hannah
Grosvenor et al.; Testimony of Silence Sessions; Hall, *Worlds of Wonder*, 174.
Alexander and Silence may have had in mind their brother Amasa's interests as a
criminal defendant when they cast doubt on Zerviah's reliability as the star pros-
ecution witness.

30. Deposition of Abigail Nightingale.

31. Testimony of Zerviah Grosvenor; Deposition of John Grosvenor. Abigail
Nightingale recalled a scene when Sarah "was just going out of the world." She
and Amasa were sitting on Sarah's bed, and Amasa "endeavour[ed] to raise her
up &c. He asked my thought of her state &c. and then leaning over her used these
words: poor Creature, I have undone you[!]"; Deposition of Abigail
Nightingale.

32. Deposition of Ebenezer Grosvenor; Testimony of John Shaw in Multiple Deposition of Hannah Grosvenor et al. See also Deposition of John Grosvenor.

33. On the centrality of confession see Hall, *Worlds of Wonder*, 173, 241.

34. Deposition of Ebenezer Grosvenor; Deposition of John Grosvenor. Although a host of witnesses testified to the contrary, Hallowell on one occasion told Amasa's brother "That Sessions never applied to him for anything, to cause an abortion and that if She was with Child he did not Think Amasa knew it"; Testimony of Alexander Sessions in Multiple Deposition of Hannah Grosvenor et al.

35. Testimony of John Shaw in Multiple Deposition of Hannah Grosvenor et al. One of these confrontations took place in the Providence jail, probably in late 1745 or early 1746.

36. It is interesting to note that Sessions claimed to have other sources for strong medicines: he told Shaw that, had he known Sarah was in danger of dying, "he tho't he could have got Things that would have preserved her Life"; ibid.

37. Ibid. Shaw here was reporting Dr. [Theodore?] Coker's account of his confrontation with Hallowell during Sarah's final illness.

38. One of the magistrates, Ebenezer West, had been a justice of the county court since 1726. The other, Jonathan Trumbull, the future governor, was serving both as a county court justice and as an assistant. The fact that the two men made the 24-mile trip from their hometown of Lebanon to preside over this Inferior Court, rather than allow local magistrates to handle the hearing, may indicate that one or both of them had insisted the alleged crime be prosecuted.

39. Record of the Inferior Court held at Pomfret, November 5–6, 1745. Hallowell was the only one of the four persons charged who was not examined at this time. He was reportedly in jail in Providence. Apprehended in Connecticut the following March, he was jailed until the Pomfret witnesses could travel to Windham for a hearing before Trumbull and West. At the second hearing, the magistrates charged Hallowell with "murdering Sarah . . . *and* A Bastard Female Child with which she was pregnant" (emphasis added). See Record of an Inferior Court held at Windham, April 17, 1746.

40. Indictment against Hallowell, September 4, 1746; Indictment against Hallowell and Sessions, September 20, 1746; Pleas of Hallowell and Sessions before the adjourned Windham Superior Court, November [18], 1746; Superior Court Records, Book 12, 112–17, 131–33.

41. Superior Court Records, Book 12, 173, 175; Indictment against John Hallowell, March 1746/47; *Rex v. Amasa Sessions*, Indictment, March 1746/47, Windham Superior Court Files, box 172. See William Blackstone, *Commentaries on the Laws of England* (Facsimile of 1st ed. of 1765–69) (Chicago, 1979), I, 125–26; IV, 198.

42. Ellen D. Larned, *History of Windham County, Connecticut* (Worcester, MA, 1874), I, 363.

43. Even in the context of the inflation of the 1740s, Hallowell's bill of costs was unusually high: £110.2s.6d. Sessions was hit hard in the pocketbook, too; he was assessed £83.14s.2d. in costs.

44. Note Blackstone's discussion of the liability of "a physician or surgeon who gives his patient a potion . . . to cure him, which contrary to expectation kills him." *Commentaries*, IV, 197.

2   Advice on Menstruation and Pregnancy

William Buchan

Printed medical manuals supplemented the knowledge of friends, kin, midwives, and physicians as an important source of information on reproductive control in antebellum America. The most popular home medical reference book in the early nineteenth century was William Buchan's Domestic Medicine. *First published in London in 1769, it was reprinted in America at least twenty-eight times between 1770 and 1850. As did other such guides of the era, it prescribed tonics and potions that could be prepared from easily obtained ingredients for a wide array of ailments. Consistent with contemporary medical thinking,* Domestic Medicine *depicted gynecological functions as the most important feature of womanhood; a woman's demeanor and disposition were thought to mirror her reproductive health. In line with most antebellum medical manuals,* Domestic Medicine *did not condone abortions; indeed, as this excerpt shows, it condemned them as egregious violations of "natural" motherhood. Paradoxically, however, by advising women of the activities and substances to avoid during pregnancy, Buchan furnished readers with information that could be used to induce miscarriages.*

Of the Menstrual Discharge

FEMALES GENERALLY BEGIN TO MENSTRUATE about the age of fifteen and leave off it about fifty, which renders these two periods the most critical of their lives. . . .

After the menses have once begun to flow, the greatest care should be taken to avoid every thing that may tend to obstruct them. Females ought to be exceeding[ly] cautious of what they eat or drink at the time they are out of order. Every thing that is cold, or apt to sour on the stomach, ought to be avoided; as fruit, butter-milk, and such like. Fish, and all kinds of food that are hard of digestion, are also to be avoided. . . .

From William Buchan, *Domestic Medicine, or a Treatise on the Prevention and Cure of Diseases by Regimen and Simple Medicines* (Boston, 1813), 345–47, 349–51, 368, 513–15.

Cold is extremely hurtful at this particular period. More of the sex date their diseases from colds, caught while they are out of order, than from all other causes. This ought surely to put them upon their guard, and to make them very circumspect in this conduct at such times. A degree of cold that will not in the least hurt them at another time, will at this period be sufficient entirely to ruin their health and constitution. . . .

From whatever cause this [menstrual] flux is obstructed, except in the state of pregnancy, proper means should be used to restore it. For this purpose we would recommend sufficient exercise in a dry, open and rather cool air; wholesome diet, and, if the body be weak and languid, generous liquors; also cheerful company and all manner of amusements. If these fail, recourse must be had to medicine.

When obstructions proceed from a weak relaxed state of the solids, such medicines as tend to promote digestion, to brace the solids and assist the body in preparing good blood, ought to be used. The principal of these are iron and the Peruvian bark, with other bitter and astringent medicines. Filings of iron may be infused in wine or ale, two or three ounces to an English quart, and after it has stood for two or three weeks, it may be filtered, and about half a wine glass of it taken twice a-day; or prepared steel may be taken in the dose of half a drachm, mixed with a little honey or treacle, three or four times a-day. The bark and other bitters may either be taken in substance or infusion, as is most agreeable to the patient.

When obstructions proceed from a viscid state of the blood, or from women of a gross or full habit, evacuations, and such medicines as attenuate the humours, are necessary. The patient in this case ought to be bled, to bathe her feet frequently in warm water, to take now and then a cooling purge, and to live upon a spare thin diet. Her drink should be whey, water, or small beer and she ought to take sufficient exercise. A teaspoonful of the tincture of black hellebore [an herb used as a purgative] may also be taken twice a day in a cup of warm water. . . .

Of Pregnancy

Though pregnancy is not a disease, yet that state is often attended with a variety of complaints which merit attention, and which sometimes require the assistance of medicine. Some women, indeed, are more healthy during their pregnancy than at any other time, but this is by no means the general case: most of them *breed in sorrow* [italics in the original], and are frequently indisposed during the whole time of pregnancy. Few fatal diseases, however, happen during that period; and hardly any, except abortion, that can be called dangerous. We shall therefore pay particular attention to it, as it proves generally fatal to the child, and sometimes so to the mother. . . .

Every pregnant woman is more or less in danger of abortion. This should be guarded against with the greatest care, as it not only weakens the constitution, but renders the woman liable to the same misfortune afterwards. Abortion may happen at any period.

The common causes of abortion are the death of the child; weakness or relaxation of the mother; great evacuations; violent exercise; raising great weights; reaching too high; jumping or stepping from an eminence; vomiting; coughing; convulsive fits; strokes on the belly; falls; fevers; disagreeable smells; excess of blood; indolence; high living, or the contrary; violent passions or affections of the mind, as fear, grief, etc. . . .

To prevent abortion, we would advise women of a weak or relaxed habit to use solid food, avoiding great quantities of tea and other weak and watery liquors; to rise early and go soon to bed; to shun damp houses; to take frequent exercise in the open air, but to avoid fatigue; and never to go abroad in damp foggy weather, if they can shun it.

Women of a full habit ought to use a spare diet, avoiding strong liquors, and every thing that may tend to heat the body, or increase the quantity of blood. Their diet should be of an opening nature, consisting principally of vegetable substances. Every woman with child ought to be kept cheerful and easy in her mind. Her appetites, even though depraved, ought to be indulged as far as prudence will permit. . . .

Sanguine robust women who are liable to miscarry at a certain time of pregnancy, ought always to be bled a few days before that period arrives. By this means, and observing the regimen above prescribed, they might often escape the misfortune.

Of Barrenness

Barrenness may be very properly reckoned among the diseases of females, as few married women who have not children enjoy a good state of health. It may proceed from various causes, as high living, grief, relaxation, etc. but it is chiefly owing to an obstruction or irregularity of the menstrual flux.

It is very certain that high living prevents fecundity. We seldom find a barren woman among the labouring poor, while nothing is more common among the rich and affluent. The inhabitants of every country are prolific in proportion to their poverty; and it would be an easy matter to adduce many instances of women, who, by being reduced to live entirely upon a milk and vegetable diet, have conceived and brought forth children, though they never had any before. . . .

Affluence begets indolence which induces a great relaxation of the solids, a state highly unfavorable to procreation. To remove this, we would recommend the following course: First, sufficient exercise in the open air; secondly, a diet consisting chiefly of milk and vegetables; thirdly, the use of astringent medicines, as steel, allum, dragon's blood, elixir of vitriol, the Spaw or Tunbridge waters, Peruvian bark, etc.; and lastly, above all, the cold bath.

Barrenness is often the consequence of grief, sudden fear, anxiety, or any of the passions which tend to obstruct the menstrual flux. When barrenness is suspected to proceed from affections of the mind, the person ought to be kept as easy and cheerful as possible; all disagreeable objects are to be avoided, and every method taken to amuse and entertain the fancy.

Rules of Conduct during Pregnancy

The dread of public shame or private scorn, though no excuse for murder, may urge the victim of seduction to commit a crime at once so abominable and so dangerous. But is it possible that a married woman should madly and wickedly attempt to procure abortion, merely from an apprehension of a large family, or to avoid the trouble of bearing and bringing up children? Can she hope to taste the joys, and yet destroy the fruits of love? What a frantic idea— The same poison puts an end to both. And in vain does she flatter herself that her guilt is concealed, or that the law exists to punish it. The laws of nature are never violated with impunity; and in the cases alluded to, the criminal is made at once to feel the horrors of late remorse. . . .

But suppose that a miscarriage brought about by such deplorable means did not endanger the health and life of the mother;

suppose that an act held in such abhorrence, both by earth and heaven, could possibly escape punishment; suppose a woman deaf to the cries of nature, incapable of tender emotions, and fearless of the immediate sufferings in her own person—I have one argument here to make her stop her murderous hand: perhaps the embryo, which she is not going to destroy, would, if cherished in her womb, and afterwards reared with due attention, prove the sweetest comfort of her future years, and repay all her maternal care with endless gratitude. It may be a daughter to nurse her in her old age, or a son to swell her heart with joy at his honourable and successful career in life. I only wish her to pause for a moment and to consider, that by the wilful extinction of the babe in her womb, all her fairest hopes are extinguished also, and that the present danger is aggravated by the certainty of future despair.

3   The Murders of Three Infants

Maryland Gazette

Infanticide, the deliberate killing of newborn infants, was the most universal method of population control in preindustrial societies. Although infanticide was illegal in colonial America, it was a regular occurrence relative to today's standards, particularly among unmarried or poor women. Indeed, harsher punishments for bastardy (the bearing of children out of wedlock) in the colonial period seem to have had the unintended effect of encouraging infanticide. Although bastardy was easily documented, infanticide was harder to determine because the burden of proof generally favored the offender: a woman could be found guilty only if the deceased infant was proven to have been murdered rather than stillborn. To make it easier to prosecute women for infanticide, many colonies instituted measures to criminalize the unwitnessed burial of bastard infants, an action that served as a telling indicator of its prevalence. The risk that a woman assumed by committing infanticide was great; if she was found guilty, the sentence was death. The following descriptions of infanticide, printed on the same page of a single edition of the Maryland Gazette *in 1761, suggest both*

From the *Maryland Gazette*, February 19, 1761.

the frequency of the crime and the concerns that its practice
engendered in eighteenth-century America.

ONE MORNING LAST MONTH, A young Infant was found Dead in a
Well at *Chester-Town* in *Kent* County. It was drawn up by the
Bucket, and had been there for some Time. It had a String round Its
Neck, was cramm'd into Part of a Stocking, and is suppos'd to have
been tied to a Pair of Pot-Hooks which was found at the Bottom, to
sink it. The suppos'd Mother is taken up and committed to Prison
there.

Last Week a Woman in *Baltimore* County, who had lived near
Deer-Creek, was committed to Prison at *Joppa* for the Murder of a
Bastard Child. She was often tax'd with being with Child, but al-
ways denied it; and at the Time of her Travail, went to the Creek
Side, and was Delivered by herself, and flung the Child in. A few
Days after, the dead Child being found by the Children of the House,
and she being charg'd, confess'd the Fact.

And on Tuesday Afternoon last, a Dead Female Child was found
floating in a Pond in this Town, sew'd up in a Linen Bag, supposed
to have been not above 4 or 5 Days since the Birth. . . . The Mother
(if Wretches of her Stamp may be call'd by that Appellation) is not
yet discovered; but it is hop'd she will soon, now being the proper
Time for Examination not only that the Guilty may suffer, but that
the Innocent and Virtuous may be cleared from the malicious Whis-
pers and Aspersions of the Ill-minded and Censorious.

4   *Commonwealth v. Luceba Parker* (1845)

Until the early nineteenth century, in deference to common law
rights, abortion prior to quickening was legal across the coun-
try. Quickening referred to the time, usually in the fourth or
fifth month of pregnancy, when a woman first felt the fetus move.
In an age when do-it-yourself pregnancy tests were still centu-
ries away, contemporaries believed that fetal movement sup-
plied the only incontrovertible proof of pregnancy. A missed
menstrual period was not regarded as an automatic indication
that conception had taken place; it could also be, contempo-
raries thought, a symptom of a dangerous medical disorder

From *Commonwealth v. Luceba Parker* 50 Mass. 263 (1845).

—an unnatural blockage or obstruction that, left unattended, might jeopardize a woman's health. Accordingly, efforts to remove blockages and restore "natural menses" before quickening (even if such a blockage was later discovered to be a pregnancy) were legal. In addition, because contemporaries regarded quickening as the point at which the fetus acquired life, actions taken to restore menstruation before quickening did not violate moral codes.

Although in 1803 the British Parliament rejected common law abortion rights by criminalizing abortion prior to quickening, courts in the United States continued to uphold the quickening doctrine. In an 1812 court decision that provided the legal framework for abortions in the antebellum period, Commonwealth v. Isaiah Bangs, *the Massachusetts Supreme Court declared legal the termination of pregnancies before quickening. This ruling was affirmed thirty-three years later in* Commonwealth v. Luceba Parker.

T HE INDICTMENT AGAINST THE DEFENDANT contained three counts. The first alleged that the defendant, at Boston, on the 6th of June 1843, unlawfully, knowingly and inhumanly, did force and thrust a sharp metallic instrument into the womb and body of a married woman, [named,] she, the said married woman, "being then and there pregnant with child, with a wicked and unlawful intent, of her the said Luceba, then and there to cause and procure the said" married woman "to miscarry, and prematurely bring forth the said child, with which she was then and there pregnant, as aforesaid, and that she, the said" married woman, "at said Boston, on the thirteenth day of the same month of June, by means of the said forcing and thrusting of said instrument into the womb and body of the said" married woman, "in manner aforesaid, did bring forth the said child, of which she was so pregnant, dead."

The second count was like the first, except in the name of the married woman therein mentioned, and the time of the alleged offence. The third count was like the first and second, except that the offence was charged to have been committed, at another time, on another married woman, who was alleged to have been "quick and pregnant.". . .

SHAW [Chief Justice]. Without stating particularly the formal grounds of the motions in arrest of judgment and for a new trial, it is sufficient to say that they resolve themselves into one question, namely, whether it is an indictable offence, at common law, to administer a drug, or perform an operation upon a pregnant woman, with her consent, with the intention and for the purpose of causing an abortion and premature birth of the foetus of which she is pregnant, by means of which an abortion is in fact caused, without averring and proving that, at the time of the administration of such drug, or the performance of such operation, such woman was quick with child. The instruction of the judge, at the trial, was, that it was not necessary to aver, or, if averred, to prove, this fact; and if this instruction was incorrect, a new trial ought to be awarded.

We must take care not to confound this case with some others, which resemble it in fact, but fall within another principle. The use of violence upon a woman, with an intent to procure her miscarriage, without her consent, is an assault highly aggravated by such wicked purpose, and would be indictable at common law. So where, upon a similar attempt by drugs or instruments, the death of the mother ensues, the party making such an attempt, with or without the consent of the woman, is guilty of the murder of the mother, on the ground that it is an act done without lawful purpose, dangerous to life, and that the consent of the woman cannot take away the imputation of malice, any more than in case of a duel, where, in like manner, there is the consent of the parties.

The case of *Commonwealth v. Bangs*, 9 Mass. 387, is relied on, as a direct authority for the defendant. It is insisted upon, however, on the part of the prosecution, that that part of the opinion, which states that it must be averred and proved that the woman was quick with child, was . . . not necessary to the decision.

The report is very short; and as no reasons are assigned, we cannot certainly infer whether the decision was placed upon that ground. The motion in arrest of judgment was upon two grounds; *first*, that no abortion, in fact, was produced; and *second*, that it was not alleged that the woman was quick with child; and the judgment was arrested, apparently, on both grounds. We are therefore inclined to consider it as an adjudication of the point now raised.

And the court are of opinion that, at common law, no indictment will lie, for attempts to procure abortion with the consent of the mother, until she is quick with child. It was only considered by the ancient common law that the child had a separate and independent existence, when the embryo had advanced to that degree of maturity designated by the terms "quick with child.". . . And the ancient authorities, which speak of this crime as an offence at common law, speak of a case where the woman is quick with child. In 3 Inst. 50, Lord Coke says, "if a woman be quick with child, and, by a potion or otherwise, killeth it in her womb, or if a man beat her, whereby the child dieth in her body, and she is delivered of a dead child, this is a great misprision, and no murder.". . .

This distinction, between a woman being pregnant and being quick with child, whatever may be the physical theory upon which it was originally founded, is well known and recognized in the law. "Life," says [the English jurist William] Blackstone, "begins, in contemplation of law, as soon as an infant is able to stir in the mother's womb." This distinction is strongly marked in *St.* 43 Geo. 3, *c.* 58, known as Lord Ellenborough's act; the first section of which declares it a capital offence to administer a drug to cause the miscarriage of any woman then being quick with child. And the same statute has another provision, declaring the same act, to procure the miscarriage of a woman not being quick with child, a felony of a mitigated character.

In the case of *Rex v. Phillips*, 3 Campb. 73, which was an indictment on this statute, it was held by that learned judge, Mr. Justice Lawrence, that, in the construction of this statute, the words "quick with child" must be taken to be according to the common understanding, which was proved to be this; that a woman is not considered to be quick with child, till she has herself felt the child alive and quick within her. It is not necessary, however, to decide, in the present case, what degree of advancement in a state of gestation would justify the application of this description to a pregnant woman; because, in this case, it was not alleged, and the court ruled that it was not necessary to prove, that she was quick with child. . . .

The indictment contains several counts, and they all charge an assault upon the woman; and there is no intimation that the applications were made with her consent, but the conclusion, from the averments, is otherwise. It is then the case of an assault at common law, with aggravations. But what is more material is, that, although the woman was not alleged to be quick with child, yet it is averred that she was pregnant and big with child, and that the act was done by the defendant wilfully, and with intent feloniously, wilfully, and of his malice aforethought, to kill and murder the child with which she was so big and pregnant. And in other counts, it is laid that drugs were administered to her, she being pregnant with another child, and with intent to cause and procure her to miscarry and bring forth said child dead, &c. The whole proceeds on the averment, that she was then pregnant with a child, then so far advanced as to be regarded in law as having a separate existence, a life capable of being destroyed; which is equivalent to the averment that she was quick with child.

There being no averment, in the first count in this indictment, that the woman was quick with child, or any equivalent averment, and the judge, who tried the case, having instructed the jury that it was not necessary to prove such averment in the third count, the court are all of opinion that, although the acts set forth are, in a high degree, offensive to good morals and injurious to society, yet they are not punishable at common law, and that this indictment cannot be sustained.

II

The Medicalization
of Reproduction

5   "Science" Enters the Birthing Room: Obstetrics in America since the Eighteenth Century

Judith Walzer Leavitt

Childbirth as a hospital- and physician-based experience is of relatively recent origin. As late as 1900 less than 5 percent of women had given birth in hospitals, and only about one-half of all children had been delivered by physicians. In early America, birthing was principally a group female activity: delivery took place at home in the company of female friends, kin, and midwives. In the post-1750 period, coincident with the rise of formal medical training and the gradual professionalization of medicine, educated male physicians (first family doctors, then obstetrical specialists) began to claim a larger role in birthing middle-class women. The medicalization of childbirth spawned fundamental shifts in how and where birthing occurred, who participated in the process, and cultural perceptions of pregnancy and labor. Judith Walzer Leavitt, a historian at the University of Wisconsin at Madison, explores the transition from social to scientific childbirth and its impact on women.

A T THE END OF THE eighteenth century, Dr. William Shippen, Jr., of Philadelphia attended all the childbearing women in the well-established Drinker family. The family members chose Shippen instead of a woman midwife, in spite of their ambivalence about having a man in the traditionally all-female birthing room, because they believed the physician offered the best hope for a successful outcome. The Drinkers, and many others like them, considered themselves fortunate to be living at a time when male physicians began replacing female midwives in the birthing rooms of the American urban elite. The families expected—and believed that they received—better care at the hands of physicians than they thought possible with traditional female attendants.[1] . . .

From Judith Walzer Leavitt, " 'Science' Enters the Birthing Room: Obstetrics in America since the Eighteenth Century," *Journal of American History* 70 (September 1983): 281–304. Figure omitted. Reprinted by permission of the *Journal of American History*.

Before 1760 birth was a women's affair in the British colonies of North America. When a woman went into labor, she "called her women together" and left her husband and other male family members outside. "I went to bed about 10 o'clock," wrote William Byrd of Virginia, "and left the women full of expectation with my wife." Only in cases where women were not available did men participate in labor and delivery, and only in cases where labor did not progress normally did physicians intervene and perhaps extricate a dead fetus. The midwife orchestrated the events of labor and delivery, and the women neighbors and relatives comforted and shared advice with the parturient.[2] Women suffered through the agonies and dangers of birth together, sought each other's support, and shared the relief of successful deliveries and the grief of unsuccessful ones. This "social childbirth" experience united women and provided, as Carroll Smith-Rosenberg has argued, one of the functional bonds that formed the basis of women's domestic culture.[3]

Within their own homes, birthing women controlled much of the experience of childbirth. They determined the physical setting for their births, the people to attend them during labor and delivery, and the aids or comforts employed. Midwives traditionally played a noninterventionist, supportive role in the home birthing rooms. As much as possible they let nature take its course: they examined the cervix or encouraged women to walk around; they caught the child, tied the umbilical cord, and if necessary fetched the placenta. In complicated cases, midwives might have turned the fetus—podalic version—or fortified women with hard liquor or mulled wine. They may have manually stretched the cervix or, rarely, administered ergot. Midwives spent most of their time, as the written record reveals, comforting the parturient and waiting. The other women attendants supported the midwife and the birthing woman, and the atmosphere in the birthing rooms—if everything proceeded normally—was congenial and cooperative. Parturient women, who felt vulnerable at the time of their confinements, armed themselves with the strength of other women who had passed through the event successfully.[4]

Despite the very positive aspects of social childbirth, a romantic image of childbirth in this period would be misleading. Women garnered support from their networks of companions, but they continued to fear their births because of the possibilities of death or debility that could and frequently did result from childbirth. Although statistics do not exist to measure these dangers precisely, women's fears were not unfounded. By all accounts maternal and infant mortality rates were high. Furthermore, postpartum gynecological problems resulting from unsutured perineal tears, prolapsed uteri, or vesico-vaginal and recto-vaginal fistulas caused some women extreme discomfort and disability throughout the rest of their lives. Women's fears of death and physical debility led them away from traditional birthing patterns to a long search for safer and less painful childbirths. Thus some women, especially those who were economically advantaged, tried to modify traditional births by incorporating new possibilities as they became available. Like the Drinkers, these eighteenth-century women readily invited physicians to attend them, despite their worries about the propriety of having men participate in intimate female events, in hopes that the "man-midwives" could provide easier and safer births.[5]

The entrance of physician-accoucheurs into the practice of obstetrics in America during the second half of the eighteenth century marked the first significant break with tradition. The story of this new midwifery, familiar to historians of American medicine, centers on Shippen, who in 1762 returned from his studies in London and Edinburgh and established the first systematic series of lectures on midwifery in America. Shippen initially trained both female midwives and male physicians in anatomy (including the gravid uterus), but he soon limited his lectures to male students. He established a private practice of midwifery and became a favorite of Philadelphia's established families. The Drinkers found him "very kind and attentive" during labor and delivery and noted that he remained with his patients even during protracted labors and "sleep't very little."[6]

Shippen was the most famous of late eighteenth-century physicians who practiced midwifery, but he was not alone. Numerous doctors expanded their practice of medicine and began to attend laboring women. The transition to male attendants occurred so easily among advantaged urban women that it can only be explained by understanding the women's impression that physicians knew more than midwives about the birth process and about what to do if things went wrong. Women overturned millennia of all-female tradition and invited men into their birthing rooms because they believed that men offered additional security against the potential dangers of childbirth. By their acknowledgment of physician superiority, women changed the fashions of childbearing and made it desirable to be attended by physicians.[7]

Women had good reason to believe that physicians could provide services that midwives could not. Many of the physicians who
practiced obstetrics at the turn of the nineteenth century had trained
in Great Britain, where a tradition of male accoucheurs had already
developed. The men had access to education then denied to women,
which provided theoretical understanding of female anatomy and
the process of parturition. Whereas women midwives relied on practical experience and an appeal to female traditions—attributes to
some extent taken for granted and unappreciated—men physicians
had the extra advantage and prestige associated with formal learning. Even though most American practitioners had not attended
medical school and were themselves apprentice trained, physicians
carried with them the status advantages of their gender and of the
popular image of superior education. Furthermore, birthing women
perceived that the male presence had already contributed opium
and forceps to obstetrics and promised even greater benefits in the
future. The appeal to overturn tradition was strong.[8]

When Shippen attended Sally Drinker Downing's 1795 birth,
which was complicated by a footling presentation, he administered
opium to relieve her suffering. Two years later, faced with another
of Downing's difficult labors, Shippen "was oblig'd to force her
mouth open to give some thing with a view of reviving her." In
1799, Downing again suffered a protracted labor, and Shippen took
fourteen ounces of blood and then gave her eighty to ninety drops
of liquid laudanum. According to Downing's mother, when labor
still did not progress, Shippen gave "an Opium pill three grains he
said, in order to ease her pain, or to bring it on more violently."
When this still did not produce the desired result, Shippen threatened to use his instruments, but finally Downing delivered without
them.[9]

Shippen's practice of allaying painful and lengthy labors by
bleeding, giving opium, and occasionally using forceps illustrates
why women wanted physicians to attend them. The prospect of a
difficult birth, which all women fearfully anticipated, and the knowledge that physicians' remedies could provide relief and successful
outcomes led women to seek out practitioners whose obstetric
armamentarium included drugs and instruments.[10]

The promise of the new obstetrics developed in part through
formal physician education in midwifery. Shippen's first lectures
covered pelvic anatomy, the gravid uterus, the placenta, fetal circulation and nutrition, natural and unnatural labor, and the use of

obstetrical instruments. He demonstrated on manikins and on patients—poor women for whom he provided accommodation—and
used drawings and textbooks. Other physicians followed his example, and courses in midwifery became available in Boston and
New York as well as in Philadelphia.[11]

During the first half of the nineteenth century medical education in obstetrics expanded. To many professors and students, the
subject was embarrassing, and students generally did not observe
women in labor but received only a theoretical education. Samuel D. Gross, a student who observed Thomas Chalkley James
teaching obstetrics at the University of Pennsylvania early in the
nineteenth century, noticed that "it was seldom that he . . . looked
squarely at his audience. His cheeks would be mantled with blushes
while engaging in demonstrating some pelvic viscus, or discussing
topics not mentionable in ordinary conversation. It was often painful to witness his embarrassment."[12]

Although the embarrassment of physicians about their role in
obstetrics soon disappeared, the question of a man's proper behavior in a woman's birthing room continued to influence the teaching
and the practice of obstetrics. Of William Potts Dewees, who succeeded James at the University of Pennsylvania, Gross observed,
"he did not hesitate to call things by their proper names. No
blush suffused his cheek in the lecture-room." But Dewees, whose
A Compendious System of Midwifery went through an influential
twelve editions, remained as horrified by the idea of ocular inspection as his most modest patients. Using manikins, he taught his
students how to perform unsighted digital explorations of parturient women. Even when applying forceps, Dewees taught, "every
attention should be paid to delicacy . . . the patient should not be
exposed . . . even for the drawing off of the urine. . . . The operator
must become familiar with the introduction of the instruments without the aid of sight."[13]

Students graduating from such didactic obstetrics courses were
forced to enter the birthing rooms of their patients in relative ignorance. Never having witnessed actual births, and armed with only
theoretical knowledge, they must have been somewhat apprehensive. Yet doctors knew that they had to be confident to gain confidence, and they forged ahead and delivered babies. One medical
graduate wrote that when he delivered his first baby he examined
the laboring woman, "but whether it was head or breech, hand or
foot, man or monkey, that was defended from my uninstructed

finger by the distended membranes, I was as uncomfortably ignorant, with all my learning, as the foetus itself that was making all
this fuss."[14] Rejecting the practical experience of the midwives'
training, those physicians who had formal medical education tried
to raise the practice of obstetrics to a higher level by emphasizing
anatomy and physiology.

Through their theoretical training, this physician elite had the
potential to expand the practice of obstetrics beyond individual
experience. Apprentice-trained midwives and physicians could develop expertise only insofar as their mentors' or their own experiences took them, and wider perspectives remained elusive. But when
some doctors took it upon themselves to study anatomy of the female pelvis and activity of the gravid uterus, they removed knowledge from its anchor in individual human experience and brought
it to a more abstract level. Learning what was possible and probable in labor and delivery, what was normal and abnormal, provided these birth attendants with knowledge to make judgments on
the individual cases they examined.

While the potential for this increased enlightenment may have
existed, the question remains whether or not individual medical
graduates related their theoretical knowledge to the actual cases
they faced in their practices. Did male physicians enhance or improve childbirth, as women believed they would? Did "science,"
the symbol of the promises of physician-directed obstetrics, come
to the aid of birthing women?

Either because of their training or because of families' expectations, male physicians, the apprentice trained and medical school
graduates alike, intervened in the birth process more than midwives.
Walter Channing, professor of obstetrics at Harvard, advised that a
doctor, when called to attend laboring women, "must do something.
He cannot remain a spectator merely, where there are many witnesses, and where interest in what is going on is too deep to allow
of his inaction. Let him be collected and calm, and he will probably do little he will afterwards look upon with regret."[15]

Physicians' favorite interventions during the first half of the
nineteenth century were bloodletting, drugs, and forceps, frequently
all used together. Dewees advocated substantial bloodletting. In one
of his difficult cases, for example, with the woman standing on her
feet, he took "upwards of two quarts" until she fainted. Dewees
remarked that "every thing appeared better. . . . I introduced the

forceps, and delivered a living and healthy child." Physicians believed that venesection could relieve pain, accelerate labor, soften a rigid cervix, ease podalic version, and reduce inflammation. They even bled patients who were hemorrhaging, using the logic that further reducing circulation would produce blood clotting and stop the hemorrhage. They also relieved puerperal convulsions by bloodletting. In fact, as one historian has concluded, "bloodletting . . . was uncritically accepted as the fashion in early American obstetric practice."[16]

The use of opium or laudanum (tincture of opium) seems to have been equally popular among physician-accoucheurs in the nineteenth century. In cases of protracted labor, as in the Shippen-Downing cases cited above, physicians tried opium to accelerate cervical dilation and ease suffering. They also employed cathartics to open the bowels, ergot to stimulate contractions, tobacco infusions to encourage the cervix to dilate, and manually breaking the waters to accelerate labor. In cases of extreme need physicians could surgically separate the pubic bones to facilitate passage of the fetus's head or they could introduce the crochet, the instrument used for fetal dismemberment and extraction.[17]

The forceps constituted the favorite instrument of physician intervention, and women both feared and respected the "hands of iron." When Shippen referred obliquely to forceps in front of Sally Downing's mother, she "was afraid to ask him, lest he should answer in the affirmative" that he needed to use it. Her confidence in its benefits, however, remained intact. Women were grateful for the tool that could extricate a fetus in compacted labors.[18] . . .

When well used, forceps could save lives; when misused, they could increase women's perineal lacerations and cause head injuries to the fetus. Dewees called attention to the "mischief" that forceps could cause and believed that their dangers were enhanced because physicians used them too often and unnecessarily. He cautioned: "The greatest care must be taken, before we begin our traction, that no portion of the mother is included in the locking of the blades—this must be done by passing a finger entirely round the place of union. . . . I was once called to a poor woman who had had a considerable portion of the internal face of the right labium removed, by having been included in the joint of the short forceps."[19] Physicians who had been trained to use forceps only on manikins and who were required by custom to perform the forceps operation without the benefit of sight ran considerable risk of creating new problems for the women whose obstructed labors they tried to ameliorate.

Countless stories testify to the severe lacerations nineteenth-century women suffered in childbirth, and they suggest an increase in the problem over what women had previously experienced. The accusation of "meddlesome midwifery" followed physician-accoucheurs, and textbooks cautioned against forceps misuse often enough to suggest that a significant problem existed. The midwifery professors repeatedly warned against unnecessary use of forceps. But their students or apprentice-trained physicians in practice in America's communities found forceps a very valuable tool, and because of their eagerness or their limited practical experience, they may have overused and misused them. Dewees observed so many cases of misused forceps that he concluded: "The forceps . . . are nearly as fatal as the crochet itself."[20]

If forceps were at fault in the "meddlesome midwifery" of the early nineteenth century, they were not the only problem. Almost any intervention by the physician created a potential for harm. If a birth could not proceed without help, the physician provided a service not available elsewhere and necessary to saving lives. If, however, as was statistically more probable, labor was proceeding normally and physicians intervened anyway, their actions introduced dangers not otherwise present. Dewees's caution about careful use of forceps inadvertently informs us about the concurrent dangers of infection. He taught his students to check that no part of the mother was caught in the blades of the forceps by "passing a finger entirely round the place of union." An unwashed and ungloved finger could have carried a higher risk to women's lives than a perineal laceration. . . .

Physicians' obstetrics courses taught them the theoretical basis of their craft, their apprenticeships gave them tools with which to effect a successful birth, but nowhere did they receive clear guidelines for the practical application of their knowledge. Doctors had numerous techniques at their command and complete leeway in their use. If physicians used forceps too often, or if they intervened in the birth process too eagerly, it was because they were more persuaded by the faces of women in agony than by the cautions of their elders. Their decisions about intervention were made on the spot and in relative isolation. Even the professors at the medical schools and the leading textbooks taught by anecdotal example, making generalizations hard if not impossible to construct. Physicians could convince themselves easily and in good conscience that their judgment to intervene in labor was in the best interests of the patient. The majority of successful outcomes in each individual's practice underlined the truthfulness of these conclusions. Early obstetric "science" provided knowledge and wherewithal, but the principles of the practical application remained at the bedside in the hands of individual, isolated doctors.[21]. . .

The decision of whether or not to employ the skills of the physician remained with women, where it had traditionally been. The parturient, her midwife, and her assistants frequently decided to call a doctor after labor had begun and then gave or withheld permission for each procedure suggested. Dewees, for example, after one successful forceps operation, was called to other cases because "the influence of this case upon many of the midwives of this city, procured me many opportunities of applying the forceps." Similarly, the young Pennsylvania doctor's success in delivering babies using forceps led women to refuse to let other doctors use the crochet. Although physicians had broken the gender barrier and birth was no longer exclusively a woman's event, women continued to hold the power to shape events in the birthing room.[22]

Despite the strength of tradition, however, birth had changed for the women who invited physicians to attend them in their homes. These women formed a minority of all birthing women, and they probably were limited geographically to the major cities and economically to the advantaged classes. Most Americans still could not afford doctors and employed midwives and delivered their babies in the same ways as their mothers and grandmothers had. But for those women who chose physicians instead of or in addition to midwives, birth became less a natural process and more an event that could be altered and influenced by a wide selection of interventions. Women and physicians realized that fate no longer held women in such a tight grip and that decisions could be made and actions could be taken that would determine what kind of a birth a woman would have and perhaps whether she and her baby lived or died. This mental perception of the ability to shape the birth experience became even more important in the second half of the nineteenth century when anesthesia emerged as the paramount birthing panacea.

Fanny Longfellow's exuberant description of her childbirth under ether in 1847 (the first in the United States) indicates just how ready women were to change their childbirth experiences. "I never was better or got through a confinement so comfortably," she wrote her sister-in-law. "I feel proud to be the pioneer to less suffering for poor, weak womankind. This is certainly the greatest blessing of this age, and I am glad to have lived at the time of its coming and in the country which gives it to the world."[23] By the middle of the century middle-class women had become accustomed to male birth attendants, although a large segment of the population—probably growing as immigration soared in the latter part of the century—remained faithful to female midwives and traditional birth procedures. Advantaged urban women sought every obstetric improvement that male physicians could offer because they continued to fear childbirth and its attendant discomforts. As one woman wrote about her fourth birth in 1885, "Between the oceans of pain, there stretched continents of fear; fear of death and dread of suffering beyond bearing."[24]

Women who experienced their childbirths as the hour in which they "touched the hand of death" eagerly sought relief from the frightful event. Ether and chloroform promised such relief, and women like Longfellow embraced anesthesia enthusiastically. One of Channing's patients told him after her etherized birth "how wonderful it was that she should have got through without the least suffering, and how grateful she was."[25]

Women, in fact, were initially more eager than physicians to use anesthesia. Among physicians, there was some uncertainty about the safety of the new drugs for midwifery practice. Charles D. Meigs of Philadelphia rejected chloroform and ether and carried on a well-published campaign against their use, claiming that he had "not yielded to several solicitations as to its exhibition addressed to me by my patients in labour." Meigs relied upon women's painful contractions to help him determine labor's progress and believed that their inhibition would make him a less effective birth attendant.[26]

Walter Channing, one of ether's most ardent supporters, in 1848 surveyed forty-six Boston-area physicians' use of anesthesia in labor and found that they held back on using the drugs except in cases when "patients have demanded it with an emphasis which could not be resisted . . . in many cases, and in the practice of some physicians, it has only been used when such demand has been made."[27] A. R. Thompson of Charlestown, Massachusetts, wrote Channing the following account, which was not unusual. "This lady had informed herself fully as to the use of ether, and had made up her mind to take it. . . . When called to her, I frankly told her that I had never used the ether, nor had I ever seen it used in any case, but that I had no prejudice against it, and would consent to its administration in her case . . . she was resolute, and demanded the ether. . . . I poured an ounce of ether into the sponge, and the lady held it to her mouth and nose." A successful outcome and a happy patient convinced this doctor to use the drug in subsequent cases. After his second trial of ether, Thompson concluded confidently, "My conviction at the time was strong, that the ether had greatly diminished the sufferings of the mother, and shortened the term of her travail for many hours."[28]. . .

Many physicians felt pressed, if their time was limited and other patients were waiting, to use forceps, anesthesia, or both to direct labor into patterns under their control. This inclination was reinforced by women eagerly seeking relief from their suffering. A Colorado physician related that after several hours of hard labor one of his patients "implored me to do something, and, with many misgivings, at last I decided to use instruments [and] chloroform."[29]

Physicians came to adopt anesthesia so generally that one physician in 1895 observed that "the profession has come to regard the use of chloroform in parturition as almost utterly devoid of danger," so that "chloroform is given in labor often recklessly, carelessly, and copiously." As physicians delivered the babies, other attendants—"ignorant nurses, husbands, bystanders, and even . . . the patients themselves"—dripped chloroform or ether onto a sponge or cloth and held it to the woman's nose. No standard procedures guarded physicians' drug dosages.[30]

Physicians' reports of their obstetric practices in the second half of the nineteenth century indicate that use of anesthesia did not necessarily lead to increased forceps use. While doctors did come to use anesthesia routinely in forceps deliveries, the reverse was not true. Physicians did not use forceps routinely on patients to whom they gave ether and chloroform. Physicians employed forceps in approximately 8 percent of their births, whereas some used anesthesia at almost every birth they attended, and on the average about 50 percent of all physician-attended births utilized chloroform or ether.[31] Thus, despite the haphazard use of open-drop ether or chloroform and the consequent potential for overdosing, actual anesthesia use must have remained light. Profound anesthesia would have caused labor to decelerate and would have made forceps necessary to lift the baby that the woman was unable to push out. But with light analgesia physicians did not require forceps, and in the nineteenth century forceps abuse did not increase as a result of increased use of anesthetics. Physicians aimed at pain relief, not total unconsciousness. If a woman administered her own drugs on a handkerchief she held up to her nose, her arm would periodically drop away, decreasing the drug dose. One physician advised maintaining what he called a "dreamy sleep, in which the patient follows in her imagination the direction of the physician." While labor progressed, he conversed with his patients about scenes from their childhood or the Sunday school picnic. One of his patients "almost immediately after the first inhalation burst out in a beautiful song, and continued singing one after another until her babe, a large boy, first child, was born."[32]

Most physicians continued to intervene in the birth process in the second half of the nineteenth century as they had earlier. Their safety record when measured by mortality matched the record of midwives, who continued to follow a basically noninterventionist birth policy. Dorothy Reed Mendenhall studied births in Wisconsin at the beginning of the twentieth century and concluded that for both physicians and midwives maternal mortality was higher than it needed to be but that "we must admit that the midwife is, on the whole, probably less culpable in regard to the deaths of parturient women than physicians in the state."[33] Similar maternal mortality rates for midwife- and physician-attended births indicate that physicians, with all their expertise and intervention techniques, did not, as they had promised, enhance the safety of the birth experience for women. Medicine may have improved comfort levels and may have rescued some women from complicated labors, but it did not, on the whole, increase women's chances of survival.

There are other indications that physicians' techniques created new problems for birthing women and actually increased the dangers of childbirth. Inappropriate forceps use and the careless administration of ether and chloroform introduced serious lacerations and breathing disorders that otherwise might not have developed. Most significant, physicians carried puerperal fever, which was potentially disastrous, to birthing women. Because their medical practices included attending patients with communicable diseases, doctors were more likely than midwives to bring with them on their hands and on their clothing the agents of infection. Epidemics of puerperal fever developed even in the practices of physicians like H. H. Whitcomb of Norristown, Pennsylvania, who did "as little meddling as possible" in normal labor and delivery. In 1886 one of Whitcomb's parturient patients developed fever because Whitcomb brought the infection from a previous patient who had scarlet fever. That winter and spring Whitcomb transmitted the fever to thirty-two more birthing women.[34]

Physicians offered some women relief from suffering and aided others through compacted labors, but because of the variations in ability and practices of their birth attendants, most women continued to experience discomfort and to fear childbirth. One woman described her physician-attended delivery as "hell. . . . It bursts your brain, and tears out your heart, and crushes your nerves to bits. It's just hell."[35] Despite their continued suffering, those middle-class women who had chosen physicians to attend them did not want to return to midwives. They believed that if birth were to be eased, improvements would come from progress in medicine. Instead of turning to tradition, these women demanded more of their physicians and continued to hope that safe and comfortable deliveries would come to them from the medical world.

As the symbol of what science had to offer, anesthesia enhanced the place and role of physicians in birthing rooms across America. Women who could afford physicians and their new panacea demanded the advantages of painlessness. Despite the presence of men and modern technology in the birthing rooms, however, the birth experience of nineteenth-century middle- and upper-class women retained many important elements from traditional births. Anita McCormick Blaine's first childbirth in 1890 illustrates this. During her pregnancy Blaine corresponded with her mother, who was in Europe seeking a cure for a hearing loss, and sought the traditional female support network to help her through the impending crisis. "If you could but be with me now, what wouldn't I give," wrote Blaine to her mother, Nettie Fowler McCormick. Despite all of Blaine's preparations and the doctor and nurse who would attend her, McCormick yearned to be with her daughter. She wrote detailed instructions about her care, advising, for example, rubbing olive oil over the abdomen and perineal area to ease delivery. She worried that only a mother could rightfully do such an intimate job. "I don't know if you have a person you could let do it," she wrote, "but I wish I were there to do it." Blaine sequestered herself in her childhood Chicago home, where "every chair and table speaks to me of dear familiar times . . . nothing is so sweet as to feel the presence of all it reminds me of." She surrounded herself with helpers, including her old friend Harriot ("Missy") Hammond, who traveled from Virginia to be with her. Strengthened by these traditional comforts, Anita delivered her baby while under the influence of chloroform, supported by her nurse and by Hammond and attended by a male physician. Her husband waited outside. She united the old and the new in obstetric experiences and planned the whole event to meet her expectations. The doctor managed the birth in the context that the woman created.[36]

The decision-making process in the turn-of-the-century birthing rooms reveals how the old and the new intermingled. Doctors, who may have had only minimal practical experience, were invited to attend women in their own homes in the presence of other women, many of whom had had considerable birth experience and had developed strong opinions about birth procedures. Within the birthing rooms, these attendants negotiated. There were desires and expectations on both sides. Women retained a lot of power in their own homes, and physicians bowed to it or risked damaging their reputations among a whole community of women and losing patients. As the new obstetrical techniques—from forceps to anesthetics—became available, they worked to the advantage of physicians, who held the monopoly over their use, while centuries of female traditions and the domestic environment in which they operated worked to the advantage of women. . . .

Women invited physicians to attend them in order to benefit from their expertise and technology, yet doctors could not obtain patients' compliance with all procedures. An Oklahoma physician explained why he could never try to shave a patient's pubic hair even though it would help prevent infection. "In about three seconds after the doctor has made the first rake with his safety [razor], he will find himself on his back out in the yard with the imprint of a woman's bare foot emblazoned on his manly chest, the window sash round his neck and a revolving vision of all the stars in the firmament presented to him. Tell him not to try to shave 'em."[37] Another practitioner realized that a doctor "has his living to make and cannot be too insistent with his patient over whom, usually, he has no control." Yet physicians could not come into the birthing room and do nothing. One Kansas doctor admitted, "Perhaps the best way to manage normal labor is to let it alone, but you cannot hold down a job and do that." Women and physicians negotiated the procedures that would be used, and the result represented a compromise between the two worlds of women's tradition and men's medicine. The compromises held until the twentieth century, when physician-directed obstetrics finally became master of the birthing room.[38]

At the turn of the twentieth century, physicians delivered approximately half of the nation's babies. Most of these births took place in the woman's home and combined aspects of traditional and modern techniques. Although most of the medical profession accepted the need for aseptic conditions—sterile gloves, shaved perineum, antiseptic infusions, sterile instruments—they could not always achieve them. Whether because of their own abilities or their patients' demands, physicians intermingled modern surgical techniques with wide individual variations and traditional practices. . . . Physician practice—susceptible to the physical environment, to the opinions of other attendants, and to the physician's own training and inclination—varied from individual to individual. Physicians acted when they were called to women in labor, but the nature of their interventions followed particular circumstances more than any predetermined science of obstetrics.

The lack of a systematic approach to the practice of obstetrics in the early twentieth century can be directly traced to the quality and emphasis of obstetric education, which had not changed substantially during the nineteenth century. After the middle of the nineteenth century, "demonstrative midwifery," or teaching students by having them observe actual laboring women, became available, but many medical schools ignored this innovation and continued their didactic teaching from textbooks and manikins. In 1910, although most practitioners now received a formal medical education, many still graduated having witnessed few or no live deliveries. Such training at best prepared students to understand birth pathology and perhaps how to intervene to rescue a woman in trouble, but it did not prepare physicians to attend women in normal labor.[39] . . .

Even as a significant portion of American women continued to be attended by midwives in their own homes, and most others continued to invite general practitioners to attend them at home, increasing numbers of women from the middle and upper classes became convinced that childbirth in the hospital offered them the safest experience. Many factors converged to encourage women to move to the hospital in the early years of the twentieth century, including the new anesthetic agent scopolamine (best monitored in the hospital), the preference of the specialists, the growth of the hospitals themselves, and the increasing technology and ease of management in the well-equipped and well-staffed hospital setting. Still seeking more comfortable births and safer deliveries with minimal negative aftereffects, many women decided to try the newest that obstetrics had to offer and go to the hospital to be attended by specialists. "I have placed myself in the hands of . . . a specialist in obstetrics," wrote Lella Secor to her mother in 1918. "I have every confidence in him, and it is a great relief."[40]

In hospital deliveries women left their family and friends at the door of the labor room and faced their birthings alone, as one account of birth in the 1930s indicated:

> Arriving [at the hospital], she is immediately given the benefit of one of the modern analgesics or pain-killers. Soon she is in a dreamy, half-conscious state. . . .
> She knows nothing about being taken to a spotlessly clean delivery room, placed on a sterile table, draped with sterile sheets; neither does she see her attendants, the doctor and nurses, garbed for her protection in sterile white gowns and gloves; nor the shiny boiled instruments and antiseptic solutions. She does not hear the cry of her baby when first he feels the chill of this cold world, or see the care with which the doctor repairs such lacerations as may have occurred. . . . Finally she awakes in smiles, a mother with no recollection of having become one.[41]

This woman was separated from the people she loved, she was in an unfamiliar environment controlled by others, and she was unconscious during her childbirth. Women did not view the stay in the hospital as a time when they lost important parts of the traditional birth experiences, but rather as a time when they gained protection for life and health, aspects of birth that had been elusive and uncertain in the past. Women gave up some kinds of control for others because on balance the new benefits seemed more important. In seeking life and health, women relinquished consciousness and self-determination.

The hospital appealed to women because it was modern, well equipped, and staffed by experts: it represented the newest medical advance. Also, it physically separated women from their domestic chores and allowed them to relax. One wrote, "My stay in that hospital was like a lovely vacation." "I can't tell you the relief I feel as I walk out my door headed for the hospital to have a baby," wrote another. "I have nothing to worry about . . . and have only to concentrate on giving birth. All this peace of mind, plus expert medical attention, makes me wonder why anybody would consider it a 'privilege' to have her baby at home." Home did not hold for mid-twentieth-century women the same comforts and sustenance that Blaine had found so reassuring. The "hospital is equipped with every modern device for the safe delivery of babies," wrote one mother. "Nursing and medical attention is available at any hour of the day or night. How much simpler—and more restful—to be in a hospital where babies are an accepted business."[42]

The move to the hospital was hastened by specialists' attempts to wrest birth away from general practitioners and to systematize birth procedures within the hospital setting. One very influential move in this direction was made in 1920 by Joseph B. DeLee of Chicago in the first volume of the new journal of specialists, the *American Journal of Obstetrics and Gynecology*. DeLee argued that birth was a "pathologic process" and that "only a small minority of women escape damage during labor." He continued, "So frequent are these bad effects, that I have often wondered whether Nature did not deliberately intend women should be used up in the process of reproduction, in a manner analogous to that of salmon, which dies after spawning." Because of its dangers, DeLee believed birth needed careful monitoring in skilled hands. He recommended reducing birth to predictable patterns by using outlet forceps and episiotomy routinely and prophylactically in normal deliveries. DeLee sedated the parturient with scopolamine, allowed the cervix to dilate, gave ether during the second stage, performed an episiotomy, and lifted the fetus with forceps. He then extracted the placenta, gave ergot to help the uterus contract, and stitched the perineal cut.[43]

DeLee's operation achieved wide acceptance. It represented the new move in the 1920s and 1930s to make obstetrics scientific, systematic, and predictable by putting it under the control of the specialist. Not all specialists wanted to use prophylactic forceps, but hospital-based obstetricians did develop routines for managing childbirth that incorporated systematic use of pain-relieving drugs, labor inducers, and technological intervention. Mothers-to-be learned they could plan when and how they would have a baby, and doctors could predict the course of labor because they controlled it. "The old way [of having a baby] was no fun," wrote one father about the 1916 birth of his first daughter. In 1938 his second daughter "was born the new way—the easy, painless, streamlined way." His wife, in consultation with her doctor, decided which day to deliver, and after a matinee and dinner went into the hospital.

Pituitrin induced her labor, Nembutal and scopolamine deadened her perceptions of it, and the doctor delivered her baby. "Why, I wouldn't mind having another baby next week," she said, "if that's all there is to it."[44] Increasing numbers of middle-class women turned to the hospital and the specialist for their childbirths, believing, as one of them put it, "the vexation of hospital routine shrinks to infinitesimal importance beside the safety of the delivery room."[45]

But was streamlined childbirth safe? Had medicine at last provided safer and more comfortable childbirth for women, as it had promised since the 1760s? Observers in the 1930s realized that while the practice of obstetrics now could relieve women of much of their discomfort, childbirth remained unsafe. Maternal mortality in the 1930s remained "unnecessarily high," according to a group of concerned physicians in New York. The physicians claimed hospital deliveries contributed to the high mortality with a "high incidence of operative interference during labor . . . undertaken when there was no indication or a plain contra-indication." Birth in the hospital encouraged interference because the equipment and staff were readily accessible, and this interference increased the number of maternal deaths. Rather than making childbirth safer, physicians in the 1920s and 1930s, according to their own evaluation, were responsible for maintaining high rates of maternal mortality.[46]

In home deliveries of the nineteenth century, increased anesthetic use had not caused an increase in forceps deliveries, but in hospital deliveries of the early twentieth century, a direct relationship existed between anesthesia and forceps. The New York doctors noted, "The frequent use of instrumentation is based upon the easy accessibility of anaesthesia . . . the increase in the use of anaesthesia is a factor in keeping the maternal mortality rate stationary." According to the New York study, use of anesthetic agents led directly to increased instrumentation because drugged women were less effective in pushing the baby out. Approximately 25 percent of hospital deliveries were operative. "The increase in the use of instrumentation brings with it an increased hazard," the doctors found. "Clearly a reduction of the mortality rate can be achieved through a reduction in operative interference."[47]

During the early 1930s the medical profession publicly confessed the shortcomings of its obstetric practices. Rudolph Wieser Holmes declared at a crowded American Medical Association meeting, "I have seen hundreds of women die on the delivery table because of the wrongful use of drugs." Holmes blamed his own role in accelerating scopolamine use for many of these deaths. The public health commissioner for the state of New York calculated that maternal deaths were actually increasing in the twentieth century and concluded that "they represent the results of meddlesome and unskillful obstetrical practice."[48] Philadelphia doctors agreed that 56 percent of preventable maternal deaths could be blamed on physician errors of judgment and technique.[49] A national study concluded similarly that "artificial delivery is becoming increasingly frequent, especially in hospital practice," and "that interference with normal labor is accompanied by some added risk to both mother and child." Although the indictment was not universally accepted by physicians in the 1930s, the statistics indicated that going to a hospital to have a baby managed by a physician and under the influence of twentieth-century drugs and instruments did not necessarily give a mother an advantage and may have put her in greater jeopardy than her neighbor who stayed home.[50]

Obstetrics by the 1930s had not achieved a record of safety commensurate with its abilities. Aided by the New York Academy of Medicine's 1933 revelations about preventable maternal and infant deaths, however, physicians moved toward regulation and standardization of hospital obstetrics practice in their attempts to decrease the overuse and misuse of drugs and operative procedures. Their success in establishing minimum standards for delivery procedures is evident in the fact that hospital births increased from 35 percent of all births in 1933 to 72 percent ten years later and "for the first time was not associated with higher rates of puerperal death." Other factors converged with hospital regulations to cause the decrease in maternal mortality after 1935. The prenatal-care movement spearheaded by middle-class women succeeded in gaining adherents and in educating the public about the importance of care during pregnancy. Probably most important in the decelerating death rates was the wide adoption of sulfonamides, blood transfusions, and, after World War II, antibiotics, which were successful in combating infection and hemorrhaging, two of the major causes of maternal deaths. After 1935 maternal mortality fell dramatically.[51]

Even though birth became safer in the 1940s and 1950s, women who went to the hospital to deliver their babies—95 percent of American women by 1955—missed some of the features of traditional social childbirth and found hospital births sterile both in the antiseptic sense and in the human dimension. Continuing to appreciate the safety factors they acknowledged to exist for hospital births, women as early as the 1950s attacked the "cruelty in maternity wards." One woman from Elkhart, Indiana, wrote to the *Ladies' Home Journal*, which exposed these conditions: "So many women, especially first mothers, who are frightened to start out with, receive such brutal inconsiderate treatment that the whole thing is a horrible nightmare. They give you drugs, whether you want them or not, strap you down like an animal." A woman from Columbus, Ohio, concurred that a new mother was "foiled in every attempt to follow her own wishes."[52] These women noticed that the physical removal of childbirth from the woman's home to the physician's institution shifted the balance of power. Birth was no longer part of the woman's domain, as it had been during all the years it remained in the home. It had become instead a medical affair run by medical professionals. Women were no longer the main actors, but instead physicians acted upon women's bodies. Women who were attended by physicians in their own homes could still determine what would happen—could refuse to be shaved or could demand ether. They still controlled much of their own births. But women who entered the birthing rooms of medicine were captured by the routine and by the expertise surrounding them. They could not decide what kind of births they would have.

Some hospitals and some doctors did not depersonalize birth with institutional routine and were able to provide satisfying birth experiences. But many women agreed with the Bozeman, Montana, mother who wrote, "The cruelest part of [hospital] childbirth is being alone among strangers." She found nothing familiar to comfort her through the difficult hours, only the routine of hospital life that she and others described as an assembly line.[53] Physician-directed hospital obstetrics had not met the expectations of American women by protecting a woman's dignity and integrity at the same time as it ensured safety. Women wanted the psychologically comforting practices of their traditional birthing rooms to be incorporated into the modern practices of the birthing rooms of science.

The two images of birthing women in America—one "brought to bed" in her own home by the women she had called together and the other drugged and "alone among strangers" in an impersonal hospital—frame the American obstetric experience. The eighteenth-century woman felt vulnerable to death and debility despite the strength she derived from her friends; the twentieth-century woman felt vulnerable to the institutional routine despite the strength she derived from encouraging maternal-mortality statistics. Neither woman had what she knew she needed at the time of her birth: the certainty of a healthy outcome with the freedom to make choices about how to conduct the important event. . . .

Each major transition in American childbirth history—from midwives to physicians, from home to hospital, from "hands of flesh" intervention to "hands of iron" interference—represents in a different form the lure of science and its promise to improve the childbirth experience.[54] As women and their attendants came to perceive birth as an event that could be shaped and manipulated, their *mentalité* of pathology and impending emergencies led each generation to seek its own kind of ideal childbirth. Ultimately it was the promise of continual advances that pushed birth into new patterns throughout American history. Women and their birth attendants believed that medicine could solve their birthing problems and make procreation safe, and they put their faith in scientific advances years before science had significant impact on obstetric practices. Systematic application of tested principles did not characterize obstetrics until the twentieth century, yet medical activities in the birthing room were valued much earlier because physicians carried an image of expertise and knowledge along with the instruments and drugs in their medical bags.

Despite the lack of a systematic practice of obstetrics, women did not want to turn back to traditional practices. Only in very recent years has any sizable group of American women tried to change direction. Today some women are trying to alter the patterns of childbirth by seeking practices that were common in the past. These women, still a minority and predominantly middle-class, search out midwives or demand that doctors turn back the clock to a time when decision making involved all the birth participants. Women in America today who are seeking to control their own births are fighting the legacy of childbirth as structured by the medical profession and are demanding that choice be reintroduced to the childbirth agenda. They are not trying to overturn science but rather to control it within the traditional female context.

The two themes of social childbirth and scientific childbirth have persisted throughout American history. In the seventeenth and eighteenth centuries, social childbirth practices prevailed. The two vied for supremacy during the nineteenth century, and not until the middle of the twentieth century did the medical model succeed in dominating American childbirth. Yet physician-directed childbirth has not met all the needs of birthing women. The pendulum swing between the two traditions has not yet found its resting place.

Notes

1. Cecil K. Drinker, *Not So Long Ago: A Chronicle of Medicine and Doctors in Colonial Philadelphia* (New York, 1937), 50–62; Jane B. Donegan, *Women and Men Midwives: Medicine, Morality, and Misogyny in Early America* (Westport, Conn., 1978); and Catherine M. Scholten, " 'On the Importance of the Obstetrick Art': Changing Customs of Childbirth in America, 1760 to 1825," *William and Mary Quarterly* 34 (July 1977), 426–45. . . .

2. Louis B. Wright and Marion Tinling, eds., *The Secret Diary of William Byrd of Westover, 1709–1792* (Richmond, 1941), 79. The phrase "called her women together" is common in early childbirth accounts. . . .

3. Carroll Smith-Rosenberg, "The Female World of Love and Ritual: Relations between Women in Nineteenth-Century America," *Signs* 1 (Autumn 1975), 1–29. For a discussion of social childbirth, see Richard W. Wertz and Dorothy C. Wertz, *Lying-in: A History of Childbirth in America* (New York, 1977), 1–26.

4. On midwives' practices, see Donegan, *Women and Men Midwives*, 9–11, 25, 127; Scholten, " 'On the Importance of the Obstetrick Art,' " 429–31, 432–34; Claire E. Fox, "Pregnancy, Childbirth and Early Infancy in Anglo-American Culture, 1675–1830" (Ph.D. diss., University of Pennsylvania, 1966), 122–27; and Janet Bogdan, "Care or Cure? Childbirth Practices in Nineteenth Century America," *Feminist Studies* 4 (June 1978), 94.

5. For more on women's perceptions of childbirth as a time of danger, see Judith Walzer Leavitt and Whitney Walton, "Down to Death's Door: Women's Perceptions of Childbirth in America," in *Proceedings of the Second Motherhood Symposium: Childbirth: The Beginning of Motherhood*, ed. Sophie Colleau (Madison, 1982), 113–36. On efforts to compute maternal mortality, see B. M. Willmott Dobbie, "An Attempt to Estimate the True Rate of Maternal Mortality, Sixteenth to Eighteenth Centuries," *Medical History* 26 (January 1982), 79–90; and Louis I. Dublin, "Mortality among Women from Causes Incidental to Childbearing," *American Journal of Obstetrics and Diseases of Women and Children* 78 (July 1918), 20–37.

6. Drinker, *Not So Long Ago*, 60–61; Lewis C. Scheffey, "The Earlier History and the Transition Period of Obstetrics and Gynecology in Philadelphia," *Annals of Medical History* 2 (May 1940), 215–16.

7. Scholten, " 'On the Importance of the Obstetrick Art,' " 434–36.

8. Bogdan, "Care or Cure?" 96–97; Donegan, *Women and Men Midwives*, 141–57.

9. Drinker, *Not So Long Ago*, 51–53, 58–61.

10. Jane B. Donegan argues that William Shippen practiced conservative obstetrics when compared to the "meddlesome midwifery" of others. Donegan, *Women and Men Midwives*, 118–19. For more on Shippen, see Betsy Copping Corner, *William Shippen, Jr.: Pioneer in American Medical Education: A Biographical Essay* (Philadelphia, 1951).

11. Lawrence D. Longo, "Obstetrics and Gynecology," in *The Education of American Physicians: Historical Essays*, ed. Ronald L. Numbers (Berkeley, 1980), 205–8.

12. *Autobiography of Samuel D. Gross, M.D., with Sketches of His Contemporaries*, ed. Samuel Weissel Gross and Albert Haller Gross, 2 vols. (Philadelphia, 1887), II, 240.

13. Ibid., 247; William P. Dewees, *A Compendious System of Midwifery, Chiefly Designed to Facilitate the Inquiries of Those Who May Be Pursuing This Branch of Study* (Philadelphia, 1843), 289. See also Irving S. Cutter and Henry R. Viets, *A Short History of Midwifery* (Philadelphia, 1964), 156–57.

14. Wertz and Wertz, *Lying-in*, 50.

15. Walter Channing, *A Treatise on Etherization in Childbirth. Illustrated by Five Hundred and Eighty-One Cases* (Boston, 1848), 229.

16. Dewees, *Compendious System*, 354, 356–57; A. Clair Siddall, "Bloodletting in American Obstetric Practice, 1800–1945," *Bulletin of the History of Medicine* 54 (Spring 1980), 101–10.

17. Bogdan, "Care or Cure?" 96–98; Scholten, " 'On the Importance of the Obstetrick Art,' " 437–39. The crochet was the classic instrument to destroy the fetus in utero and permit extraction.

18. Drinker, *Not So Long Ago*, 60–61.

19. Dewees, *Compendious System*, 290.

20. Ibid., 286.

21. See, for example, H. B. Willard Obstetrical Journal, October 27, 1849, p. 3, H. B. Willard Papers, State Historical Society of Wisconsin, Madison; ibid., December 25, 1849, p. 2; ibid., May 7, 1850, p. 4.

22. Dewees, *Compendious System*, 281; Robert P. Harris, "History of a Pair of Obstetrical Forceps Sixty Years Old," *American Journal of Obstetrics and Diseases of Women and Children* 4 (May 1871), 57.

23. Edward Wagenknecht, ed., *Mrs. Longfellow: Selected Letters and Journals of Fanny Appleton Longfellow, 1817–1861* (New York, 1956), 129–30.

24. Elizabeth H. Emerson, *Glimpses of a Life* (Burlington, N.C., 1960), 4–5.

25. Mrs. Hal Russell, "Memoirs of Marian Russell," *Colorado Magazine* 21 (January 1944), 35–36; Channing, *Treatise on Etherization*, 165. For more on women's fears of death and debility, see Leavitt and Walton, "Down to Death's Door."

26. "Dr. Meigs' Reply to Professor Simpson's Letter," *Medical Examiner and Record of Medical Science* 11 (March 1848), 148–51. See also John Duffy, "Anglo-American Reaction to Obstetrical Anesthesia," *Bulletin of the History of Medicine* 38 (January–February 1964), 32–44.

27. Channing, *Treatise on Etherization*, 300. Walter Channing did not report what proportion of these physician-attended births used anesthesia.

28. Ibid., 334–35. The woman who insisted on using ether was forty-three years old and had had five children.

29. Charles Fox Gardiner, *Doctor at Timberline* (Caldwell, Idaho, 1938), 211. See also D. M. Barr, "Anaesthesia in Labor," *Medical and Surgical Reporter* 42 (March 13, 1880), 227.

30. Bedford Brown, "The Therapeutic Action of Chloroform in Parturition," *Journal of the American Medical Association* 25 (August 31, 1895), 354; Duffy, "Anglo-American Reaction," 38. See also J. F. Ford, "Use of Drugs in Labor," *Wisconsin Medical Journal* 3 (October 1904), 257–65.

31. Ford, "Use of Drugs," 257–58; A. D. Bundy, "Obstetrics in the Country," *Medical and Surgical Reporter* 56 (February 12, 1887), 200–201. In 91,000 births in Iowa, physicians used forceps in 7 percent of cases. E. D. Plass and H. J. Alvis, "A Statistical Study of 129,539 Births in Iowa, with Special Reference to the Method of Delivery and the Stillbirth Rate," *American Journal of Obstetrics and Gynecology* 28 (August 1934), 297.

32. Barr, "Anaesthesia in Labor," 226–27. In the twentieth century, obstetricians appear to have used anesthesia with the intent to produce unconsciousness, and forceps use consequently increased.

33. Dorothy Reed Mendenhall, "Prenatal and Natal Conditions in Wisconsin," *Wisconsin Medical Journal* 15 (March 1917), 353. See also the comments of Dorothy Reed Mendenhall and Florence Sherbon, in American Association for Study and Prevention of Infant Mortality, *Transactions of the Seventh Annual Meeting, Milwaukee, October 19–21, 1916* (Baltimore, 1917), 67–68, 63–64.

34. H. H. Whitcomb, "A Report of 616 Cases of Labor in Private Practice," *Medical and Surgical Reporter* 56 (February 12, 1887), 201. Puerperal sepsis caused the largest proportion of maternal deaths at the beginning of the twentieth century. See American Association for Study and Prevention of Infant Mortality, *Transactions of the Seventh Annual Meeting*, 67.

35. Russell Kelso Carter, *The Sleeping Car "Twilight": or, Motherhood without Pain* (Boston, 1915), 10–11.

36. Anita McCormick Blaine to Nettie Fowler McCormick, August 24, 1890, folder 2B, box 46, Nancy Fowler McCormick Papers, State Historical Society of Wisconsin; McCormick to Blaine, August 1890, folder 1E, box 459, ibid.

37. S. H. Landrum to editor, *Journal of the American Medical Association* 58 (February 24, 1912), 576. See also George S. King, *Doctor on a Bicycle* (New York, 1958), 61–63; Marcus Bossard, *Eighty-One Years of Living* (Minneapolis, 1946), 39–40; and Mary Bennett Ritter, *More than Gold in California, 1849–1933* (Berkeley, 1933), 219.

38. J. H. Mackay to editor, *Journal of the American Medical Association* 58 (March 9, 1912), 720; J. H. Guinn to editor, ibid. (March 23, 1912), 880.

39. Longo, "Obstetrics and Gynecology," 211–14; Virginia G. Drachman, "The Loomis Trial: Social Mores and Obstetrics in the Mid-Nineteenth Century," in *Health Care in America: Essays in Social History*, ed. Susan Reverby and David Rosner (Philadelphia, 1979), 67–83; American Association for Study and Prevention of Infant Mortality, *Transactions of the Seventh Annual Meeting*, 63–64; Francis A. Long, *A Prairie Doctor of the Eighties: Some Personal Recollections and Some Early Medical and Social History of a Prairie State* (Norfolk, Nebr., 1937), 29.

40. Barbara Moench Florence, ed., *Lella Secor: A Diary in Letters, 1915–1922* (New York, 1978), 170.

41. Roy P. Finney, *The Story of Motherhood* (New York, 1937), 6–7. See also Alan Frank Guttmacher, *Into This Universe: The Story of Human Birth* (New York, 1937), 192–267.

42. Gladys Denny Shultz, "Journal Mothers Report on Cruelty in Maternity Wards," *Ladies' Home Journal* 75 (May 1958), 44; M. F. Ashley Montagu, "Babies Should Be Born at Home!" ibid., 72 (August 1955). See also Betty MacDonald, *The Egg and I* (Philadelphia, 1945), 108, 163. Betty MacDonald found the hospital a place of luxury, wonderful food, and good care—almost, she said, enough to keep her pregnant the rest of her life. Hospital stays may have looked attractive because women's own networks of home helpers were diminishing in this period. This hypothesis needs further research.

43. Joseph B. DeLee, "The Prophylactic Forceps Operation," *American Journal of Obstetrics and Gynecology* 1 (October 1920), 40–41, 34–35.

44. J. P. McEvoy, "Our Streamlined Baby," *Reader's Digest* 32 (May 1938), 15–16. For reaction to prophylactic forceps, see J. Whitridge Williams, "A Criticism of Certain Tendencies in American Obstetrics," *New York State Journal of Medicine* 22 (November 1922), 493–99.

45. "I Had a Baby, Too: A Symposium," *Atlantic Monthly* 163 (June 1939), 768. See also Lenore Pelham Friedrich, "I Had a Baby," ibid. (April 1939), 461–65. Clara Rust delivered five babies at home before going to the hospital to have her sixth in 1926. She was apprehensive about leaving home but went to the hospital on the doctor's advice. Jo Anne Wold, *This Old House: The Story of Clara Rust* (Anchorage, 1976), 207–8.

46. New York Academy of Medicine Committee on Public Health Relations, *Maternal Mortality in New York City: A Study of All Puerperal Deaths, 1930–1932* (New York, 1933), 213–15, 125–27.

47. Ibid., 113–17, 126–27. An Iowa study found that 11.8 percent of all births and 23 percent of hospital births were operative statewide. Plass and Alvis, "Statistical Study," 293–305.

48. "Childbirth: Nature v. Drugs," *Time* (May 25, 1936), p. 36; Matthias Nicoll, Jr., "Maternity as a Public Health Problem," *American Journal of Public Health* 19 (September 1929), 967. See also R. W. Holmes, R. D. Mussey, and F. L. Adair, "Factors and Causes of Maternal Mortality," *Journal of the American Medical Association* 93 (November 9, 1929), 1440–47.

49. Philadelphia County Medical Society, Committee on Maternal Welfare, *Maternal Mortality in Philadelphia, 1931–1933* (Philadelphia, 1934), 130. See also New York Academy of Medicine, *Maternal Mortality*, 32–38.

50. White House Conference on Child Health and Protection, *Fetal, Newborn, and Maternal Morbidity and Mortality: Report of the Subcommittee on Factors and Causes of Fetal, Newborn, and Maternal Morbidity and Mortality* (New York, 1933), 14, 220.

51. Joyce Antler and Daniel M. Fox, "The Movement toward a Safe Maternity: Physician Accountability in New York City, 1915–1940," in *Sickness and Health in America: Readings in the History of Medicine and Public Health*, ed. Judith Walzer Leavitt and Ronald L. Numbers (Madison, 1978), 386; Lawrence D. Longo

and Christina M. Thomsen, "The Evolution of Prenatal Care in America," in *Proceedings of the Second Motherhood Symposium*, ed. Colleau, 29–70.

52. Shultz, "Journal Mothers Report on Cruelty," 44–45.

53. Ibid., 44.

54. The dichotomy between hands of flesh and hands of iron is used particularly effectively by Adrienne Rich, *Of Woman Born: Motherhood as Experience and Institution* (New York, 1976), 128–55.

6   Indispositions of Women with Child

François Mauriceau

As the number of formally trained physicians increased, doctors sought ways to secure their professional identity as experts. Medical textbooks reflected the conflict over defining expertise. The Diseases of Women with Child, and in Childbed, *a gynecology and obstetrics textbook written by Paris physician François Mauriceau and circulated in the American colonies in its English translation, identifies as early as 1697 the struggle between female midwives and male doctors over what constituted "legitimate" knowledge. First published in Paris, the center of Western obstetrical training in the seventeenth and eighteenth centuries, the book reveals the scientific claims that doctors made to assert their authority. This selection highlights the ease with which subjective interpretations of women's reproductive functions were presented by physicians as impartial, scientific truths.*

The Author's Epistle Dedicatory

GENTLEMEN, . . . I HOPE YOU WILL not judge amiss of my publishing this Book to the World, which I present to you; in which I endeavour to demonstrate exactly the means of remedying many Indispositions of Women with Child and in Child-bed, with an exact method of well practicing the Art of Midwifery; being persuaded it may be very profitable to young Chirurgeons living in the Country, where but few sufficiently instructed in all things necessary to

From François Mauriceau, *The Diseases of Women with Child, and in Childbed*, trans. Hugh Chamberlen, M.D. (London, 1697), iii, v, 4–6, 13–16, 33, 104–6, 108–9.

be known can be met with. I have the rather undertaken [*sic*] this that Midwives may find therein what they ought to know, the better to exercise their Art, and undergo the Examination, at present obliged to before you for their Reception. I hope likewise (Gentlemen) you will have the goodness to excuse it, tho not in so fair a Form as the Matter requires, and tho I express not the Contents so perfectly as you conceive them; for I have (I confess with a little too much confidence) undertaken to open diverse Secrets of Nature, which (being abstruse and difficult to be comprehended) create yet greater trouble to explain them significantly, so as to be well understood: notwithstanding, as a dark Body reflects the Light it receives; so, I hope, this small Work may (by the reflection of the Sun of your Doctrine, of which I have received many Rays) enlighten the Young Chirurgeons and Midwives in the Difficulties they often meet with Labours. . . .

On the Signs of Conception

As it is very hard, and belonging to expert Gardeners to know Plants so soon as they begin to spring forth of the Earth; so likewise there are none but expert Chirurgeons can give a Woman certain assurance of conception from its beginning; altho some of the suppression of the Terms [menstruation] and other maladies in Women, cause many to be deceived in it. . . .

These are the signs of Conception which may be known at the Moment it happens, and yet more certainly if you perceive the inward Orifice exactly close, besides these Signs, there are others that cannot be known until some time after, as when she begins to have Loathing having no other Distemper; loseth her Appetite to Men which she loved; longs to eat strange things, to which not accustomed, according to the quality of the Humours predominating in her, and with which her stomach abounds; she hath often Nauseatings and Vomitings, which continue a long time; the Terms stopping no other cause appearing, having always before been cause for good Order; her Breasts swell, are hard, and cause pain from the flowing of Blood and Humours to them. . . . Moreover, there is a Sign which all the Women esteem and hold in this doubtful case for very certain, which is . . . in a flat Belly there is a Child. Indeed, there is Rime in this Proverb, and something of Reason, but not as they imagine, that the Womb closing itself after Conception, draws in a manner the Belly inwards, and flattens it; which cannot be, because the Womb is free and wavering, not fastened forwards to the Belly, whereby to draw it back after the manner; but it may possibly be by reason Women grow lean by the Indispositions of their Pregnancy, and wax thinner and smaller, not only in their Belly, but also throughout their whole Body, as may be known the first Months of their Pregnancy, during which time that contained in the Womb, is yet very small; but when the Woman's Blood begins to flow to it in abundance, then the Belly waxes daily bigger and bigger afterwards, until her Reckoning be out.

All these Signs concurring in a Woman who hath used copulation, or the most part of them together, and successively according to their Seasons; we may pass judgment, that she hath conceived, notwithstanding many of them may happen upon the suppression of the Terms, which usually produce the like: for every one knows, that it causeth also in virgins, Disgusts, Nauseatings, and Vomitings, but not so frequently; the Swelling, Hardness, and Pains of the Breasts, as also extravagant Appetites, a livid colour of the Eyes, and others, to which you must have regard. The Matrix may be yet exactly close, and the Woman not conceived; yea, there are some, in whom they almost never open, unless very little, to give passage to the Terms, which happens to some naturally, to others by accident, as by some callosity proceeding from an Ulcer, or other Malady.

If all these signs of Conception (which sometimes may deceive us, tho rarely) when they concur, do not give us a sufficient Assurance of it, but that we desire the time they stay in the Womb, and also according to the quantity of Blood with which they are always soaked. Women expel these false conceptions sooner or later, according as they cleave to the Womb, which makes them almost always flood in great quantity at those times. . . .

Whether it can be known that a Woman is with Child of a Boy or a Girl, and the Signs whether she shall have many Children

It is no great matter to satisfy the Curiosity and disquiet of a Woman, who desires to know whether she be with Child or no: but there are many, if not most, that would have one proceed further, and tell whether that be a Boy or a Girl, which is absolutely impossible; tho there is hardly a Midwife that will not boast herself able to resolve it (in effect it is easier to guess, than to find the Truth); for when it

happens, it is certainly rather by chance, than by any Knowledge or
Reason they could have to enable them to foretell it. . . .

Of Abortion, and its Causes

The particular Causes of Abortion, are all the Accidents mentioned
in the preceding Chapters, [such] as violent and frequent Vomitings;
because there is not only want of sufficient Nourishment for Mother
and Child when the Food is so continually vomited up, but also
great Reachings and Endeavours, by which the Womb being often
compressed, and as it were shaken, is at last constrained to dis-
charge itself before its time. Pains of the Reins, great Cholicks and
Gripes may likewise cause the same Accident . . . for there are then
made strong Compressions of the Belly every moment to expel the
Urine. Great Coughs, by their frequent Agitation, suddenly thrusting the Diaphragm with force downwards, give also violent Shocks
to the Womb. . . . And whatever very much agitates and shakes the
Big-bellied woman's Body, is subject to make her miscarry, as great
labour, strong Contortions, or violent Motions, of what manner
soever, in falling, leaping, dancing, and running or riding, going in
a Coach or Waggon, crying aloud, or laughing heartily, or any Blow
received on the Belly; because that by such Agitations and Com-
motions, the Ligaments of the Womb are relaxed, yea, and sometimes broken, as also the After-Birth and Membranes of the Fetus
are loosened. A great Noise suddenly and unexpectedly heard, may
make some Women miscarry; as the Noise of a Cannon, and chiefly
Thunderclaps; and yet more easily, if to this Noise be added the
Fear they usually have of such things, which happens rather to the
young than elderly Women; because their Bodies being more tender and transpirable, the Air, which is strongly forc'd by that Noise,
being introduc'd into all her Pores, offers a great Violence by its
Impulsion of the Womb, and on the child within it; which
the elder being more robust, thicker and closer, resist with more
ease. . . .

They that are subject to Abortion, ought above all to take their
ease, and keep in Bed if they can, observing a good Diet, and re-
fraining from Copulation as soon as they believe themselves to be
with Child, avoiding the use of all Diureticks and Apertives, which
are very pernicious; as also violent Passions of the Mind, because
they are very prejudicial. She ought likewise to be loose in her
Dress that she may breathe the freer, and not strait-laced, and rack'd,

as most of them are ordinarily with their Busks [corsets] under their Clothes, to make their Bodies strait; and amongst other things, they have need [to] take heed of slipping and falling in their Walking, to which Big-bellied Women are very subject, because the bigness of their Bellies hinders them from feeling their way; they will therefore do well to wear low-heel'd Shoes with large Soals, to prevent hurting themselves, as too many daily do. I admire in this case the superstition of many Midwives, and some Authors, who order a Woman with Child, to take as soon as she hath hurt her Belly with a Fall, some Crimson Silk, small minced in the yolk of an Egg, or the Grains of Scarlet, and Treddles [treadles, or chalazas] of several Eggs put into the Yolk of one, as if that entering the Stomach were able to fortify the Womb and the Child in it, and to keep it there, for which there is no appearance of Reason or Truth.

7   Quackery and Abortion

Boston Medical and Surgical Journal

The founding in 1847 of the American Medical Association, the country's first national medical organization, helped cement physicians' claims to expertise. By 1840 the prolific expansion in the number of medical schools and physicians had given the practice of medicine in the United States a bad reputation. Medical schools typically admitted anyone who could pay and required students to complete only eight months of formal training. To restore professional prestige, the AMA waged an aggressive campaign to require lengthy education and state licensing of medical practitioners—actions intended, in part, to discredit lay healers.

The tension between regulars (formally trained and licensed physicians) and irregulars (unlicensed practitioners and healers, including female midwives) led to the AMA's 1850s campaign against abortion. In 1859 the AMA passed a resolution condemning abortions, including those performed before quickening (the point at which a woman first feels fetal movement; see Document 4). One reason for the campaign was the discov-

From "Quackery and Abortion," letter from J. P. Leonard, Greenville, Rhode Island, *Boston Medical and Surgical Journal* 43, no. 24 (January 15, 1851): 477–79.

ery that fetal development preceded quickening, a realization that made quickening as a physiological marker largely irrelevant. An equally important explanation, however, was the desire of regulars to gain professional status by distancing themselves from lay practitioners, including abortionists.

T HE MEDICAL PROFESSION TAKES RANK with the other learned professions; and is justly regarded by all enlightened nations as one of the most useful, liberal and noble of the sciences. Our profession, for centuries, has been advancing. It has, indeed, accomplished that which its most ardent admirers could not reasonably have expected, and *now* it is no way inferior to law or theology. . . . When the history of our times shall be recorded, the names of those who distinguish themselves in medicine and surgery will shine as brightly as those of the jurist, the divine, the military chieftain, and others, who have also been useful to their race, and shed lustre and renown upon the nations of their birth place or adoption.

For the last half century the progress of medicine has been, in all civilized countries, remarkable; but nowhere more marked than in the United States. . . . This [American Medical] Association has not only for its object the *expurging* of worthless material and the supplying of sound doctrines, but it also aims at the establishment of good regulations and *ethics*, with a view that justice, honorable conduct, and moral integrity, shall govern and preserve the medical men of this country (thus indirectly but really benefiting the sick and all others throughout the land), and if possible, eradicate every vestige of quackery with which our country has been scourged.

While the Association, through its committees, has made excellent suggestions, pointed out valuable improvements, and discountenanced quackery in most of its forms and devices, it has not yet struck any decided blow on that most diabolical kind of quackery, that high-handed villainy, which characterizes the *abortionist.* That this kind of charlatanism is rife, and is practised by regular members of the profession, that is, men who have *diplomas*, there can be no doubt; and I believe that some who are promoted to *office in our medical societies* are of this order of quacks. That such men *are quacks*, no one will question—the *epithet* belongs to the *unprincipled* as well as to the *ignorant.* . . .

I wish to warn the young practitioner, who is about to make his *debut* in his profession, as he values his future usefulness, as he values principle, as he values reputation and a good name, to abstain from the infernal performance under *every* circumstance, let the inducement be what it may. . . . This is a dangerous situation for many young men, and if they fall here, just as they are to be introduced into legitimate practice, they fall forever; their sins will surely find them out. . . .

[Abortionists] are better known than they would like to be. It is said that a woman cannot keep a secret. Whether this is so or not, the man who procures abortions is generally well known. He needs no hand-bills, placards, or other advertisement; he is soon notorious. Inglorious fame! Who would have such a disgraceful notoriety? Who would thus disgrace his profession; who would sell his claim to honor and principle; who would shed innocent blood for a few pieces of silver? After a man has thus degraded himself, after he has sunk so low, can he expect to retrieve his character? Who ever knew such a man to reform? If he is susceptible to feelings of remorse, like Judas he will go out and hang himself to hide his own shame.

8   Prize for an Antiabortion Essay

American Medical Association

The American Medical Association's antiabortion campaign targeted not only abortionists but also women who wanted or had had abortions. In 1864 the AMA established an annual prize for the best essay written to educate women. The first prize, awarded in 1865, was given to Boston gynecologist and antiabortion crusader Horatio Storer for an essay later published under the title Why Not? A Book for Every Woman. *This excerpt from the transactions of the AMA's 1864 meeting records the reason for offering the prize.*

"WHEREAS, CRIMINAL ABORTION HAS BECOME an alarmingly common evil, we need some means to educate the community as to its criminality and physical evils; therefore,

"*Resolved*, That our delegates be requested to ask the American Medical Association to offer a premium for the best *short and comprehensive* tract calculated for circulation among females, and

From *Transactions of the American Medical Association* 15 (Philadelphia, 1865), 50.

designed to enlighten them upon the criminality and physical evils of forced abortion.". . . .

On motion, the resolution was adopted by this Association, and the following added: Moved, that the subject be referred to the Committee on Prize Essays. Carried.

9   On Insane Women and the Reproductive System

Horatio Storer

In addition to campaigning against abortion, many regulars promoted what would become axiomatic in late nineteenth-century medical thinking: the belief that the reproductive organs were the source of female physical and psychological disorders. In an 1865 article on medical treatments for female insanity, none other than Horatio Storer proposed surgical intervention to correct "deviant" female behavior. Many physicians accepted Storer's recommendation. The most common sexual surgery performed in the late nineteenth century was an ovariotomy, the removal of one or both of the ovaries. By 1906 doctors had performed an estimated 150,000 ovariotomies on American women under the guise of protecting their emotional stability and mental health.

IN WOMEN MENTAL DISEASE IS often, perhaps generally, dependent upon functional or organic disturbance of the reproductive system. . . .

The necessity of removing a cause to prevent or to cure its effect is as decided in mental pathology as in physical. We recognize it everywhere else; we must recognize it in the treatment of insane women. . . .

During the past year I have had charge of a young lady afflicted with that not uncommon disease, mechanical dysmenorrhoea. This patient, unmarried and formerly a schoolteacher, was sent to me by a physician and had previously consulted several others. She

From Horatio Storer, "The Relations of Female Patients to Hospitals for the Insane: The Necessity on Their Account of a Board of Consulting Physicians to Every Hospital," *Transactions of the American Medical Association* 15 (Philadelphia, 1865): 125, 127–28.

confessed to me that while she never had had sexual intercourse, she had experienced, from a period long preceding her first seeking medical aid, excessive sexual desire, amounting indeed to what is technically termed nymphomania—a symptom merely, as are most of the mental disturbances of women. The attacks of this were very clearly coincident with the menstrual period, and so extreme that the patient could with difficulty restrain herself from soliciting the approach of the other sex. She could not restrain herself from frequent and excessive masturbation. There was little irritability about the clitoris or other external organs, the patient herself being inclined to recognize a deeper and inner origin for her suffering. The morbid desires and the disgusting propensity thence arising ceased together with the dysmenorrhoeal pain, upon freely incising the cervix uteri and dilating its canal. They have not since returned, save in one single instance, when an acute attack of the erotic desire, plainly resulting from indulgence in so-called pepper tea, was at once allayed by the application of potassa fusa to the cervix. . . . The above case must not be thought more pertinent than others of a similar reflex character, where, however, there is no erotic desire or other direct symptom of genital irritation. However masked, they all instance a single law.

10 A Questionnaire for Professors of Obstetrics

J. Whitridge Williams

Although physicians claimed the right to care for gynecological and obstetrical matters because of their superior education, the availability of formal training in these fields was minimal until the mid-twentieth century. In 1912 a comprehensive survey conducted by Dr. J. Whitridge Williams, professor of obstetrics at Johns Hopkins University, and published as a call to educational reform, revealed that obstetrics was the most neglected specialty of medical education in the country. An excerpt from that survey speaks both to the inadequacy of obstet-

From J. Whitridge Williams, "Medical Education and the Midwife Problem in the United States," *Journal of the American Medical Association* 58, no. 1 (January 6, 1912): 1–7.

*rical training and to the profession's disregard for female mid-
wifery as an alternative to male practice.*

W HEN REQUESTED BY THE CHAIRMAN of the Committee on Midwifery of the Association for the Study and Prevention of
Infant Mortality to prepare a paper on the midwife problem, I felt
that important information on the subject might be elicited by interrogating the teachers of obstetrics throughout the country. Accordingly, I prepared a questionnaire, containing some fifty
questions, which is appended, and which was sent to the professors
in the 120 medical schools giving a full four-year course. Forty-
three professors, representing schools in every section of the country, were good enough to reply.

As some of the queries were decidedly personal in character, I
promised not to mention the names of those replying, or the schools
with which they are connected; but at the same time I stated that I
should feel free to use whatever information might be supplied. It
is with great pleasure that I take this opportunity to thank those
who replied for their courtesy and frankness, and at the same time
to express the hope that their cooperation has not been in vain, as I
feel that it will bear fruit by arousing general interest, not only in
the midwife problem, but also in the much broader question of
medical education, by showing that we have as yet failed to train
practitioners competent to meet the emergencies of obstetrical
practice.

While the responses were not so general as might be desired,
they are nevertheless sufficiently numerous to give a fair idea of
the conditions existing throughout the country. Thirty-one replies
came from the sixty-one schools which are designated as "acceptable" by the Council on Medical Education of the American Medical Association, as compared with eleven from the fifty-nine
non-acceptable schools, not including one from Canada. . . .

For many years I have regarded the general attitude toward
obstetrical teaching as a very dark spot in our system of medical
education, and the majority of the replies to my questionnaire indicate that my pessimism was more than justified. Briefly stated, they
indicate (a) that many professors are inadequately prepared for their
duties and have but little conception of the obligations of a professorship; (b) that a considerable proportion are not competent to
cope with all obstetrical emergencies; (c) that nearly all complain
that their teaching and hospital equipment is inadequate for the

proper training of students; and (d) most serious of all, that a large proportion admit that the average practitioner, through his lack of preparation for the practice of obstetrics, may do his patients as much harm as the much-maligned midwife.

In the first part of this report I shall attempt to set forth the condition of affairs as revealed by my questionnaire; while in the second part I shall venture to indicate some of the reforms necessary to place obstetrical teaching on a proper basis, and incidentally touch on certain features of the midwife problem, in an attempt to indicate how the public may obtain better obstetrical treatment. . . .

Are you engaged in general practice, or do you limit your work to gynecology and obstetrics, or to obstetrics alone?

Seventeen professors replied that they were in general practice in addition to their college duties; twenty-one that they limited their work to obstetrics and gynecology, and five others solely to obstetrics. Accordingly, considerably more than one-third of the professors, including four in the so-called high-standard schools, are not specialists in any sense, and owing to the obligations of a large general practice have not sufficient leisure to become thoroughly versed in all of the problems of obstetrics and must necessarily take their professorial duties lightly. Moreover, five professors, including three in high-standard schools, limit their work exclusively to obstetrics; and as several of them admit that they are not competent to perform major operations, it is apparent that they cannot be ideal teachers. . . .

Why did you take up obstetrics?

The forty-one answers to this question may be divided into four categories. Eight professors deliberately chose obstetrics as their life work and endeavored to obtain as ideal a training for its pursuit as possible. Thirteen stated that they were always interested in the subject, and nine that they were very much interested before taking it up seriously. On the other hand, eleven stated that chance alone led them to teach this branch of medicine. Several accepted the professorship merely because it was offered to them, but had no special training or liking for it, while others succeeded to it after having taught various other branches with more or less success.

What was your preparation for teaching?

Prior to assuming their professorial duties, twenty-one, or slightly less than one-half of the entire number of professors, served for varying periods in lying-in hospitals. In eleven instances the service varied from one to five months, in five it extended over six months, while in five others it covered one or more years.

Such a confession appears highly depressing, but on further consideration it must be admitted that it is about what might be expected in this country; as twenty-five of the professors graduated twenty or more years ago, when very few lying-in hospitals were in existence, and those poorly equipped and offering but slight opportunity for clinical observation. Such conditions, however, are in marked contrast with those obtaining in Germany and France, where the first requirement for a professorial career is a long period of preparation in a well-equipped lying-in hospital with abundant clinical material. At the same time, it must be noted that the preparation of a considerable number of our professors was augmented by service for varying periods in more or less well-organized out-patient departments.

Even more serious than the lack of rigorous hospital training, is the appallingly slight experience which many had before being appointed to professorships. The replies indicate that only nine of the entire number had seen 1,000 or more cases of labor, and twenty-one others considerably less, while eleven obtained their practical experience solely from an indefinite number of cases in private practice. Moreover, it is interesting to note that one professor admits that he had never seen a woman delivered before assuming his professorship, while five state that they had seen less than 100 cases, and thirteen others less than 500 cases.

Think of becoming a professor of obstetrics with an experience of less than 100 cases!

After considering the answers to this question, I think that it is difficult to avoid the conclusion that the majority of our professors entered on their duties with a comparatively poor equipment from a practical point of view, while their attainments in the underlying sciences were usually extremely faulty. . . .

Is a lying-in hospital connected with your school?

The answers to this question are in general very depressing, and show that six schools have no connection with a lying-in hospital. Of the other thirty-seven, nine have hospital accommodations for less than 100 patients per year, fifteen for more than 100 but less than 250, four for 250 but less than 500; and nine for 500 or more patients per year, including two schools with accommodations for over 1,000 patients. These figures indicate that most schools are very poorly equipped in this regard, as only nine have anything like adequate clinical material for the instruction of their students. Moreover, with a few exceptions, even the best of our lying-in hospitals are vastly inferior, as far as the number of patients and equipment for teaching are concerned, to the clinics in the smaller German universities. . . .

In order to give an idea of the deplorable dearth of clinical material, I have tabulated the figures from ten of the smaller lying-in hospitals with from twenty-five to 125 deliveries per year, including two connected with high-standard schools. Together they have only 553 cases for the instruction of 575 students; and when it is remembered that, owing to the long summer holiday and other causes, practically one-half of the cases are lost for purposes of instruction, it is apparent that each student on an average has an opportunity to see only one woman delivered, which is manifestly inadequate. Moreover, the conditions are only slightly better, when the combined facilities of all of the twenty hospitals owned by the medical colleges are considered, as together they present a total of 5,655 deliveries per year for 1,400 students requiring clinical instruction, which means an average of only four cases per student. . . .

Are you competent to operate on any complications arising from the female generative tract?

To this thirty-five professors answered "yes," and eight "no"; and these figures, I imagine, are much more favorable than the actual facts. Several professors frankly admit that they are not prepared to perform Cesarean section.

Consider that such a condition of affairs means that the professor is merely a man-midwife, who is unable to carry a complicated case of labor to its legitimate conclusion! Or, imagine the effect on a patient, who places herself in the hands of a professor of obstetrics in a respectable medical school, when she is told that he can conduct the case satisfactorily if it is ended by the unaided efforts of Nature, or merely requires some slight interference, but in case radical interference is demanded he will be obliged to refer her to a gynecologist or surgeon. Think of the impression such an admission must make on the student, who cannot be blamed for believing that obstetrics is a pursuit unworthy of broadly educated men, but is suitable only for midwives or physicians of mediocre intelligence. This is not the place to go into the details of this question, but I have no hesitation in asserting that a professor of obstetrics who is not prepared to perform a Cesarean section or other radical operation is not competent to undertake the care of a case of labor complicated by pelvic contraction, and is not fitted [*sic*] to teach modern obstetrics. . . .

Do you consider your hospital and teaching equipment satisfactory?

To this fourteen respondents answered "yes," and twenty-nine unhesitatingly "no." In other words, the professors in two-thirds of the schools frankly admit that the conditions are highly unsatisfactory. If this were all, it would be a grave admission; but the actual conditions are worse, and there is no justification for many of the affirmative answers. . . .

Do you consider that the ordinary graduate from your school is competent to practice obstetrics?

Eleven teachers, or one-quarter of the entire number, promptly answered "no"; while the remainder replied in the affirmative, although in many instances in a somewhat qualified manner. Thus, one replied: "Well, yes in a way; that is, some of them." It appears to me that the affirmative answers, as a rule, are more positive the poorer the school and the smaller its clinical material. That this is not an exaggeration is shown by the fact that affirmative replies came from several of the schools without lying-in hospitals, as well as from two others with only twenty-five cases per year available for the instruction of fifty students.

At the same time, most of the teachers qualify their affirmative answers by stating that their graduates are competent to conduct normal cases, while several others designate them as fairly efficient men-midwives. Moreover, most of them admit that their graduates are not competent to conduct operative labors, while several state that they deteriorate rapidly in technic after leaving the medical school. . . .

What proportion of labor cases in your city are attended by midwives?

The replies indicate great variations in different localities. Midwives are almost unknown in Montreal, and I am informed that only twenty-five practice in Boston. On the other hand, in most of our large cities including New York, Chicago, St. Louis and Atlanta, they conduct from 40 to 60 percent of all labor cases.

In regard to their licensure, eight teachers pleaded ignorance of conditions, while twenty-five stated that they were licensed and ten that they were not. . . .

After analysis of the replies to this question, it is apparent that midwives attend many cases in most of our large cities, but that their employment is dependent on local conditions rather than general necessity; as is shown by the replies from Boston and Montreal. In most localities some attempt is made to control them in a feeble way, but nowhere effectively, while the teachers of obstetrics throughout the country are about equally divided as to their necessity.

Do you believe that more women die from puerperal infection in the practice of midwives or of general practitioners?

This question, as well as the one immediately following, cannot be answered with accuracy; consequently the replies must be taken as the general impression of the respondents rather than as precise statements based on exact statistics. . . .

Eight teachers replied that they did not possess sufficient data on which to base an opinion; while of the thirty-five who answered, fifteen stated physicians, thirteen midwives and five that the deathrate is almost equal.

Accordingly, it appears that somewhat more than one-half of the teachers replying consider that general practitioners lose proportionately as many women from puerperal infection as do midwives. Even if based on somewhat faulty premises, such a conclusion is appalling, and is a railing indictment of the average practitioner and of our methods of instruction in obstetrics, more particularly as one of the main arguments urged against the midwife is the prevalence of infection in her practice.

Do as many women die as the result of ignorance, or of ill-judged and improperly performed operations, in the hands of general practitioners, as from puerperal infection in the hands of midwives?

Eight teachers state that they are not prepared to answer the question; while of the thirty-five who do so, twenty-six answer against the general practitioner, six against the midwife and three hold that the two are equally bad. Moreover, many direct attention to the unnecessary death of large numbers of children, as the result of unnecessary or improper operating, and from the failure to recognize the existence of contracted pelvis.

If it appears necessary to reform anything, here is the opportunity. Why bother about the relatively innocuous midwife, when the ignorant doctor causes quite as many absolutely unnecessary deaths? From the nature of things, it is impossible to do away with the physician, but he may be educated in time; while the midwife can eventually be abolished, if necessary. Consequently, we should direct our efforts to reforming the existing practitioner, and to changing our methods of training students so as to make the physician of the future reasonably competent.

How do you consider that the midwife problem can best be solved?

Thirty-four answers to this question gave the following result: Eighteen advocated the regulation and education, and fourteen the abolition of midwives, while one advocated that the question be left *in statu quo*, and another held that the only solution lay in better-trained doctors.

On analyzing the replies several interesting facts were elicited. Thus, a thoroughly competent professor in one of the large western cities, in which more than one-half of all labors are conducted by midwives, states that, although the smaller portion of the obstetrical work in his city is in the hands of physicians, his experience forces him to conclude that the latter nevertheless lose from infection many more women than do the midwives.

Again, one of the respondents from New York City states that owing to the extension of lying-in charities, midwives now attend many less women than formerly, notwithstanding the rapid increase in the population of the city. A similar statement comes from Cincinnati, where, without stringent regulation, the number of women attended by midwives has decreased from 70 percent in 1880 to 30 percent in 1909, thus tending to indicate that prolonged residence in this country gradually overcomes the prejudices of our foreign-born population against the employment of physicians.

Those who advocate regulation and education vary greatly in their ideas, some advocating mere general regulation, while others demand extensive education in properly equipped hospitals, as in Germany and Italy, with constant supervision by the board of health, which should have power to revoke licenses whenever necessary.

Equally divergent arguments are advanced by those favoring the abolition of midwives. One group regards as hopeless any attempt to train them efficiently, while another holds that they may be entirely done away with by educating the laity, by extending lying-in charities, and by supplying better doctors and cheaper nurses. . . .

I am convinced that no fair-minded person who is interested in the welfare of the women and children of our country, or in the problems of medical education, can read the foregoing analysis without feelings of profound depression, or without admitting that we are facing a condition urgently in need of reform.

The replies clearly demonstrate that most of the medical schools included in this report are inadequately equipped for their work, and are each year turning loose on the community hundreds of young men whom they have failed to prepare properly for the practice of obstetrics, and whose lack of training is responsible for unnecessary deaths of many women and infants, not to speak of a much larger number, more or less permanently injured by improper treatment, or lack of treatment. Moreover, the spontaneous admission by most of the respondents that poor training of medical men is responsible for many unnecessary deaths in childbirth, forces us to acknowledge that improvement in the status of the midwife alone will not materially aid in solving the problem. . . .

If midwives are to be educated, it should be done in a broad sense, and not in a makeshift way. Even then disappointment will probably follow.

III

Fertility Control in Nineteenth-Century America

11 Family Limitation, Sexual Control, and Domestic Feminism in Victorian America

Daniel Scott Smith

Between 1800 and 1900 the birth rate for white women in the United States dropped almost in half, from 7.04 children to 3.56. By 1900 only France had a lower birth rate in the Western world. The decline in family size was not exclusive to whites; in the 1880s the fertility rates of African-American women began an even sharper decline. The rise in abortions and the more frequent use of birth control caused the demographic revolution. Historian Daniel Scott Smith of the University of Illinois at Chicago examines nineteenth-century fertility control, highlighting the social meanings of coitus interruptus, *the favored method of contraception of middle-class families in the era.*

T HE HISTORY OF WOMEN IS inextricably connected with the social evolution of the family. The revitalization of the American feminist movement and the surge of interest in social history among professional historians during the past decade have combined to make the study of women in the family a crucial concern. . . .

An examination of three rather well-established quantitative indicators showing the relationship of the entire population of American women to the family suggests the hypothesis that over the course of the nineteenth century the average woman experienced a great increase in power and autonomy *within* the family. The important contribution women made to the radical decline in nineteenth-century marital fertility provides the central evidence for this hypothesis. Empirical data on the details of family limitation and the control of sexuality in the nineteenth century unfortunately are limited. However, an analysis of nineteenth-century sexual ideology supports the theory that women acquired an increasing power over sex and reproduction within marriage. The hypothesis that women's power increased within the nineteenth-century family also accords well with such important themes as the

From Daniel Scott Smith, "Family Limitation, Sexual Control, and Domestic Feminism in Victorian America," *Feminist Studies* 1, no. 3–4 (Winter/Spring 1973): 40–57. Reprinted by permission of Feminist Studies, Inc., c/o Women's Studies Program, University of Maryland, College Park, MD 20742.

narrow social base of the women's movement in America before the late nineteenth century, the flourishing of women's groups opposed to female suffrage, and the centrality of the attack on aspects of male culture in such movements as temperance. A long-term perspective is essential for understanding the history of women in the family. I shall suggest how the situation of women varied in three periods: the preindustrial (seventeenth and eighteenth century); industrial (nineteenth century); and the postindustrial (recent) phases of American society.

From the colonial period to the present, *an overwhelming majority—from 89 to 96 percent—of American women surviving past the age of forty-five have married* (Table 1). The proportion who never married was highest for those born in the last four decades of the nineteenth century. Small percentage changes represent, of course, thousands of women. While marriage was overwhelmingly the typical experience for American women, before the present century roughly a third of all females did not survive long enough to be eligible for marriage.[1] In addition, the numerically tiny minority who remained single had a far larger historical importance than their percentage would suggest. For example, 30.1 percent of 45- to 49-year-old native-white female college graduates in 1940 were unmarried.[2] Before the marked increase in life expectancy in the late nineteenth and early twentieth century, the average American woman married in her early- to mid-twenties, survived with her husband for some three decades, and, if widowed, spent an additional decade or so in widowhood.[3]. . .

Table 1. Percentage of American Women Who Never Married

Census or survey, and birth cohort		Age at enumeration	Percentage never married
1910	1835–38	70–74	7.3
	1840–44	65–69	7.1
	1845–49	60–64	8.0
	1850–54	55–59	7.7
	1855–59	50–54	8.9
	1860–64	45–49	10.0
1940	1865–69	70–74	11.1
	1870–74	65–69	10.9
	1875–79	60–64	10.4
	1880–84	55–59	8.7

	1885–89	50–54	8.8
	1890–94	45–49	8.6
1950	1895–99	50–54	7.7
	1900–04	45–49	8.0
1960	1905–09	50–54	7.6
	1910–14	45–49	6.5
1965	1915–19	45–49	4.8
1969	1921–25	45–49	4.5
	1926–30	40–44	5.0

Source: Calculated from Irene B. Taeuber, "Growth of the population of the United States in the Twentieth Century," Table 11, p. 40 in *Demographic and Social Aspects of Population Growth*, eds. Charles F. Westoff and Robert Parke, Jr., vol. 1, U.S. Commission on Population Growth and the American Future (Washington, DC: Government Printing Office, 1972).

While nearly all American women have married, *married American women did not work outside the home until the twentieth century*, with the major increase coming in the last three decades (Table 2). Only one white married woman in forty was classified in the labor force in 1890 and only one in seven in 1940; today two-fifths of all married women are working according to official definition.[4] The increase in labor-force participation for single women in the twentieth century has been less dramatic. More generally, many indicators (an increase in single-person households for the young and widowed, the disappearance of boarders and lodgers from family units, the decline in the age at marriage, an increase in premarital intercourse, and the legalization of abortion and no-fault divorce) point to an emerging postindustrial family pattern in the post-World War II period. This major shift in the family has important implications for the periodization of women's history.

Table 2. Female Participation in the Labor Force (in percentage)

Year	Total	White only		Native-white, age 35–44	
		Single	Married	Single	Married
1830[a]	(7)	—	—	—	—
1890[a]	12.1	35.2	2.5	39.3	2.3
1940[a]	26.9	47.9	14.6	73.6	17.9
1960[a]	34.1	45.5	29.6	76.5	29.9

| | | All Women | | | Age 35–44 | |
	Single	Married, husband present	Widowed, divorced, separated	Single	Married, husband present	Widowed, divorced, separated
1950[b]	50.5	23.8	37.8	83.6	28.5	65.4
1960[b]	44.1	30.5	40.0	79.7	36.2	67.4
1972[b]	54.9	41.5	40.1	71.5	48.6	71.7

[a]Stanley Lebergott, *Manpower in Economic Growth* (New York: McGraw Hill, 1964), Table A-10, p. 519.
[b]Bureau of Labor Statistics, summarized in the *New York Times*, January 31, 1973, p. 20.

The statistical trend presents an interesting historical problem. During the nineteenth century, some 90 percent of women got married, over 95 percent of the married were not employed outside the home, *yet women progressively bore fewer and fewer children*. The average number born to a white woman surviving to menopause fell from 7.04 in 1800 to 6.14 in 1840, to 4.24 in 1880, and finally to 3.56 in 1900 (Table 3). The same decline is also apparent in U.S. census data on completed fertility.[5] Between 1800 and 1900 the total fertility rate decreased by half. By the late nineteenth century, France was the only European country whose fertility rate was lower than America's.[6] Despite the demographic effects of a later marriage age and of more women remaining permanently single, from one-half to three-fourths of the nineteenth-century decline in fertility may be attributed to the reduction of fertility within marriage.[7]

Table 3. Total Fertility Rates (TFR) for Whites, 1800–1968

Year	TFR	Year	TFR	Year	TFR
1800	7.04	1860	5.21	1920	3.17
1810	6.92	1870	4.55	1930	2.45
1820	6.73	1880	4.24	1940	2.19
1830	6.55	1890	3.87	1950	3.00
1840	6.14	1900	3.56	1960	3.52
1850	5.42	1910	3.42	1968	2.36

Sources: For 1800–1960, Ansley J. Coale and Melvin Zelnik, *New Estimates of Fertility and Population in the United States* (Princeton: Princeton University Press, 1963), Table 2, p. 36; 1968 calculated from Irene B. Taeuber, "Growth of the Population of the United States in the Twentieth Century," in *Demographic and Social Aspects of Population Growth*, eds. Charles F. Westoff and Robert Parke, Jr., U.S. Commission on Population Growth and the American Future (Washington, DC: Government Printing Office, 1972), Table 7, p. 33.

The decline in marital fertility is of critical importance in structuring the possibilities open to the average woman. A fifteen-to-twenty-year cycle of conception-birth-nursing-weaning-conception (broken not infrequently by spontaneous abortions) at the height of active adulthood obviously limits chances for social and economic participation as well as for individual development. Child-rearing must be added to this onerous cycle. The great transition in fertility is a central event in the history of woman. A dominant theme in the history is that women have not shaped their own lives. Things are done to women, not by them. Thus it is important to examine the extent to which nineteenth-century women did gain control over their reproductive lives.

Many forces, to be mentioned later, were clearly at work in curbing fertility, but the power of the wife to persuade or coerce her husband into practicing birth control deserves examination. While women did employ contraceptive methods in the nineteenth century (principally douching and the sponge), the major practices involved the control of male sexuality—*coitus interruptus* (withdrawal) and abstinence.[8] Following [Aileen] Kraditor's excellent definition of the essence of feminism as the demand for autonomy, sexual control of the husband by the wife can easily be subsumed under the label of "domestic feminism."[9]

Before marshalling empirical data showing the strengthening of the position of women within the nineteenth-century American family, it is first necessary to consider certain misconceptions about women's place in the industrial and preindustrial periods. Many of the recent interpretations of the history of American women have been devoted to an autopsy of the "failure" of women's suffrage. According to Kraditor, late nineteenth- and early twentieth-century American women became conservative and were co-opted into the general progressive movement.[10] In [Carl] Degler's view, women lacked an ideology that could properly guide them to full status as human beings.[11] For [William] O'Neill, the "failure" lay in the refusal of the movement to assault the ideology and reality of the conjugal family structure that sustained women's inferior position.[12] This "what-went-wrong" approach implicitly assumes the constancy of woman's role within the family, and, more damagingly, interprets the behavior and responses of women as deviations from a preconceived standard rather than as responses to their actual situations. The turn toward conservatism in the leadership of active

American women, for example, is seen as a tactical mistake rather than as the result of interaction between the leaders and their female constituency.

The extremely low percentage of married women in the nineteenth-century labor force suggests that the domestic-sphere versus social-participation dichotomy is not appropriate for the interpretation of women's history during the industrial period. If the average woman in the last century failed to perceive her situation through the modern feminist insight, this did not mean she was not increasing her autonomy, exercising more power, or even achieving happiness within the domestic sphere. Rather than examining Victorian culture and especially the Victorian family at its heart through a twentieth-century perspective, it is more useful and revealing to contrast nineteenth-century values and institutions with their preindustrial antecedents.

Misconceptions about women in the preindustrial family fit integrally into the pessimistic view of the Victorian era derived from the modern feminist perspective. Having portrayed the nineteenth century as something of a nadir for women, by implication, all other eras must be favorable by comparison. In order to show that women are not inevitably entrapped by the family, it has seemed important to emphasize that somewhere or sometime the status and role of women were quite different. While cross-culture evidence supports this argument adequately, more compelling are conclusions drawn from as little as two centuries ago in American or Western culture. Historians, however, have been properly cautious about more than hinting at a Golden Age for the preindustrial American woman. There is, to be sure, a sharp difference between the preindustrial and industrial family and the corresponding position of women in each. A conjugal family system, in the sense of the centrality of the married pair, in contrast to the dominance of the family line, did emerge in the United States during the early nineteenth century.[13]

The effects of this shift for women are complex. The conventional belief in the more favorable position of the average woman in preindustrial society rests on three arguments: the intimacy and complementary nature of sex roles in an undifferentiated economy; [Philippe] Aries's thesis that the boundary between the preindustrial family and society was very permeable; and finally, in the American case, the favorable implications for women of the relative female and labor scarcity on the frontier. The first argument may be compared to George Fitzhugh's defense of slavery, but extreme sub-ordination and superordination do not require a highly differenti-ated economy and society. The very absence of complexity in the preindustrial family doubtless contributed to the subordination of women. While the identity of the place of work and residence in an agricultural economy inevitably meant some sharing of productive tasks by husband and wife, the husband's presence, given the pre-vailing ideological and cultural values, deterred the wife from gain-ing a sense of autonomy. Just as the gender stereotypes of masculine and feminine were not as rigidly defined as in the Victorian period, the prestige attached to the status of wife and mother was less than in the nineteenth century. Social prestige depended on the position of the woman's family in the hierarchical structure of preindustrial society. Daughters and wives shared in the deference paid to im-portant families. When this system collapsed in the nineteenth cen-tury, women of high-status families experienced considerable deprivation compared to their high-ranking colonial counterparts. Women born to more modest circumstances, however, derived en-hanced status from the shift away from deference and ascription.

Although Aries has little to say about women, his thesis that the line between the Western preindustrial family and community was not sharply delineated is of considerable importance here.[14] There does exist scattered evidence of women's nonfamilial activ-ity, e.g., voting, operating businesses, etc., in the preindustrial period. The incidence of women's nonfamilial activity over time, its relationship to family and conventional sex roles, and finally, its importance in the social structure as a whole have not been ex-plored. The existing social history of colonial women has success-fully demonstrated that wider participation was not unknown.[15] The details of such nonfamilial participation have been much more fully researched for the colonial period than for the nineteenth century. Spinsters almost certainly were more marginal and deviant in pre-industrial American society than during the nineteenth century. Only widows who controlled property may have been in a more favor-able position. While changes in colonial America law permitted a married woman to exercise certain rights, these innovations related mainly to acting as a stand-in for a husband.[16] By negating the im-pact of male absence because of travel and death, these modifica-tions in colonial law made the family a more efficient economic unit; historians should not confuse a response to high mortality and slow transportation with normative support for women's being outside the family. In fact, nonfamilial participation by preindustrial women must generally be viewed as a substitution for the activities of absent husbands. In effect, a woman's activity outside the pre-industrial family was a *familial* responsibility.

Systematic evidence comparing the position of women in the preindustrial and industrial phases of American society is scarce; what exists points to the comparatively unfavorable place of women in the earlier stage. In most populations, for example, women live considerably longer than men. Yet this was not the case in four (Andover, Hingham, Plymouth and Salem) of the five seventeenth-century New England communities studied to date. Only in seventeenth-century Ipswich did the typical pattern of longer sur-vival for adult females exist.[17] In Hingham, furthermore, an inverse relationship between family wealth and mortality is apparent only for eighteenth-century married women, not for their husbands or children.[18] Literacy is a good index of the potential to perform com-plex tasks. The scattered published data on the frequency of signa-tures on documents suggest that there may have been some narrowing of the historic differential between male and female lit-eracy during the eighteenth century. The gap, however, was not fully closed until the nineteenth century.[19] The sex differential in literacy is, of course, also a class differential. Compared to those of preindustrial men, the burdens of life were harsh for women, particularly those of low status. Finally, the resemblance in that era of the sexual act itself to the Hobbesian state of nature is revealing. Marital sex, succinctly summarized by [Edward] Shorter as "simple up-and-down, man on top, woman on bottom, little foreplay, rapid ejaculation, masculine unconcern with feminine orgasm,"[20] per-haps mirrored the broader social relationship between men and women.

It may be argued that America was not Europe and that the rela-tive strength of the woman's movement in nineteenth-century America can be attributed to a decline from a more favorable situ-ation during the colonial period. The existence of protest, however, is not an index of oppression, but rather a measure of the ambigu-ities and weaknesses of the system of control. It is ironic that the Turnerian frontier theory, implicitly biased by its emphasis on male experience, survives most strongly in the field of women's history.[21] As [Evsey] Domar has shown, however, labor scarcity and free land are intimately related to the institutions of slavery and serfdom.[22]

The economic factor associated with the exceptional freedom of white American males was a precondition of the equally exceptional degree of suppression of blacks. For a group to gain from favorable economic conditions, it must be able to benefit from the operation of the market. While this was true for single women in the nineteenth century (but not in the preindustrial period), it decidedly was not true for married women. Wives were not free to strike a better bargain with a new mate. What appears to be crucial in determining the turn toward freedom or suppression of the vulnerable group are the ideology and values of the dominant group.[23] Neither the position of the labor force nor of women can be mechanistically reduced to simple economic factors.[24]

The empirical basis for the importance of the frontier in the history of women is not impressive. On the nineteenth-century frontier at least, the high male-to-female sex ratio was a transitory phenomenon.[25] For the entire American population, the high rate of natural increase during the colonial period quickly narrowed the differential in the sex ratio created by immigration.[26] The truth left in the frontier argument is also ironic. Women's suffrage undeniably came earlier in the West. That development, as [Alan] Grimes has argued, reflected the potential usefulness of women as voters along the conservative wife-mother line rather than a recognition of Western women as citizens per se.[27] [Bernard] Farber's interesting analysis of the East-Midwest variation in marriage prohibition statutes points to a relative emphasis on the conjugal family in the newer areas of the country. Midwestern states tend to prohibit marriages of cousins while certain affinal marriages are illegal in the East and South.[28] In summary, then, the frontier and the general newness of social institutions in America benefitted women chiefly as part of the elevation of conjugality in family structure.

The majority of women in nineteenth-century families had good reason to perceive themselves as better off than their preindustrial forebearers. This shift involved not merely the level of material comfort but, more importantly, the quality of social and familial relationships. Since being a wife and mother was now evaluated more positively, women recognized an improvement within their "sphere" and thus channeled their efforts within and not beyond the family unit. It is not surprising that contemporary and later critics of the Victorian family referred to it as patriarchal, since that was the older form being superseded. If a descriptive label with a

Latin root is wanted, however, "matriarchal" would be more suitable for the nineteenth-century family. Men had inordinate power within the Victorian family, but it was as husbands—not as fathers. The conservative conception of woman's role focused, after all, on the submissive wife rather than the submissive daughter.[29] Nineteenth-century women, once married, did not retain crucial ties to their family of birth; marriage joined individuals and not their families.[30]

While the interpretation being advanced here stresses the significance of the new autonomy of women within the family as an explanation of the decline of fertility during the nineteenth century, this is not to deny the importance of economic, instrumental, or "male" considerations. The shift from agriculture, the separation of production from the family, the urbanization of the population, and the loss of child labor through compulsory education doubtless also contributed. Indeed, the wife's demand for a smaller family may have been so successful precisely because it was not contrary to the rational calculations of her husband. Since the fertility decline was nationwide and affected urban and rural areas simultaneously, attitudes and values as well as structural factors are obviously of relevance.[31] The romantic cult of childhood, for example, may have induced a change from quantitative to qualitative fertility goals on the part of parents.

The social correlates of lower fertility found in modern populations are relevant to this discussion of the history of American fertility. A common finding of cross-national studies, for example, is a strong negative relationship between fertility and female participation in the labor force.[32] The American historical record, however, does not provide much support for this theory. During the 1830–1890 period, there was probably only a slight increase in the labor-force participation of married women, and yet marital fertility continuously declined.[33] During both the post-World War II baby boom and the fertility decline since 1957, labor-force activity of married women increased.[34] For lower fertility, what is important is the meaning women assign to themselves and their work, either in or out of the home.[35] Since work is compatible with a traditional orientation for women,[36] the converse may also be true. Finally, the strong relationship between lower fertility and the educational attainment of a woman may involve more than a response to the higher financial return of nonfamilial activity for the better educated.[37]

Education may be a proxy variable for the degree to which a woman defines her life in terms of self rather than others.

Some quantitative support for the hypothesis that the wife significantly controlled family planning in the nineteenth century derives from a comparison of sex ratios of last children in small and large families, and an analysis of the sex composition of very small families in Hingham, Massachusetts. Most studies indicate that men and women equally prefer boys to girls.[38] Given a residue of patriarchal bias in nineteenth-century values, it is not an unlikely assumption that women would be more satisfied than men with girl children. A suggestive psychological study supports this notion. In a sample of Swedish women expecting their first child, those preferring a boy were found to have less of a sense of personal autonomy. Of the eleven of the eighty-one women in the sample who considered themselves dominant in their marriages, only two wanted sons. The "no-preference" women were better adjusted psychologically and scored higher on intelligence tests.[39] In short, the less autonomous and adjusted the woman, the more likely she is to want her first child to be a boy.

In Hingham marriages formed between 1821 and 1860, the last child was more likely to be a girl in small families and a boy in the larger families (see Table 4). The difference between the sex ratios of the final child in families with one to four children as compared to those with five and more is statistically significant only at the 0.1 level. Given the complexity of the argument here, this is not impressive. Small families, however, tended to contain only girls. Sixty percent of only children were girls (21 of 35); 27 percent and 17 percent of two-child families were both girls (14) and boys (9) respectively; and 14 percent and 6 percent of three-child families were all girls (9) and all boys (4) respectively. The independent probability of these differences is less than one in ten, one in four, and one in twenty respectively. With a slight biological tendency toward males in births to young women, these figures suggest that differing sex preferences of husbands and wives may explain the pattern. On the other hand, twentieth-century sex-ratio samples show either no difference or a bias toward males in the sex ratio of the last-born child.[40] In the absence of very marked differences in the preference of husbands and wives and with less than perfect contraceptive methods available to nineteenth-century couples, no extreme relationship should appear. This quantitative pattern does suggest that the Victorian family had a domestic-feminist rather than a patriarchal orientation.

Table 4. Sex Ratio of Last versus Other Children of Stated Parity and the Probability of Having Another Child According to Sex of the Last Child (Hingham women in complete families marrying before age twenty-five between 1821 and 1860)

| Parity | Sex ratio | | Parity progression ratios | | |
	Last	Not last	Male last	Female last	Difference
1	57 (22)	124 (242)	.944	.885	+.059
2	113 (32)	82 (211)	.848	.855	-.037
3	69 (49)	83 (165)	.789	.756	+.033
4	83 (42)	114 (124)	.776	.716	+.060
5	107 (31)	114 (94)	.758	.746	+.012
6	237 (22)	74 (66)	.596	.826	-.230
7	150 (20)	77 (46)	.625	.764	-.139
8&+	124 (47)	105 (86)	.628	.667	-.039

Source: Daniel Scott Smith, "Population, Family, and Society in Hingham, Massachusetts, 1635-1880" (unpublished Ph.D. diss., University of California, Berkeley, 1973), p. 360.
Note: Sample sizes in parentheses. Chi-Square (1–4) vs. (5 and more) 2,882, significant at 0.1 level.

Recognition of the desirability and even the existence of female control of marital sexual intercourse may be found in nineteenth-century marital advice literature. In these manuals, "marital excess," i.e., too-frequent coitus, was a pervasive theme. Although conservative writers, such as William Alcott, proclaimed that "the submissive wife should do everything for your husband which your strength and a due regard to your health would admit,"[41] women rejected submission. In fact, Dio Lewis claimed that marital excess was the topic best received by his female audience during his lecture tours of the 1850s. The Moral Education Society, according to Lewis, asserted the right "of a wife to be her own person, and her sacred right to deny her husband if need be; and to decide how often and when she should become a mother."[42] The theme of the wife's right to control her body and her fertility was not uncommon. "It is a woman's right, not her privilege, to control the surrender of her person; she should have pleasure or not allow access unless she wanted a child."[43]

It should be emphasized that both the husband and the wife had good (albeit different) reasons for limiting the size of their family. In most marriages, perhaps, these decisions were made jointly by the couple. Nor is it necessarily true that the wife imposed abstinence on her husband. While *coitus interruptus* is the male contraceptive par excellence, the wife could assist "with voluntary [though unspecified] effort."[44] Withdrawal was, according to one physician, "so universal it may be called a national vice, so common that it is unblushingly acknowledged by its perpetrators, *for the commission of which the husband is even eulogized by his wife and applauded by her friends* [italics added]."[45] In the marriage manuals, withdrawal was the most denounced means of marital contraception and, it may be inferred, the most common method in actual practice.

There are serious questions about the applicability of this literary evidence to actual behavior. Even among the urban middle classes (presumably the consumers of these manuals and tracts) reality and ideology probably diverged considerably. Historical variation in sexual ideology doubtless is much greater than change in actual sexual behavior.[46] The antisexual themes of the nineteenth century should not, however, be ignored. One may view this ideology as the product of underlying social circumstances—the conscious tip, so to speak, of the submerged iceberg of sexual conflict. While the influence of this literature is difficult to assess, its functions can be examined. It can be argued that antisexual themes had little to do with family limitation. Nor was contraception universally condemned by respectable opinion. The *Nation* in June 1869 called family limitation "not the noblest motive of action, of course; but there is something finely human about it."[47] Male sexual self-control was necessary, it has been suggested, to produce ordered, disciplined personalities who could focus relentlessly on success in the marketplace.[48] The conventional interpretation of these antisexual themes, of course, is that Victorian morality was but another means for suppressing women. The trouble with these arguments is that men more than women should be expected to favor, support, and extend the operation of this morality.

To understand the function of this ideology we must examine the market system involving the exchange of services between women and men. In historical, preindustrial, hierarchical society, male control and suppression of female sexuality focused especially on the paternal control of daughters. This system of control existed for the establishment of marriage alliances and for the protection of one's females from the intrusions of social inferiors. Sexual restrictiveness need not, however, imply direct male domination. In a system of equality between males in which females are denied access to other resources, a sexually restrictive ideology is predictable. Nineteenth-century mate choice was more or less an autonomous process uncontrolled by elders. American women, as de Tocqueville and others noted, had considerable freedom before marriage. Lacking economic resources, however, they could bargain with their only available good—sex. The price of sex, as of other commodities, varies inversely with the supply. Since husbands were limited by the autonomy of single women in finding sexual gratification elsewhere, sexual restrictiveness also served the interests of married women. Furthermore, in a democratic society, men could not easily violate the prerogatives of their male equals by seducing their wives. Thus Victorian morality functioned in the interest of both single and married women.[49] By having an effective monopoly on the supply of sexual gratification, married women could increase the "price" since their husbands still generally expressed a traditional uncontrolled demand for sex. Instead of being "possessed," women could now bargain. Respectable sexual ideology argued, it is true, that men should substitute work for sex. This would reduce the price that wives could exact. At the same time, according to the prevailing sexual ideology, marital sex was the least dangerous kind. In contrast to masturbation or prostitution, marital intercourse was evaluated positively. But, contrary to these ideological trends, prostitution appears to have increased during the nineteenth century. Whether or not prostitution was a substitute for marital sex or merely a reflection of the relative increase in the proportion of unattached males created by late marriage and high geographical mobility is uncertain. This brief economic analysis of the supply and demand of sex at least suggests the possibility that Victorian morality had distinctly feminist overtones.

In principle, Victorian sexual ideology did advance the interest of individual women. Whether or not this represented a genuine feminist ideology depends to some extent on the behavior of women as a group. The evidence seems to be fairly clear on this point. If women as individuals had wished to maximize their advantage, they could have furthered the devaluation of nonmarital sex for men by drawing more firmly the line between "good" and "bad" women, between the lady and the whore. While mothers may have done this on an individual basis, for example, by threatening their daughters with the dishonor of being a fallen woman, collectively they tended to sympathize with the prostitute or fallen woman and condemn the male exploiter or seducer.[50] The activity of the New York Female Moral Reform Society is an instructive case in point.[51]

Historians have had some difficulty in interpreting the anti-sexual theme in nineteenth-century women's history. Although [Carroll Smith-]Rosenberg recognizes the implicit radicalness of the assault on the double standard and the demand for a reformation in male sexual behavior, she tends to apologize for the failure of sexual reformers to link up with the "real" feminism represented by Sarah Grimke's feminist manifesto.[52] More serious is the distortion of the central question of the periodization of women's history. [Nancy] Cott's labeling of the first half of the nineteenth century as a question of "the cult of domesticity vs. social change," Kraditor's similar choice of "the family vs. autonomy," and [Gerda] Lerner's dichotomy of "the lady and the mill girl" all perpetuate the half-truth that the family served only as a source of social stability and change for women occurred only outside of the family.[53] I am arguing here, however, that the domestic roles of women and the perceptions that developed out of these roles were not an alternative to social change but presented a significant and positive development for nineteenth-century women.

Linking the decline of marital fertility to women's increasing autonomy within the family—the concept of "domestic feminism"—conflicts with several other theories held by scholars. To stress the failure of the woman's movement to support family limitation, as [J. A. and Olive] Banks do in their analyses for England, ignores the possibility of a parallel domestic feminist movement. It may be more to the point that antifeminists blamed the revolt against maternity and marital sexual intercourse on the public feminists.[54] The Bankses suggest that individual feminists may have fought a battle to gain control over their own reproduction.[55] The nineteenth-century neo-Malthusians and the woman's movement had different purposes; the former attempted to control the fertility of "others," i.e., the working classes, while the latter sought reforms in its own interest. Since mechanical means of contraception were associated with nonmarital sex of a kind exploitative of women, the opposition of women to these devices was an expression of the deeper hostility to the double standard.

A more serious objection to identifying the increasing power and autonomy of women within the family as feminism is, of course, the existence of the parallel tradition of "real" or "public" feminism. This tradition—linking Wollstonecraft, Seneca Falls, Stanton, Anthony, and Gilman—at least partially recognized the centrality of the role and position of women in the family to the general subjugation of women in society. In contrast, the goals of domestic feminism, at least in its initial stage, were situated entirely within marriage. Clearly some explanation is needed of why both strands of feminism existed. A possible answer relates to the evolution of the family in the process of modernization. With the democratization of American society, prestige ascribed by birth declined. Women born into families of high social status could not obtain deference if they remained single; even if a woman married a man of equally high status, his position would not assure her prestige; his status depended on his achievement. The satisfactory and valued performance in the roles of wife and mother could not compensate for the loss of status associated with the family line in preindustrial society. Thus public feminism would be most attractive to women of high social origin.[56] This conception of the woman as an atomistic person and citizen naturally drew on the Enlightenment attack on traditional social ties. The modeling of the Seneca Falls manifesto on the Declaration of Independence is suggestive in this regard.[57]

The liberal origins of public feminism were both its strength and its weakness. Because it emphasized a clear standard of justice and stressed the importance of human individuality, it was consistent with the most fundamental values in American political history. But it was also limiting as a political ideology in that it cast its rhetoric against nearly obsolete social forms that had little relevance in the experience of the average American woman, i.e., patriarchalism and arbitrary male authority. Paradoxically, public feminism was simultaneously behind and ahead of the times. Resting on eighteenth-century notions, it clashed with the romantic and sentimental mood of the nineteenth century. The social basis of the appeal of public feminism—the opportunity for married women to assume both family and social roles—would not be created for the average woman until the postindustrial period.

Domestic feminism, on the other hand, was a nineteenth-century creation, born out of the emerging conjugal family and the social stresses accompanying modern economic growth. Instead of postulating woman as an atom in competitive society, domestic feminism viewed woman as a person in the context of relationships with others. By defining the family as a community, this ideology allowed women to engage in something of a critique of male, materialistic, market society and simultaneously proceed to seize power within the family. Women asserted themselves within the family much as their husbands were attempting to assert themselves outside the home. Critics such as de Tocqueville concluded that the Victorian conjugal family was really a manifestation of selfishness and a retreat from the older conception of community as place. As one utopian-communitarian put it, the basic social question of the day was "whether the existence of the marital family is compatible with that of the universal family which the term 'Community' signifies."[58]

Community—"that mythical state of social wholeness in which each member has his place and in which life is regulated by cooperation rather than by competition and conflict"[59]—is not fixed historically in one social institution. Rather, as Kirk Jeffrey has argued, the nineteenth-century home was conceived of as a utopian community—at once a retreat, refuge, and critique of the city.[60] Jeffrey, however, does not fully realize the implications of his insight. He admits that the literature of the utopian home demanded that husbands consult their wives, avoid sexual assault on them, and even consciously structure their own behavior on the model of their spouses. Yet he still concludes that "there seems little doubt that they (women) suffered a notable decline in autonomy and morale during the three-quarters of a century following the founding of the American republic."[61] He suggests that women who engaged in writing, social activities, political reform, drug use, and sickliness were "dropping out" of domesticity. On the contrary, these responses reflect both the time and autonomy newly available to women. The romantic ideal of woman as wife and mother in contrast to the Enlightenment model of woman as person and citizen did not have entirely negative consequences—particularly for the vast majority of American women who did not benefit from the position of their family in society.

The perspective suggested above helps to explain why the history of the suffrage movement involved a shift from the woman-as-atomistic-person notion toward the ideology of woman as wife-and-mother. Drawing on the perceptions gained from their rise within the family, women finally entered politics in large numbers at the turn of the twentieth century. Given the importance of family limitation and sexual control in domestic feminism, it is not surprising that women were involved in and strongly supported the temperance and social purity movements—reform attempts implicitly attacking male culture. Since these antimale responses and attitudes were based on the familial and social experience of women, it seems beside the point to infer psychological abnormality from this emphasis.[62]

In an important sense, the traditions of domestic and public feminism merged in the fight for suffrage in the early twentieth century. In a study of "elite" women surveyed in 1913, [Richard] Jensen found that mothers of completed fertility actually exhibited more support for suffrage than childless married women.[63] Women in careers involving more social interaction, for example, medicine, law, administration, tended to favor suffrage more strongly than women in more privatistic occupations, for example, teaching, writing, art.[64] In short, the dichotomy between women trapped or suppressed within marriage and women seeking to gain freedom through social participation does not accurately represent the history of American women in the nineteenth century.

It has been argued that historians must take seriously the changing roles and behavior of women within the Victorian conjugal family. That women eventually attained a larger arena of activity was not so much an alternative to the woman-as-wife-and-mother as an extension of the progress made within the family itself. Future research doubtless will qualify, if not completely obviate, the arguments presented in this essay. Although power relationships within contemporary marriages are poorly understood by social scientists, this critical area very much needs a historical dimension.[65] The history of women must take into account major changes in the structure of society and the family. During the preindustrial period, women (mainly widows) exercised power as replacements for men. In the industrializing phase of the last century, married women gained power and a sense of autonomy within the family. In the postindustrial era, the potentiality for full social participation of women clearly exists. The construction of these historical stages inevitably involves oversimplification. Drawing these sharp contrasts, however, permits the historian to escape from the present-day definition of the situation. Once it is clear just what the long-run course of change actually was, more subtlety and attention to the mechanism of change will be possible in the analysis of women's history.

Notes

1. For a suggestive illustration of the impact of changing mortality on the average female see Peter R. Uhlenberg, "A Study of Cohort Life Cycles: Cohorts of Native-Born Massachusetts Women, 1830–1920," *Population Studies* 23 (November 1969): 407–20.

2. Wilson H. Grabill, Clyde V. Kiser, and Pascal K. Whelpton, *The Fertility of American Women* (New York: John Wiley & Sons, 1958), Table 67, p. 145.

3. Robert V. Wells, "Demographic Change and the Life Cycle of American Families," *Journal of Interdisciplinary History* 2 (Autumn 1971): Table 2, p. 282.

4. Some working women may have been counted as housewives by the census takers. Stanley Lebergott, *Manpower in Economic Growth* (New York: McGraw Hill, 1964), pp. 70–73, however, makes a cogent case for accepting the census figures.

5. Grabill et al., *Fertility*, Table 9, p. 22.

6. Ansley J. Coale and Melvin Zelnik, *New Estimates of Fertility and Population in the United States* (Princeton: Princeton University Press, 1963), p. 41.

7. Yasukichi Yasuba, *Birth Rates of the White Population in the United States, 1800–1860* (Baltimore: Johns Hopkins University Press, 1961), Table IV-9, p. 119, attributes 64.3 percent of the Connecticut fertility decline between 1774 and 1890 and 74.3 percent of the New Hampshire decline between 1774 and 1890 to change in marital fertility. Longer birth intervals and an earlier age at the termination of childbearing contributed nearly equally to the decrease in marital fertility. See Daniel Scott Smith, "Change in American Family Structure before the Demographic Transition: The Case of Hingham, Massachusetts" (unpublished paper presented to the American Society for Ethnohistory, October 1972), p. 3.

8. For a summary of the importance of withdrawal in the history of European contraception see D. V. Glass, *Population: Policies and Movements in Europe* (New York: Augustus M. Kelley, Booksellers, 1967), pp. 46–50.

9. For this definition see Aileen S. Kraditor, *Up from the Pedestal* (Chicago: Quadrangle Books, 1968), p. 5.

10. Aileen S. Kraditor, *The Ideas of the Woman Suffrage Movement* (New York: Anchor Books, 1971).

11. Carl N. Degler, "Revolution without Ideology: The Changing Place of Women in America," *Daedalus* 93 (Spring 1964): 653–70.

12. William L. O'Neill, *Everyone Was Brave* (Chicago: Quadrangle Books, 1969).

13. My use of the term "conjugal" is intended to be much broader than the strict application to household composition. On the relatively unchanging conjugal (or nuclear) structure of the household see Peter Laslett, ed., *Household and Family in Past Time* (Cambridge: Cambridge University Press, 1972). For an empirical demonstration of the types of changes involved see my article, "Parental Power and Marriage Patterns: An Analysis of Historical Trends in Hingham, Massachusetts," in the special historical issue of *Journal of Marriage and the Family* 35 (August 1973).

14. Philippe Aries, *Centuries of Childhood: A Social History of Family Life*, trans. Robert Baldick (New York: Vintage Books, 1962).

15. Julia Cherry Spruill, *Women's Life and Work in the Southern Colonies* (Chapel Hill: University of North Carolina Press, 1938); and Elisabeth Anthony Dexter, *Colonial Women of Affairs* (Boston: Houghton Miffin Company, 1924).

16. Richard B. Morris, *Studies in the History of American Law*, 2nd ed. (Philadelphia: Joseph M. Mitchell Co., 1959), pp. 126–200.

17. Maris Vinovskis, "Mortality Rates and Trends in Massachusetts before 1860," *Journal of Economic History* 32 (March 1972): 198–99. In the eighteenth century women began to live longer than men with the exception again of Ipswich.

18. Daniel Scott Smith, "Population, Family, and Society in Hingham, Massachusetts, 1635–1880" (unpublished Ph.D. diss., University of California, Berkeley, 1973), pp. 225–27.

19. Scattered American data are available in Lawrence A. Cremin, *American Education: The Colonial Experience, 1607–1783* (New York: Harper Torchbooks, 1970), pp. 526, 533, 540. Also see Carlo M. Cipolla, *Literacy and Development in the West* (Baltimore: Penguin Books, 1969), Table 1, p. 14, Professor Kenneth Lockridge of the University of Michigan, who is undertaking a major study of literacy in early America, has written me, however, that women using a mark may have been able to read.

20. Edward Shorter, "Capitalism, Culture, and Sexuality: Some Competing Models," *Social Science Quarterly* 53 (September 1972): 339.

21. David M. Potter, "American Women and the American Character," in *History and American Society: Essays of David M. Potter*, ed. Don E. Fehrenbacher (New York: Oxford University Press, 1973), pp. 227–303.

22. Evsey D. Domar, "The Causes of Slavery or Serfdom: A Hypothesis," *Journal of Economic History* 30 (March 1970): 18–32.

23. See Edmund S. Morgan, "Slavery and Freedom: An American Paradox," *Journal of American History* 59 (June 1972): 3–29.

24. Stanley Eagerman, "Some Considerations Relating to Property Rights in Man," *Journal of Economic History* 33 (March 1973): 56–65.

25. Jack E. Eblen, "An Analysis of Nineteenth-Century Frontier Populations," *Demography* 2 (1965): 399–413.

26. See Herbert Moller, "Sex Composition and Correlated Culture Patterns of Colonial America," *William and Mary Quarterly* 2 (April 1945): 113–53 for data on sex ratios.

27. Alan P. Grimes, *The Puritan Ethic and Woman Suffrage* (New York: Oxford University Press, 1967).

28. Bernard Farber, *Comparative Kinship Systems* (New York: John Wiley & Sons, 1968), pp. 23–46.

29. Walter E. Houghton, *The Victorian Frame of Mind* (New Haven: Yale University Press, 1957), pp. 348–53.

30. See Smith, "Parental Power and Marriage Patterns," *Journal of Marriage and the Family* (August 1973).

31. Grabill et al., *Fertility*, pp. 16–19. For insights based on differentials in census child-woman ratios see Yasuba, *Birth Rates*, as well as Colin Forster and G. S. Tucker, *Economic Opportunity and White American Fertility Ratios, 1800–1860* (New Haven: Yale University Press, 1972). For a brief statement of the

structural argument see Richard Easterlin, "Does Fertility Adjust to the Environment?" *American Economic Review* 61 (1971): 394–407.

32. John D. Kasarda, "Economic Structure and Fertility: A Comparative Analysis," *Demography* 8 (August 1971): 307–17.

33. Lebergott, *Manpower*, p. 63.

34. Kingsley Davis, "The American Family in Relation to Demographic Change," in *Demographic and Social Aspects of Population Growth*, eds. Charles F. Westoff and Robert Parke, Jr. (Washington, DC: Government Printing Office, 1972), p. 245.

35. One study involving seven Latin American cities has suggestively concluded that the "wife's motivation for employment, her education, and her preferred role seem to exert greater influence on her fertility than her actual role of employee or homemaker." Paula H. Hass, "Maternal Role Incompatibility and Fertility in Urban Latin America," *Journal of Social Issues* 28 (1972): 111–27.

36. Virginia Yans McLaughlin, "Patterns of Work and Family Organization: Buffalo's Italians," *Journal of Interdisciplinary History* 2 (Autumn 1971): 299–314.

37. For the relationship between fertility and individual characteristics see the special issue of the *Journal of Political Economy* 81, pt. 2 (March/April 1973) on "new economic approaches to fertility."

38. See the summary by Gerald E. Markle and Charles B. Nam, "Sex Determination: Its Impact on Fertility," *Social Biology* 18 (March 1971): 73–82.

39. N. Uddenberg, P. E. Almgren, and A. Nilsson, "Preference for Sex of Child among Pregnant Women," *Journal of Biosocial Science* 3 (July 1971): 267–80.

40. In a study of early twentieth-century *Who's Who*, cited by Markle and Nam, the sex ratio of the last child was 117.4 in 5,466 families. No differences appear in Harriet L. Fancher, "The Relationship between the Occupational Status of Individuals and the Sex Ratio of Their Offspring," *Human Biology* 28 (September 1966): 316–22.

41. William A. Alcott, *The Young Man's Wife, or Duties of Women in the Marriage Role* (Boston: George W. Light, 1837), p. 176.

42. Dio Lewis, *Chastity, or Our Secret Sins* (New York: Canfield Publishing Company, 1888), p. 18.

43. Henry C. Wright, *Marriage and Parentage* (Boston: Bela Marsh, 1853), pp. 242–55.

44. Anon., *Satan in Society* (Cincinnati: C. V. Vent, 1875), p. 153.

45. Ibid., p. 152.

46. For a discussion of the gradualness of change in sexual behavior see Daniel Scott Smith, "The Dating of the American Sexual Revolution: Evidence and Interpretation," in *The American Family in Social-Historical Perspective*, ed. Michael Gordon (New York: St. Martin's Press, 1973), pp. 321–35.

47. Quoted by George Humphrey Napheys, *The Physical Life of Women* (Philadelphia: H. C. Watts Co., 1882), p. 119.

48. Peter C. Cominos, "Late Victorian Sexual Respectability and the Social System," *International Review of Social History* 8 (1963): 18–48, 216–50.

49. Although the basic argument here was formulated independently, Randall Collins, "A Conflict Theory of Sexual Stratification," *Social Problems* 19 (Summer 1971): 3–21; and David G. Berger and Morton C. Wenger, "The Ideology of Virginity" (paper read at the 1972 meeting of the National Council on Family Relations) were very helpful in developing this theme.

50. On attitudes toward prostitution see Margaret Wyman, "The Rise of the Fallen Woman," *American Quarterly* 3 (Summer 1951): 167–77; and Robert E. Riegel, "Changing American Attitudes toward Prostitution," *Journal of the History of Ideas* 29 (July–September 1968): 437–52.

51. Carroll Smith-Rosenberg, "Beauty, the Beast and the Militant Woman: A Case Study in Sex Roles in Jacksonian America," *American Quarterly* 23 (October 1971): 562–84.

52. Ibid.

53. Nancy F. Cott, *Root of Bitterness* (New York: E. P. Dutton & Co., 1972), pp. 11–14; Kraditor, *Up from the Pedestal*, p. 21; Gerda Lerner, "The Lady and the Mill Girl: Changes in the Status of Women in the Age of Jackson," *Midcontinent American Studies Journal* 10 (Spring 1969): 5–14.

54. J. A. and Olive Banks, *Feminism and Family Planning in Victorian England* (Liverpool: Liverpool University Press, 1964), esp. pp. 53–57.

55. Ibid., p. 125.

56. In his book, *Daughters of the Promised Land* (Boston: Little, Brown, 1970), Page Smith argues that many prominent feminists had strong fathers. It might be that the true relationship, if any in fact exists, is between public feminism and high-status fathers.

57. Robert A. Nisbet, *The Sociological Tradition* (New York: Basic Books, 1966), chap. 3, esp. pp. 47–51.

58. Quoted by John L. Thomas, "Romantic Reform in America, 1815–1865," *American Quarterly* 17 (Winter 1965): 677.

59. Charles Abrams, *The Language of Cities* (New York: Viking Press, 1971), p. 60.

60. Kirk Jeffrey effectively develops this theme in "The Family as Utopian Retreat from the City: The Nineteenth-Century Contribution," in *The Family, Communes and Utopian Societies*, ed. Sallie Teselle (New York: Harper Torchbooks, 1972), pp. 21–41.

61. Ibid., p. 30.

62. For a psychological emphasis see James R. McGovern, "Anna Howard Shaw: New Approaches to Feminism," *Journal of Social History* 3 (Winter 1969–70): 135–53.

63. Richard Jensen, "Family, Career, and Reform: Women Leaders of the Progressive Era," in *The American Family in Social-Historical Perspective*, Table 7, p. 277.

64. Ibid., Table 2, p. 273.

65. An analysis of recent literature of this important topic is presented by Constantina Safilios-Rothschild, "The Study of Family Power Structure: A Review, 1960–1969," *Journal of Marriage and the Family* 32 (November 1970): 539–52.

12   Three Newspaper Advertisements

Cleveland Plain Dealer

Nineteenth-century women used commercial products as well as natural methods to prevent unwanted pregnancy. Before the enactment of the Comstock Act in 1873 (see Document 19), advertisements for commercial birth control and abortifacients appeared frequently in newspapers. These notices, published on the front page of the Cleveland Plain Dealer *in 1863, reveal the centrality of reproductive issues to Victorian culture.*

DR. WADSWORTH'S
Uterine Elevators
For Sale Wholesale and Retail by C. S. Mackenzie.

~

IMPORTANT TO THE LADIES!
THE GREAT FRENCH PREVENTIVE PILL,
Invented and prepared by an eminent French Physician, a graduate of the COLLEGE LES FEMMES DE LYONS, and practitioner in the Royal Hospitals of France and Germany.

This Pill contains no injurious drugs, but is compounded of PURELY VEGETABLE EXTRACTS, by a process known only to the inventor, Prof. M. BEIYROYE.

Their effect on the person is only on the Generative Organs, and does not effect the ordinary routine of business of the one using them; they regulate the organs and leave them in a state of perfect health.

This pill is, as its name implies, a preventive of gravidity or conception (but produces no abortion, remember that), and can be taken with the most perfect safety.

The inventor has used this Pill in his extensive practice in over 3000 cases, and always with the desired result. . . .

These Pills sent by mail in a secure and safe manner, post paid, on receipt of one dollar for single box, or six for 5 dollars.

Communications strictly confidential.

From the *Cleveland Plain Dealer*, July 1, 1863.

~

DR. VICHOIS' FEMALE MONTHLY PILLS,
The only genuine Female Pills in the world.
NOTICE TO LADIES.—No article of medicine intended for the exclusive use of Females, that has ever made its appearance, has met with such universal success as these celebrated Pills. No disease is so little understood, and consequently so badly treated, as female diseases. These Pills are the result of much study and careful experience in all varieties of female complaints, and in all cases of irregularities, suppression, lucorrhoea [*sic*] or whites, inflammation of the bladder, kidneys, and womb, and loss of nervous energy. Their use is above all praise. . . .
N.B.—Married ladies who have reason to believe themselves in the family way should not use them, as by their action on the womb, miscarriage would be the consequence.
Price $1.00 per box. Persons sending for Pills will enclose one dollar and two postage stamps.

13   On Disgraceful Advertisements

Boston Medical and Surgical Journal

The prevalence of birth control and abortion ads in nineteenth-century newspapers can be gauged not only by their appearance but also by the inflamed reaction that their publication provoked. In 1851 regular physicians condemned "utterly shameless" advertisers.

NO BETTER EVIDENCE OF THE corruption of the times and the boldness of those who live by imposition, and even crime, could be adduced, than many of the advertisements in this and all the great Atlantic cities. The advertisers seem utterly shameless, besides being thoroughly unprincipled. These shocking specimens of ingenious corruption, under the guise of Samaritan efforts for suffering humanity, are a disgrace to the newspapers, the medium through which the concentrated vileness of a mighty host of depredators on health obtains an introduction to the ignorant commu-

From "Disgraceful Advertisements," *Boston Medical and Surgical Journal* 44, no. 15 (May 14, 1851): 265.

nity. Look at the advertiser's description of the *Portuguese Female Pills*.—"The combination of ingredients of which these pills are composed, have made them the wonder and admiration of the world." "They must not be used during pregnancy, for though always mild, safe and healthy, they are certain to produce miscarriage, if used during that period." This false caution creates a positive demand for them for the most wicked purposes. And so of a multitude of others which we have neither time nor patience further to allude to. These advertisements are admitted into papers which circulate in families and lie on parlor tables, and the mischief which is done in various ways through their means is incalculable.

14   Madame Restell's Preventive Powders

New York Herald

The notices of individual abortionists enjoyed pride of place in newspaper advertising in the 1840–1870 period. The most notorious were those promoting the services of New York City's Madame Restell, the most famous abortionist of the era. She began performing abortions in the 1830s in relative anonymity. Publicity surrounding her arrest for malpractice in 1841, however, soon catapulted Restell to fame and wealth. By 1850 she had branch offices in Boston and Philadelphia, a traveling sales staff, and a capacious advertising budget (alleged to exceed $60,000 yearly by 1861). This ad in the New York Herald *for Restell's abortifacients typified those that she placed in Eastern newspapers in the 1840s.*

IMPORTANT TO MARRIED FEMALES—Madame Restell's Preventive Powders. These valuable powders have been universally adopted in Europe, but France in particular, for upwards of thirty years, as well as by thousands in this country as being the only mild, safe and efficacious remedy for married ladies whose health forbids a too rapid increase of family.

Madame Restell, as is well known, was for thirty years Female Physician in the two principal female hospitals in Europe—those

From Meade Minnegerode, *The Fabulous Forties, 1840–1850: A Presentation of Private Life* (New York: G. P. Putnam's Sons, 1924), 103–4.

of Vienna and Paris—where, favored by her great experience and opportunities, she attained that celebrity in those great discoveries in medical science so specially adapted to the female frame for which her medicines now stand unrivalled, as well in this country as in Europe. Her acquaintance with the physiology and anatomy of the female frame enabled her—by tracing the decline and ill health of married females scarce in the meridian of life, and the consequent rapid and often apparently inexplicable causes which consign many a fond mother to a premature grave, to their true source—to arrive at a knowledge of the primary cause of female indisposition—especially of married females—which in 1808 led to the discovery of her celebrated Preventive Powders. Their adoption has been the means of preserving not only the health but even the life of many an affectionate wife and fond mother.

Is it not wise and virtuous to prevent evils to which we are subject by simple and healthy means within our control? Every dispassionate, virtuous and enlightened mind will unhesitatingly answer in the affirmative. This is all that Madame Restell recommends, or ever recommended. Price five dollars a package, accompanied with full and particular directions.

15   The Evil of the Age

New York Times

Exact abortion rates for the nineteenth century are impossible to calculate. Historians agree, however, that the number rose steadily after the 1830s, possibly as much as 500 percent between 1830 to 1860—from one in twenty-five pregnancies to one in five. Of particular concern to many contemporaries was the demographic profile of the majority of women who had abortions: middle-class, native-born, and married. The popularity of the procedure among women who were expected by many to be guardians of morality and virtue set the stage for the public outcry and regulation that followed. A newspaper article in 1871 denounces New York City's abortion trade under the headline "The Evil of the Age."

From "The Evil of the Age," *New York Times*, August 23, 1871.

THE ENORMOUS AMOUNT OF MEDICAL malpractice that exists and flourishes, almost unchecked, in the city of New-York, is a theme for most serious consideration. Thousands of human beings are thus murdered before they have seen the light of this world, and thousands upon thousands more of adults are irremediably ruined in constitution, health and happiness. So secretly are these crimes committed, and so craftily do the perpetrators inveigle their victims, that it is next to impossible to obtain evidence and witnesses. Facts are so artfully concealed from the public mind, and appearances so carefully guarded, that very meagre outlines of the horrible truth have thus far been disclosed. But could even a portion of the facts that have been detected in frightful profusion, by the agents of the TIMES, be revealed in print, in their hideous truth, the reader would shrink from the appalling picture. . . .

The men and women who are engaged in this outrageous business are, with few exceptions, the worst class of impostors. Very few have genuine medical diplomas. Some are, or have been, nurses, and thus picked up fragments of knowledge, but are lamentably devoid of scientific education; in some cases they are ridiculously ignorant of the commonest rudiments or ordinary branches of learning. Some are said to have purchased diplomas, which it is reported can be obtained at certain Pennsylvania and Vermont institutions for $40 each. One man procured the diploma of a deceased physician, erased the name by some chemical process, and inserted his own. These documents are framed and conspicuously displayed in the "office," to attract the first glance of the dupes who may enter.

Very rarely do these persons use their true names. Nearly all have one or more aliases. One fellow who appends "M.D." to his circulars, was recently a cobbling shoemaker—and a very poor one at that. Suddenly he closed his shop, moved to another part of town, and was metamorphosed into a "doctor.". . . The female practitioners generally have been nurses or midwives. Almost invariably they are in partnership with a man "doctor," and are titled "madame," or in some cases "doctor." Lady patients, of course, prefer to call upon a "madame" in delicate cases, and are willing to converse freely with her. The ice being broken, the forbidden subject fully broached, and the purposes of the visit all developed, the "madame" calls in her "husband," the "doctor," who really then assumes charge of all that is afterward done. . . .

There are a great number of educated male and female physicians in or near this City, who live and thrive by these criminal practices. There are others who are the vilest of quacks. Of the latter there are about two hundred. Most of these have offices where they receive, consult with, and examine patients, but have no nursing rooms attached. The place is cunningly arranged. The outer hall door is open; the inner one is closed. Over the glass is a thick lace curtain, through which a keen-eyed attendant peers. When the patient enters, he sums up in his mind what his or her circumstances may be. He then steps into the hall, opens the front room door, and politely ushers them in. Two eye-holes in the folding doors afford the "doctor" a full view from the back room. Similar arrangements are provided at other places, so that a dissatisfied or an incurable dupe may be seen, and the "doctor" can slip out of the back door and be "not in." Sometimes an ostentatious display of instruments, bottles, and drugs is made for effect. The preliminary conversation is cheerful and polite, but brief. Then to business. A smatter of medical talk follows, then an explanation of symptoms, an examination, and the payment of the fee. A box of "pills," a phial of liquid "drops," or sometimes powders, are given, and the patient is bowed out.

A retired practitioner told the writer: "I never did any harm to these patients. I knew they were determined to get some one to do what they wished. If it was done, one, or perhaps two, lives would be sacrificed. So I pretended, and thus saved life. I gave them pills of paste, rhubarb and sugar; and colored water slightly flavored. . . ."

Undoubtedly a large number of quacks in the country, as well as in the City, practice the same method, and thus the fools and their money are parted. There are others, however, who pursue a widely different course. They compound and prescribe the most dangerous drugs, with reckless disregard of human suffering and life, and venture upon operations that are always hazardous, and not unfrequently fatal. The case of most recent notoriety was that of Dr. "Lookup" EVANS, who was recently convicted and sentenced in the Court of General Sessions to five years' imprisonment in the State Prison. . . . The evidences of guilt . . . were of the most conclusive nature. Human flesh, supposed to have been the remains of infants, was found [in his office] in barrels of lime and acids, undergoing decomposition. He came here from Scotland about twenty years ago, with no medical education whatever. Stubborn energy, active perseverance, and undaunted boldness appear to have forced his guilty success. . . . The reckless bravado of this wretch may be inferred from the circumstance that when he was released on bail upon the charge that looked so black against him, he opened an office . . . and continued to transact a brisk business. It is said that he advertised to the extent of $1,000 per week, and received a daily average of 400 letters, most of which enclosed money for "pills." In this nefarious business he had amassed a fortune of $100,000, a portion of which is invested in a splendid farm near Jamaica, Long Island. . . .

Only the Police authorities have anything like an adequate idea of the gigantic dimensions of this evil. Every day adds new indications. That the number of murders from this cause is not generally known is easily accounted for. All the parties interested have the strongest motives to unite in hushing the scandal.

IV

Regulating Reproduction

16 "About to Meet Her Maker": The State's Investigation of Abortion in Chicago, 1867–1940

Leslie J. Reagan

During the nineteenth century, legislation regulating abortion was passed for the first time in American history. Although legislative enactment occurred at different stages in different states, by 1900 all states, except Kentucky, had passed antiabortion measures. (In Kentucky, court rulings rather than legislation outlawed abortions.) Leslie Reagan, a historian at the University of Illinois at Urbana-Champaign, emphasizes the roles played by state officials and the medical profession to enforce in Chicago the new Illinois law.

IN MARCH 1916, CAROLINA PETROVITIS, a Lithuanian immigrant to Chicago, married and the mother of three, was in terrible pain following her abortion. Her friends called in Dr. Maurice Kahn. The doctor asked her, "Who did it for you?" He "coaxed" her to answer, then told her, "If you won't tell me what was done to you I can't handle your case." When Petrovitis finally revealed that a midwife had performed an abortion, Dr. Kahn called for an ambulance, sent her to a hospital, told the hospital physician of the situation, and suggested he "communicate with the Coroner's office." Three police officers soon arrived to question Petrovitis. With the permission of the hospital physician, Sgt. William E. O'Connor "instructed" an intern to "tell her she is going to die." The sergeant and another officer accompanied the intern to the woman's bedside. As the doctor told Petrovitis of her impending death, she "started to cry—her eyes watered." Sure that Petrovitis realized she was about to die, the police then collected from her a "dying declaration" in which she named the midwife who performed her abortion, told where and when it was done and the price paid, and described the instruments used. Later the police brought in the

From Leslie J. Reagan, " 'About to Meet Her Maker': Women, Doctors, Dying Declarations, and the State's Investigation of Abortion, Chicago, 1867–1940," *Journal of American History* 77 (March 1991): 1240–64. Figures omitted. See original article for full text of notes. Reprinted by permission of the *Journal of American History*.

midwife and asked Petrovitis "if this was the woman," and she nodded "yes." A third police officer drew up another dying statement "covering the facts." He read that statement back to Petrovitis as she lay in bed "in pain, vomiting," and she made her "mark" on the statement. Then she died.[1]

Carolina Petrovitis's experience in 1916 provides an example of the standard medical and investigative procedures used in criminal abortion cases. This account, drawn from the Cook County coroner's inquest into Petrovitis's death, illustrates this essay's major themes: the state's interest in obtaining dying declarations in order to prosecute abortionists; the intimate questioning endured by women during official investigations into abortion; and the ways in which physicians and hospitals served the state in collecting evidence in criminal abortion cases.

~

Abortion had not always been a crime. During the eighteenth and early nineteenth centuries, early abortions were legal under common law. Abortions were illegal only after quickening, the point at which a pregnant woman could feel the movements of the fetus (at approximately sixteen weeks' gestation). In the 1840s and 1850s abortion became commercialized and was increasingly used by married, white, native-born, Protestant women of the middle and upper classes. In 1857 the newly organized American Medical Association (AMA) initiated the ultimately successful crusade to make abortion illegal. Regular physicians, such as those who formed the AMA, were motivated to organize for the criminalization of abortion in part by their desire to win professional power, control medical practice, and restrict their irregular competitors, including homeopaths, midwives, and others. Hostility toward feminists, immigrants, and Catholics fueled the medical campaign against abortion and the passage of criminal abortion laws by state legislatures. In response to the physicians' campaign, in 1867 Illinois criminalized abortion and in 1871 outlawed the sale of abortifacients (drugs used to induce abortions) without a prescription. The new statutes permitted only therapeutic abortions performed when pregnancy threatened a woman's life. By the end of the century, every state had restricted abortion.[2]

The history of the nineteenth-century criminalization of abortion has been well studied, as has the movement to decriminalize it in the 1960s and 1970s. We know very little, however, about the practice or control of abortion while it was illegal in the United States.

This is the first study to address a crucial question in the history of reproduction: How did the state enforce the criminal abortion laws? I examine the methods of enforcement in Chicago from 1867, when Illinois made abortion illegal, to 1940, when changing conditions of abortion during the depression brought changes in the control of abortion. This study is based on research in legal records from the city of Chicago, Cook County, and Illinois and in the national medical literature. Coroners' inquests have been especially rich sources. The evidence shows continuity in the patterns of control followed by government officials in Chicago, and across the nation, for over half a century. In that period, in cases involving abortion, the state prosecuted chiefly abortionists, most often after a woman had died, and prosecutors relied for evidence on dying declarations collected from women near death due to their illegal abortions. Furthermore, the state focused on regulating the use of abortion by working-class women.[3]

The history of abortion reveals the complexity of the medical profession's role in sexual regulation. Feminists, writing primarily in the 1970s, have tended to portray the medical profession as intent on controlling female sexuality. My analysis of the regulation of abortion shifts the focus away from the medical profession and to the state as the regulator of sexual and reproductive behavior. To obtain evidence against abortionists, the state needed to have physicians reporting abortions and collecting dying declarations from their patients, which many doctors were reluctant to do. Without doctors' cooperation, police and prosecutors could do little to enforce the criminal abortion laws. Illinois law did not require doctors to report evidence of abortions. But by threatening physicians with prosecution, officials successfully pulled doctors into a partnership with the state in the suppression of abortion. In cases of illegal abortion, doctors were caught in the middle between their responsibilities to their patients and the demands of government officials.[4]

My analysis of the actual workings of lower-level government agencies in the control of abortion changes our understanding of legal processes and punishment. Most historians of crime and punishment have focused on police and prisons, while historians of women and the law have focused mainly on marriage and property rights, rather than on crime. Few have studied law in practice. This essay analyzes the experience of ordinary people caught in criminal investigations, the routine procedures of the legal system, rather than analyzing the volume of cases that reached the courts or judicial rulings. In abortion cases, the investigative procedures themselves constituted a form of punishment and control.

Although women were not arrested, prosecuted, or incarcerated for having abortions, the state nonetheless punished working-class women for having illegal abortions through official investigations and public exposure of their abortions. Recognizing the impact of the criminal abortion laws on women requires looking closely at the details of women's experiences: especially the interactions between women and their doctors and between women and police and petty state officials. Our understanding of what punishment is needs to be refined and redefined, particularly in cases of women who violate sexual norms, to include more subtle methods of disciplining individuals. The penalties imposed on women for having illegal abortions were not fines or jail sentences, but humiliating interrogations about sexual matters by male officials— often conducted at women's deathbeds. During investigations of abortion, police, coroner's officers, and prosecutors followed standard procedures in order to achieve the larger end of putting abortionists out of business. No evidence suggests that officials consciously designed their investigative procedures to harass women, yet the procedures were punitive, and this punishment became a central aspect of the state's efforts to control abortion. For government officials, the procedures were routine; for women subjected to them, the procedures were frightening and shameful once-in-a-lifetime events. Moreover, media attention to abortion deaths warned all women that those who strayed from marriage and motherhood would suffer death and shameful publicity.

This essay also highlights the gendered character both of legally enforced standards of behavior and of punishment. The criminalization of abortion not only prohibited abortion but demanded conformity to gender norms, which required men and women to marry, women to bear children, and men to bear the financial responsibility of children. Although most women who had abortions were married, state officials focused on unwed women and their partners. Coroners' inquests into the abortion-related deaths of unwed women reveal the state's interest in forcing working-class men to marry the women they had impregnated. Historians of sexuality have given little attention to the regulation of male heterosexuality, concentrating instead on the sexual control of women and "deviants." Yet in the late nineteenth and early twentieth centuries, I was surprised to find, the state punished unmarried working-class men whose lovers died after an abortion. The sexual double standard certainly existed, but the state imposed penalties on men, in certain unusual situations, when they failed to carry out their paternal obligation to marry their pregnant lovers and head a "nuclear" family. Unmarried men implicated in abortion deaths were, like women, punished through embarrassing questions about their sexual behavior; in general, the state punished men in more conventionally recognized ways: arresting, jailing, and prosecuting them.[5]

The state's attempt to control abortion reflected a turn-of-the-century trend toward growing intervention by the state in medical practice as well as in sexual and family matters. The regulation of doctors by the state in abortion cases coincided with expanding governmental control of medicine through licensing laws and medical practice acts. The state's interest in enforcing marriage when premarital sex led to pregnancy reveals another area where it took over the functions of the male patriarch. The punishment of unmarried men for the abortion-related deaths of unmarried women may also have reflected the influence of feminist critiques of male sexual irresponsibility.[6]

Despite legal prohibitions, each year thousands of women around the country had abortions. In 1904, Dr. Charles Sumner Bacon estimated that "six to ten thousand abortions are induced in Chicago every year." Both midwives and physicians performed abortions in the early twentieth century, and many women induced their own abortions at home. At drugstores, women could buy abortifacients and instruments, such as rubber catheters, to induce abortions. Most women survived their abortions, and most abortions remained hidden from state authorities. Yet the number of deaths following illegal abortions was significant. In the late 1920s a Children's Bureau study documented that at least 11 percent of deaths related to pregnancy and childbearing followed illegal abortion.[7]

Working-class women's poverty—in both wealth and health care—made it more likely that they, rather than middle-class women, would reach official attention for having abortions. All forty-four Cook County coroner's inquests that I have examined recorded investigations into the abortions and deaths of white, working-class women. Over half of the women were immigrants or daughters of immigrants. Working-class women may have had more abortions than did middle-class women. In addition, poor women, lacking funds, often used inexpensive, and often dangerous, self-induced measures and delayed calling in doctors if they had complications. By the time poor women sought medical attention, they had often reached a critical stage and, as a result, had come to the attention of officials. Affluent women avoided official investigations into their abortions because they had personal relations with private physicians, many of whom never collected dying statements, destroyed such statements, or falsified death certificates. If necessary, wealthier families might be able to pressure or pay physicians, coroners, the police, and the press to keep quiet about a woman's abortion-related death.[8]

I found only one case in which the Cook County coroner investigated the abortion-related death of a black woman, in 1916, and, unfortunately, there is no record of the coroner's inquest into it. Despite a tremendous increase in Chicago's black population after World War I, I did not find any cases involving black women in the 1920s or 1930s. The paucity of information on the abortion-related deaths of black women may be an artifact of bias in the sources or may reflect the relatively small size of Chicago's black population. Black women who called in doctors or entered hospitals after their abortions would presumably have been questioned as Petrovitis was. They might have found it particularly upsetting to be questioned by white police officers or coroner's staff. A black physician prosecuted for abortion complained of racist treatment by the coroner's office; black women dying due to abortions or their family members may have suffered similar incidents.[9]

~

From the late nineteenth century through the 1930s, the state prosecuted abortionists primarily after a woman died. Popular tolerance of abortion tempered enforcement of the laws. Prosecutors discovered early the difficulty of winning convictions in criminal abortion cases. Juries nullified the law and regularly acquitted abortionists. As a result, prosecutors concentrated on cases where they had a "victim"—a woman who had died at the hands of a criminal abortionist. In 1903 attorney H. H. Hawkins reviewed Colorado's record and concluded, "No one is prosecuted in Colorado for abortion except where death occurs . . . the law only applies to the man who is so unskilful as to kill his patient." Thirty-seven out of the forty-three different abortion cases on which the Supreme Court of Illinois ruled between 1870 and 1940 involved a woman's death. Because prosecutors focused on abortionists responsible for abortion-related deaths, they relied for evidence on dying declarations, such as those obtained from Petrovitis, and coroner's inquests. In almost a third of the Illinois Supreme Court cases in which a woman had died because of an abortion, the opinions commented on dying declarations.[10]

Simply counting the convictions for abortion underestimates and obscures the state's significant effort to enforce the criminal abortion laws; analysis of the entire investigative process brings it to light. Police arrests for abortion and inquests into abortion deaths indicate a greater degree of interest in repressing abortion than suggested by the number of convictions. Between 1902 and 1934 in Chicago, the state's attorney's office prosecuted at most a handful of criminal abortion cases a year and never won more than one or two of them. In one ten-year period, less than one-quarter of the prosecutions for murder by abortion resulted in a conviction. In contrast, police made at least ten arrests annually for abortion after 1905 and averaged twenty-five or twenty-six arrests annually during the 1910s and 1920s and almost forty arrests annually in the early 1930s. Police stepped up their arrests under political pressure. The coroner conducted even more inquests into abortion deaths every year. Between 1901 and 1919, the years for which figures are available, the Cook County coroner investigated an average of over 60 abortion deaths a year, from a low of 18 in 1903 to a high of 103 in 1917. Not all of those deaths followed criminal abortions. Some deaths followed "accidental," "self-induced," or "spontaneous" abortions or ones due to an "undetermined" cause, but because the coroner had to determine the cause of death, those deaths were investigated like criminal cases. Between 1905 and 1919 the coroner sent an average of twelve suspects a year to the grand jury. The level of legal action against abortion steadily increased, but the number of convictions did not change at all. While most of the rise in abortion arrests and inquests is probably explained by Chicago's growing population, the increase may also reflect intensified efforts by state officials to control abortion or an increase in police surveillance and control of the populace in general or of abortion specifically. Sorting out the role and relative importance of those factors in causing the rise in arrests and investigations is difficult, though perhaps possible with additional research.[11]

Abortion investigations began, as in the Petrovitis case, when physicians or hospital staff members noticed "suspicious" cases and reported them to the police or the Cook County coroner. In the first stage of an investigation, a woman was questioned by her doctor. She might be questioned again by police officers or special investigators sent from the coroner's office. Each interrogation was an attempt to obtain a legally valid dying declaration, in which the woman admitted her abortion and named her abortionist. A dying declaration not only led police to suspects; it also was crucial evidence that could be introduced at criminal trials. As one lawyer observed, it was almost "impossible" to obtain evidence of criminal abortion in any other way.[12]

The dying declaration was an unusual legal instrument that allowed the words of the dead to enter the courtroom. Legally, a dying declaration is an exception to the hearsay rule, which excludes the courtroom use of information that has been received secondhand. Common law allowed the admission of dying declarations as evidence in homicide cases, and states permitted this exception in abortion cases as well. Courts treated dying declarations as though given under oath based on the common law assumption that a dying person would not lie since she was, as the coroner put it during the inquest on Petrovitis, "about to leave the world—to meet her maker." The exception allowed prosecutors to present the dying declaration, in court, as the dead woman's own accusation of the person who had killed her.[13]

If the woman died, the abortion investigation proceeded to a second stage: an autopsy performed by coroner's physicians and an official coroner's inquest into the woman's death. During the inquest the coroner or his deputy questioned witnesses and attempted to collect the facts in the case. There the police for the first time presented the dying statements they had collected, other information uncovered during their investigation, or individuals possessing information. Family members, lovers, friends, midwives, physicians, and hospital staff all testified at the inquests. A coroner's jury then deliberated on the proceedings and decided the cause of death. Although the legal purpose of an inquest was simply to determine the cause of death, the coroner in fact wielded significant power. The coroner's inquest was a highly important stage in the legal process since it generally determined whether anyone would be criminally prosecuted. The jury decided the guilt or innocence of various people involved in a case, and if the jury determined that the woman's death resulted from "murder by abortion," it ordered the police to hold the suspected abortionist and accomplices. The suspects remained in jail or out on bail until the case was concluded. Once the coroner's jury made its determination, prosecutors brought the case before the grand jury, which then indicted the suspects. Both prosecutors and the grand jury tended to follow the findings of the coroner's jury; if the coroner's jury failed to accuse anyone of criminal abortion, prosecutors generally dropped the case. Abortion cases did not come to trial exclusively after inquests into abortion-related deaths; some abortionists were caught during raids, and sometimes women testified in court against them, but most prosecutions for criminal abortion followed the death or injury of a woman.[14]

A visible and vocal minority of physicians actively assisted state officials in efforts to suppress abortion in Chicago. At various times, members of the Chicago Medical Society's criminal abortion committee worked to remove abortion advertising from the pages of local newspapers, assisted coroner's investigations, and joined efforts to investigate and control midwives in order to end abortion in their city. The AMA, headquartered in Chicago, collected information on abortionists and abortifacients and shared it with local and federal officials investigating violations of the criminal law.[15]

Not all physicians wanted to help prosecutors bring abortionists to trial, however. Publicly, the leaders of the medical profession opposed abortion; privately, many physicians sympathized with women's need for abortions, performed abortions, or referred patients to midwives or physicians who performed them. Dr. Rudolph Holmes discovered during his work on the criminal abortion committee that physicians often decline to testify against abortionists. He reported that "so-called reputable members of our Chicago Medical Society regularly appear in court to support the testimony of some notorious abortionist." Furthermore, he concluded, "the public does not want, the profession does not want, the women in particular do not want any aggressive campaign against the crime of abortion." Dr. Charles H. Parkes, chairman of the Chicago Medical Society's criminal abortion committee in 1912, confessed that state authorities believed the society's members to be "apathetic in the extreme" regarding abortion. Some members were abortionists.[16]

The illegality of abortion made caring for patients who had had abortions not only a medical challenge but also a legal peril. In abortion cases, physicians performed emergency curettements, repaired uterine tears and wounds, tried to stop hemorrhaging, and, most difficult in an age without antibiotics, fought infections. Once a woman had a widespread, septic infection (characterized by chills and fever), it was very likely that she would die. If a woman died despite a doctor's efforts, he became a likely suspect in the criminal abortion case. According to the New York attorney Almuth C. Vandiver, police arrested physicians "simply because they were the last physician attending the patient and they had not made their report to the coroner."[17]

The state could not investigate abortion cases without medical cooperation; state officials won doctors' help by threatening them. Physicians learned that if they failed to report criminal abortion cases, the investigative process could be turned against them. At a 1900 meeting of the Illinois State Medical Society, Dr. O. B. Will of Peoria warned his associates of the "responsibilities and dangers" associated with abortion by relating his own "very annoying experience" when a patient died because of an abortion. He was indicted as an accessory to murder in an abortion case for "keeping the circumstances quiet, . . . not securing a dying statement from the patient, and . . . not informing the coroner." Will declared that he was not required to notify the coroner and that the woman had refused to make a statement, but his story implied that cooperation with the authorities might help other doctors avoid similar notoriety. One doctor told his colleagues horror stories of Boston physicians who had been arrested, tried, and, though acquitted of abortion charges, nonetheless ousted by the Massachusetts Medical Society. Doctors who were associated with illegal abortion also risked losing their medical licenses. In Illinois a physician had to be convicted of abortion to lose his or her license, but some states revoked medical licenses without a trial. Physicians learned from tales like these that if they treated women for complications following abortions, they should report the cases to local officials or collect dying declarations themselves in order to avoid being arrested and prosecuted.[18]

Coroners' inquests into abortion deaths and the negative publicity coroners could cause helped enmesh doctors and hospitals in the enforcement system. At inquests into abortion-related deaths, the Cook County coroner regularly reminded attending physicians of the unwritten "rule" (emanating from the law enforcers) requiring them to call the police or coroner whenever there was evidence that a woman had been "tampered with" and reprimanded those who failed to follow this policy. The fragile reputations of hospitals and physicians could be damaged if they were even named or associated with an abortion case in the newspapers. At a 1915 inquest into the death of a woman due to abortion, the coroner's jury suggested that Rhodes Avenue Hospital, which had cared for the woman, "be severely censured for lax methods in not complying with the rules required in notifying the proper officials . . . and the seeming indifference on the part of physicians and assistants . . . to ascertain[ing] who performed said abortion." The hospital's superintendent strongly objected to this censure and the notoriety the hospital subsequently received in Chicago's newspapers. Its superintendent wrote that the hospital had always cooperated with the coroner's office and that "the hospital was not on trial." Such publicized reproofs warned hospitals and physicians that if they failed to cooperate with state officials, their institutions and their individual careers could be hurt.[19]

By 1917, perhaps earlier, state authorities had persuaded Chicago's hospitals to pledge their cooperation in the investigation of abortion cases. The city's hospital superintendents reached an agreement with the coroner, chief of police, and state's attorney's office to notify the coroner's office when they saw patients who had had abortions. Furthermore, if it seemed that the woman would die before an official investigator arrived, hospitals agreed to collect the dying declaration themselves. The coroner even provided hospitals with a "blank form" for dying declarations. Although the official expectation that doctors would report abortion cases to the coroner was not codified, in the minds of both doctors and state officials, reporting abortions was, as one doctor described it in court, "compulsory."[20]

A few New York physicians voiced the indignation that many doctors may have felt toward coroners and the treatment they received from them. Doctors who were the last attending physicians in abortion cases resented being pursued by the police and subjected to "disagreeable inquest[s]." New York physicians felt harassed by the city's coroners, who were, doctors complained, far too ready to arrest and investigate physicians in criminal abortion cases.[21]

One way to protect themselves from legal trouble and notoriety in abortion cases, physicians learned, was to secure dying declarations. In 1912 the chairman of the Chicago Medical Society's criminal abortion committee, Dr. Parkes, reminded the society that "it is extremely easy for anyone to become criminally involved when connected with these cases, unless properly protected." Parkes presented to the medical society a model dying declaration drafted by State's Attorney John Wayman that would be legally admissible as evidence, that would "stand the supreme court test." Wayman advised the doctors to ask the dying woman the following questions: "*Q*. Do you believe that you are about to die? . . . *Q*. Have you any hope of recovery? . . . *Q*. Do you understand these questions fully? . . . *Q*. Are you able to give a clear account of the causes of your illness?"[22]

The state's attorney also provided a standardized format for the dying woman's answer. She should answer, "I am Miss ———. Believing that I am about to die, and having no hope of recovery, I make the following statement, while of sound mind and in full possession of my faculties." To be considered valid in court, the statement had to establish that the woman believed she was near death. The woman was then expected to name her abortionist; to tell when, where, and how the abortion was done; and to name the man "responsible" for her pregnant "condition." Although most women who had abortions were married, the state's prosecutors focused on abortions by unwed women, and this formulaic dying declaration assumed that the dying woman would be unmarried.[23]

Physicians advised each other to deny medical care to a woman who had had an abortion until she made a statement. In 1902 the editors of the *Journal of the American Medical Association* endorsed this policy of (mis)treating abortion patients. The *Journal*'s editorial quoted a physician who counseled his colleagues to "refuse all responsibility for the patient unless a confession exonerating him from any connection with the crime is given." Twenty years later, Dr. Palmer Findley gave the same advice to obstetricians and gynecologists. "It is common experience," he reported, "that the patient will tell all she knows when made to realize her danger and a double purpose is attained—the physician in charge is protected and the guilty party is revealed."[24]

If a woman refused to give information, the smart doctor, according to these advisers, would walk out and refuse to attend her. And some physicians, like Dr. Kahn in the Petrovitis case, threatened to do just that. In 1916 a Chicago fireman called in Dr. G. P. Miller to attend his wife who had been sick for three weeks following her abortion. Dr. Miller told her, "If I take this case . . . I want you to tell me the truth and who did it, who it was. Under the understanding that I was going to leave the house and have nothing to do with it, she told me the whole story." Physicians' refusals to treat abortion cases seem to have reached women's consciousness. In 1930, Mathilde Kleinschmidt, ill from her abortion, rejected her boyfriend's plan to call in a second doctor and insisted that he instead find the doctor who had performed the abortion. "Another doctor won't look at me," she explained. "He won't take the case."[25]

Fear of undeserved prosecution encouraged physicians to distrust their female patients. New York attorney Vandiver warned doctors, "Unscrupulous women and their accomplices have it within their power . . . to successfully blackmail the reputable practitioner, who omits the essential precautions for his protection." Dr. Henry Dawson Furniss told a story that encapsulated doctors' worst fears. He had "absolutely refused" to perform an abortion for a woman who later died from one. Under questioning, she got even with Furniss for spurning her plea by blaming him for her abortion.[26]

It seems that women rarely falsely accused physicians, and many, perhaps the majority, protected their abortionists by refusing to name them to doctors or policemen. The prosecuting attorney for St. Louis, Ernest F. Oakley, marveled at the loyalty of women who refused to reveal their abortionists' names. Dying declarations, he thought, were obtained in only "four out of ten cases." One New York woman, who was hospitalized following her abortion, told the doctors who pressed her to name her abortionist, "She was the only one who would help me, and I won't tell on her."[27]

Because the illegality of abortion compelled doctors to regard all miscarriages as suspect and to protect themselves against prosecution, women's health care suffered. Fearing prosecution, many physicians treated their female patients badly—rudely questioning them in attempts to gain dying declarations or delaying or refusing to provide needed medical care. For example, in 1915 when city, state, and federal officials began a "war" on abortion in Chicago following an abortion-related death, the *Chicago Tribune* discovered that "publicity has changed the attitude of hospital authorities in regard to the handling of abortion victims." One hospital superintendent would neither admit an abortion patient nor allow an operation "until he had received orders from the police." In this case, the hospital allowed police officers to make medical and legal decisions as a result of a local antiabortion campaign. "It was not until detectives had assured the superintendent that an operation was necessary to save Mrs. Lapinski's life and that there would be no trouble for the hospital," the newspaper reported, "that Dr. G. M. Cushing . . . was permitted to take the sufferer to the operating room." In a less dramatic fashion, doctors regularly avoided caring for abortion patients by sending them to hospitals instead. In 1929, when Dr. Julius Auerbach was called in to care for a woman who had had an abortion, he refused to examine her and sent her to the county hospital to avoid being "implicated" in the case.[28]

While some frightened doctors threatened to deny medical care to women who had abortions and insisted that they make statements, others agreed with one physician who said that he refused "to act as a policeman" for the state. Dr. Parkes reported that Chicago officials "believe that the best hospitals now smother these cases and hinder in every way the work of investigation." Dr. William Robinson, a radical who advocated legalized abortion, scorned physicians who "badger[ed]" sick women to make dying statements. "The business of the doctor is to relieve pain, cure disease and save life," he declared, "not to act as a bloodhound [for] the state."[29]

Other doctors found a middle ground between compliance with and rejection of the state's rules. Dr. Henry Kruse asked Edna Lamb about her abortion but did not inform her that she was about to die, omitting the explicit statement needed to make a dying declaration valid. He later explained, "We don't do that to patients because sometimes it is ver[y] discouraging and the result is bad." Other doctors questioned their patients about their abortions but only reported cases to authorities when women died. When women survived, the doctors destroyed their statements and kept the abortions confidential. In fact, the Cook County coroner accepted this practice as one that protected the interests of women who survived their abortions, shielded physicians from possible prosecution, and provided information to authorities in cases of death.[30]

Making a patient's medical history public undermined the private and personal relationships physicians had with their patients. Some physicians expressed their intention of maintaining patients' confidentiality, regardless of the wishes of authorities. Dr. Louis Frank of Louisville, Kentucky, commented on the issue in 1904, "If I was called in I would not give testimony compromising a young lady, and I would not put it on record, no matter what the facts were, and I would not 'give away' a girl, but would attempt to protect her." Doctors Richard C. Norris and A. C. Morgan of Philadelphia strongly believed in the patient's right to confidentiality and proclaimed that medical ethics barred them from testifying against abortionists if such testimony violated their relationships with patients.[31]

The names of women who had had illegal abortions and the intimate details of their lives periodically hit the newspapers. Press coverage of abortion-related deaths warned all women of the dangers of abortion: death and publicity. Sometimes newspapers covered abortion stories on the front page and included photos; often abortion-related deaths and arrests of abortionists appeared in small announcements. The story of an unwed woman's seduction and abortion-related death made exciting copy and could dominate local newspapers for days. In 1916, Chicago and Denver newspapers published Ruth Merriweather's love letters to a Chicago medical student, who was on trial for his involvement in her abortion-related death. In 1918 the *Chicago Examiner* ran a series of "*tragedies*," excerpted from coroners' inquests, that told the stories of unwed women "*who were killed through illegal operations*." The articles in this series, and others like them, warned young women of the dangers of seduction and abortion and also warned rural fathers of the need to protect their daughters from the dangers of city life. The names and addresses of married women who had abortions often appeared in the press too, but their stories were not presented as seduction tales. Newspapers sometimes highlighted police officers' discovery of thousands of women's names in an abortionist's patient records. In doing so, they implicitly threatened women who had had abortions with the danger that they too could be named and exposed in the newspaper.[32]

Public exposure of a woman's abortion—through the press or gossip—served as social punishment of women who had abortions and members of their families. A Chicago police officer recalled that when he questioned Mary Shelley, she "remark[ed] that she didn't want the statement in the newspapers." Some women whose abortions had been reported in the local press lived to face the shame of public exposure. Doctors observed that even when a woman died after an abortion, families did not want authorities to investigate because they wanted "to shield her reputation." Some families invited state investigation of abortions and pursued prosecution, yet even they may have resented publicity about the case. One mother whose daughter had died as a result of an illegal abortion cried at a public hearing that her whole family had "keenly felt the disgrace" of the crime. When Frances Collins died, police visited "all houses on both sides" of her home as well as "some ladies" in her old neighborhood and questioned them in hopes of finding a "woman confidant." The police failed to find any information, but they had informed the woman's entire community of her death by abortion and displayed the state's interest in controlling abortion.[33]

To the women whose abortions attracted the attention of medical and legal authorities, the demands of physicians and police for dying statements felt punitive. One woman described her hospital experience after an abortion as "very humiliating. The doctors put me through a regular jail examination." In their efforts to obtain dying declarations, policemen and physicians, usually male, repeatedly questioned women abour their private lives, their sexuality, and their abortions; they asked women when they last menstruated, when they went to the abortionist, and what he or she did. Were instruments introduced into "their privates"? If so, what did the instruments look like and how were they used? If the woman was unmarried, she was asked with whom she had been sexually intimate and when, precisely the information that she may have hoped to conceal by having an abortion. Furthermore, as in the Petrovitis case, the police routinely brought the suspected abortionist to the bedside of the dying woman for her to identify and accuse. Hundreds of women who had abortions may have been questioned annually by physicians, police, or coroner's officers without their names ever entering official records because they survived their abortions.[34]

An investigation into a woman's abortion-related death was a shameful event for her relatives and friends because state officials required that they speak publicly about sexual matters that they ordinarily kept private and rarely discussed. At the Petrovitis inquest, police officer John A. Gallagher recalled that Petrovitis's sister had translated his questions, but when he reached the questions "about using instruments on her privates . . . the sister could not interpret anymore, didn't want to." To document a pregnancy and abortion, the coroner asked questions about menstruation, sexual histories, and women's bodies. Family and friends often evaded such questions, but the coroner simply repeated his questions until he received an answer. Female witnesses, who may have discussed sexual topics only with other women, sometimes hesitated to speak before male officials, attorneys, and a jury of six men. At a 1917 inquest into an abortion death, the dead woman's sister perjured herself during questioning. At a later trial, she explained, "I knew everything but I could not answer all of them on account of all the men around. . . . Because there was so many men around I hated to talk about my poor sister more than I had to." The question she could not answer was, she explained, "about her body. . . . He asked me if the doctor had used any instrument, and I said no at that time." One immigrant woman commented during questioning by the coroner about her friend's abortion, "I am ashamed to tell." Despite her shame, she was forced to tell and to repeat her testimony at a criminal trial of the midwife-abortionist.[35]

The members of the coroner's staff understood that female family members often shared intimate knowledge about women's bodies and sexual behavior, and they tried to crack that female network to obtain information. The questioning of nineteen-year-old Julia McElroy at the 1928 inquest into the death of her sister Eunice McElroy is a vivid example of how the coroner's office expected sisters to have specific information, asked personal and shaming questions, and threatened those suspected of not cooperating. The deputy coroner questioned Julia intensively about the sisters' dating practices and Eunice's sexual behavior. He began with an offer to proceed in "a private chamber" because his questions might embarrass Julia, but he immediately denied the validity of her feelings in the legal arena. As he explained to Julia, "I may put some question to you that you may think is embarrassing, but it is not. I am just merely questioning you because I am an officer of the law, the coroner." Julia denied knowing anything. The coroner established that the sisters shared a bed and asked, "When was the last time your sister had her last menstrual period? You tell the truth," he ordered. Julia told him that Eunice had menstruated over three months earlier and denied knowing of a pregnancy. "Well, you know they are supposed to come around and flow once a month unless a person is flowing irregularly? . . . you would know when your sister is unwell. She wears a napkin and you probably wear a napkin when you are not well on account of the odor, isn't that a fact?" Julia responded only with silence. The coroner continued to press her for information about Eunice's periods and sexual history. When Julia still maintained her ignorance a few days later, the deputy warned her, "If you don't tell a true story, you are going to get into a jam for a year." On the final day of the inquest, the deputy coroner told Julia that he knew that she had shielded the abortionist. With that, Julia revealed her knowledge and explained that she had been repeating the false story begun by her sister to protect her abortionist. The coroner concluded, "You are lucky you are telling the truth. I would sure send you to jail." The coroner eventually obtained from Julia McElroy evidence helpful in the prosecution of Eunice McElroy's abortionist, but he had also put Julia through a grueling experience, asked her graphic sexual questions, questioned her closely about her sister's and her own dating behavior, and threatened her with jail.[36]

Criminal abortion investigations reveal the importance of marriage—and especially of the lack of it—in the eyes of state officials. When police collected dying statements, they routinely asked about the woman's marital status, and at inquests into the deaths of unmarried women, many of the coroner's questions focused on marital status. At inquests the coroner probed to discover whether the man had offered marriage. To a man, all claimed to have "promised to marry her." Perhaps men understood that this was the only way they could redeem themselves in the eyes of the law and the community. Yet there is evidence of genuine intention to marry. One man had bought a wedding ring; some even married after the abortion. In some cases, the woman wanted to delay marriage; in others, couples found marriage and children financially impossible. At the trial occasioned by the abortion-related death of his girlfriend, William Cozzi testified "that he went to Dr. Rongetti to get rid of the baby because he could not afford it."[37]

Just as dying women endured intrusive questioning about their abortions, their unmarried lovers endured similar interrogations at inquests. For both unmarried women and men, the official prying into their private sexual lives, and their own mortification, served as punishment for their illicit sexual behavior. The coroner's questions to Marshall Hostetler about his sexual relationship with his sweetheart (who died in 1915) were not unusual at inquests into abortion deaths. The coroner asked Hostetler, "When did you become intimate with her? . . . have any relations with her? . . . When did that occur? . . . Had you been intimate with her before? . . . How many times? . . . Where did it occur?"[38]

During public investigations into abortion, men, too, tried to avoid answering questions about sex. Charles Morehouse, for example, readily answered numerous questions about his girlfriend's abortion, how they borrowed money from an aunt, and how the family had tried to avoid an investigation. He also explained that the doctor had used "a spray." But when the coroner asked, "Where?" Morehouse was silent. "*A*. No Response. *Q*. What portion of the body? *A*. Well, the private parts."[39]

The "sweetheart of the dead girl" could be punished severely for having transgressed sexual norms. When an unwed woman died because of an abortion, her lover was automatically arrested, jailed, interrogated by the police and coroner, and sometimes prosecuted as an accessory to the crime. Bob Berry's experience in 1931 was typical. When Alma Bromps died, policemen arrived at Berry's door, arrested him, and jailed him. The next morning he identified the body of his girlfriend and was questioned at the inquest into her death. He remained in jail for at least a week and ultimately became a witness for the state against the accused abortionist. Unmarried men involved in abortion deaths often spent at least one night in jail before the inquests. If they had no money to bail themselves out, they might spend several days or weeks, depending on the length of the inquest. Some spent months in jail waiting for their cases to come to trial. In 1917, Charles Morehouse spent four months in jail after the death of his girlfriend. The state prosecuted Partick O'Connell, a poor laborer, along with Dr. Adolph Buettner, for the abortion that led to Nellie Walsh's death. Although O'Connell was acquitted, it appears that he spent the nine months between Walsh's death and his criminal trial in the Cook County Jail. Other men were convicted and sentenced to prison for their part in an abortion.[40]

The actions of state officials toward unmarried men implicated in criminal abortion deaths reveal the state's stake in enforcing marriage in cases where an unwed woman became pregnant. The state punished young men for the moral offense of engaging in premarital intercourse and then failing to fulfill the implicit engagement by marrying the women they had made pregnant. Police routinely arrested and incarcerated unmarried men as accomplices in the crime of abortion, and the state's attorney sometimes prosecuted them. In contrast, husbands, who often had been just as involved as unmarried men in obtaining abortions, were very rarely arrested or prosecuted as accomplices when their wives died.[41]

Bastardy cases heard in Chicago also demonstrate the state's policy of coercing couples into marrying when pregnancy occurred. In bastardy cases, the unwed woman brought the father to court to register paternity and to gain minimal financial support for the child. If the couple did not marry, the man could be fined up to $550 or sentenced to six months in jail. Of 163 bastardy cases studied by Hull House leader Louise DeKoven Bowen in 1914, a third ended in marriage. Fourteen couples "settled out of court" by marrying, while forty "married in court." A man who reconsidered his situation once in jail could gain his freedom if he decided to marry the woman and legitimate their child.[42]

The official response to unmarried men in abortion cases, as in bastardy cases, warned other young men of the dangerous consequences of avoiding marriage and children when pregnancy occurred. The newspaper story of an abortion-related death often told of the arrest, imprisonment, and interrogation of the "sweetheart of the dead girl," and young men probably traded detailed information about the events that transpired during abortion investigations. Newspaper coverage of abortions warned women that they could die and men that they could be thrown in jail—some may have concluded that it was better to marry.[43]

Jilted women could exploit the state's readiness to hold unmarried men accountable in illegal abortions as a weapon to strike back at their lovers. Alice Grimes of southern Illinois actively encouraged official investigation into her abortion for this reason. As she was dying in 1896, Grimes told her mother that her boyfriend, James Dunn, "ought to suffer some" as she had. When Grimes learned that her uncle had had Dunn arrested, she told her brother she was "glad of it."[44]

∼

From the late nineteenth century through the 1930s, the state concentrated on collecting dying declarations and on prosecuting abortionists when a woman had died, but the experience of the 1930s changed the state's methods of abortion control. During the depression, abortion increased just when advances in medicine were making it possible to save the lives of women who, in earlier decades, would have died from their abortion-related injuries and infections. The changes in the conditions and practice of abortion in the 1930s presaged changes in the investigation and control of abortion in the 1940s. Abortion control in the 1940s took two forms. First, hospitals took over much of the control of abortion through newly created therapeutic abortion committees; second, police and prosecutors stepped up raids on abortionists' offices. Rather than waiting for a death, the state's attorney's office sent police to raid the offices of suspected abortionists where they arrested abortionists and patients and collected medical instruments and patient records. In criminal trials of accused abortionists, the prosecution relied for evidence on testimony from women who had been patients of the abortionist, rather than on dying declarations. In the 1940s the system changed, but the process remained punitive for the women caught in it; criminal trials of abortionists required public exposure of women's sexual histories and abortions.[45]

The state's control of abortion was by no means entirely successful, but neither was it insignificant. Thousands of women regularly defied the law and had the abortions they needed. When questioned by doctors or police about their abortions, many defied their interrogators and refused to provide the information needed to prosecute abortionists. Yet the state punished women for having abortions, damaged the relationships between women and their doctors, and undermined women's health care. Officials focused on regulating the sexual behavior of working-class women and men, and especially the unmarried. Investigations and inquests into abortions forcefully reminded all involved not only of the illegality of abortion but also of the power of the state to intervene in the private lives of ordinary people in order to prevent and punish violations of sexual codes that demanded marriage and maternity.

Medicine played a complicated role in the enforcement of the criminal abortion laws. Physicians both participated in the suppression of abortion and helped women obtain abortions. Organized medicine acted as part of the state in policing the practice of abortion by women *and* by physicians. While some physicians actively sought an alliance with the state in enforcing the criminal abortion laws, most physicians who cooperated with the state's investigations did so out of their very real fears of being arrested as suspects in abortion cases. By arming themselves with dying declarations naming others as the abortionists, doctors could avoid prosecution and help the state prosecute the real abortionists. The agreement in Chicago to notify the coroner of abortions became a "law," in a sense. Physicians who did not comply with the informal regulations were treated with suspicion by both their colleagues and state officials.[46]

This study of the investigation of abortion in Chicago calls attention to the social punishment inherent in the state's routine process of investigation and illuminates the ways in which punishment has been gendered. The state may not have prosecuted women for having abortions, but it did punish women through persistent questioning by doctors and police and through public exposure of their abortions. The harassment of sick or dying women in the name of criminal investigation continued until the decriminalization of abortion.[47]

At inquests into abortion deaths, the state reinforced the norms requiring men to marry the women they had made pregnant. Through arrests, incarceration, interrogation, and prosecution, unmarried women's lovers were punished for illegal abortions as well as for their illicit sexual behavior. The treatment of unmarried men in these cases reveals the implicit assumption of state authorities that the unwed women who had abortions had been forced to do so because their "sweethearts" had refused to marry. This underlying assumption ignored the evident agency of many women who sought abortions and delayed marriage. The punishment of unmarried men maintained age-old patriarchal standards that gave community support to fathers when they forced men to marry the women they had impregnated.

At a time when abortion is a political issue of national importance, the history of the enforcement of the criminal abortion laws should serve as a warning against recriminalizing abortion. If abortion is made illegal again, we can expect that the punitive procedures of the past will be revived. The antifeminist movement, which is pressuring the state to recriminalize abortion, will pressure the state to punish women if abortion is made illegal. We can expect that women will once again besiege doctors with requests for abortions and that the state will threaten to prosecute physicians who fail to report women who have, or perhaps even seek, abortions. As in the past, doctors are likely to be roped into assisting the state by interrogating and reporting women who have had abortions. Some women, like Carolina Petrovitis, will be injured or die from abortions induced by themselves or by inept practitioners. Many more may be interrogated, captured by police during raids of abortionists' offices, or publicly exposed. Today, as in the past, enforcement of any criminal abortion law will target the most powerless groups—poor and working-class women, women of color, and teenage women—and their health care will be harmed the most. The history of illegal abortion is a history that should not be repeated.

Notes

1. Inquest on Carolina Petrovitis, March 21, 1916, case 234-3-1916, Medical Records Department (Cook County Medical Examiner's Office, Chicago, Illinois). For another example of a physician closely questioning a woman about an abortion, see Inquest on Matilda Olson, April 30, 1918, case 289-4-1918, ibid.

2. James C. Mohr, *Abortion in America: The Origins and Evolution of National Policy, 1800–1900* (New York, 1978), 205–6, 325. The Illinois statute, passed in 1867, read: "If any person shall, by means of any instrument or instruments, or any other means whatever, cause any pregnant woman to miscarry, or shall attempt to procure or produce such miscarriage, the person so offending shall be deemed guilty of a high misdemeanor, and, upon conviction thereof, shall be confined in the penitentiary for a period not less than two nor more than ten years. 2. If any person shall, in the attempt to produce the miscarriage of a pregnant woman, thereby cause and produce the death of such woman, the person so offending shall be deemed guilty of murder, and shall be punished as the law requires for such offense. 3. The provisions of this act shall not apply to any person who procures or attempts to produce the miscarriage of any pregnant woman for *bona fide* medical or surgical purposes." 1867 Ill. Laws 89. The 1872 law read: "No druggist, dealer in medicines, or any other person in this state, shall sell to any person or persons any drug or medicine known or presumed to be ecbolic or abortifacient, except upon the written prescription of some well known and respectable practicing physician. . . . Any person or persons violating any of the provisions of this act, shall, upon conviction thereof, be punished by a fine of not less than fifty nor more than five hundred dollars, or by imprisonment in the county jail for not less than thirty days or more than six months, for each and every offense, or by both." 1872 Ill. Laws 369.

3. I have examined 44 Cook County coroner's inquests into abortion deaths between 1907 and 1937, which can be found in the Cook County Medical Examiner's Office. Cook County coroner's inquests can only be located with a name and date of death; they cannot be located by topic. I found the names of women who had died following abortions through two sources: in published Illinois Supreme Court opinions on abortion and in the large collection of clippings from Chicago newspapers in the Abortionists Files in the Historical Health Fraud Collection (American Medical Association, Chicago, Illinois). Two of the inquests were found in transcripts of criminal abortion trials: Inquest on Nellie Walsh, 1907, in Transcript of *People v. Buettner*, 233 Ill. 272 (1908), Case Files, vault no. 30876, Supreme Court of Illinois, Record Series 901 (Illinois State Archives, Springfield, Illinois); and Inquest on Lena Benes, 1919, in Transcript of *People v. Heisler*, 300 Ill. 98 (1921), Case Files, vault no. 39077, ibid. I have also examined all of the Illinois Supreme Court opinions on abortion cases (45)

from 1867 to 1940, 20 selected transcripts of criminal abortion trials in Illinois criminal and circuit courts that were appealed to the Illinois Supreme Court (held at the Illinois State Archives), and Chicago, Cook County, and Illinois government reports for the same period at the Municipal Reference Library, Chicago, Illinois.

4. Ann Douglas Wood, " 'The Fashionable Diseases': Women's Complaints and Their Treatment in Nineteenth-Century America," in *Women and Health in America: Historical Readings*, ed. Judith Walzer Leavitt (Madison, 1984), 222–38. For a critical response to Wood, see Regina Markell Morantz, "The Perils of Feminist History," ibid., 239–45; Adrienne Rich, *Of Woman Born: Motherhood as Experience and Institution* (New York, 1976); Barbara Ehrenreich and Deirdre English, *For Her Own Good: 150 Years of the Experts' Advice to Women* (Garden City, 1978). For a different view, see Judith Walzer Leavitt, *Brought to Bed: Childbearing in America, 1750–1950* (New York, 1986).

5. Minnie C. T. Love, "Criminal Abortion," *Colorado Medicine* 1 (1903–1904), 57; Paul Titus, "A Statistical Study of a Series of Abortions Occurring in the Obstetrical Department of the Johns Hopkins Hospital," *American Journal of Obstetrics and Diseases of Women and Children* 65 (June 1912), 979; Raymond M. Spivy, "The Control and Treatment of Criminal Abortion," *Journal of the Missouri State Medical Association* 15 (January 1918), 3; Frederick J. Taussig, *Abortion, Spontaneous and Induced: Medical and Social Aspects* (St. Louis, 1936), 391; Endre K. Brunner and Louis Newton, "Abortions in Relation to Viable Births in 10,609 Pregnancies," *American Journal of Obstetrics and Gynecology* 38 (July 1939), 88. In Minneapolis between 1927 and 1936, 57 percent of 109 women who died because of criminal abortion were married, according to Calvin Schmid, *Social Saga of Two Cities: An Ecological and Statistical Study of Social Trends in Minneapolis and St. Paul* (Minneapolis, 1937), 410–11.

6. Paul Starr, *The Social Transformation of Medicine: The Rise of a Sovereign Profession and the Making of a Vast Industry* (New York, 1982), 102–12, 118, 184–97; William G. Rothstein, *American Physicians in the Nineteenth Century: From Sects to Science* (Baltimore, 1972), 305–12; Richard Harrison Shryock, *Medical Licensing in America, 1650–1965* (Baltimore, 1967).

7. For the estimate by Dr. C. S. Bacon, see "Chicago Medical Society. Regular Meeting, Held Nov. 23, 1904," *Journal of the American Medical Association*, December 17, 1904, p. 1889. On self-induced abortions, see Maximilian Herzog, "The Pathology of Criminal Abortion," ibid., May 26, 1900, p. 1310; J. E. Lackner, "Serological Findings in 100 Cases, Bacteriological Findings in 50 Cases, and a Résumé of 679 Cases of Abortion at the Michael Reese Hospital," *Surgery, Gynecology, and Obstetrics* 20 (May 1915), 537; G. D. Royston, "A Statistical Study of the Causes of Abortion," *American Journal of Obstetrics and Diseases of Women and Children* 76 (October 1917), 572–73; and Schmid, *Social Saga of Two Cities*, 411. On rubber catheters, see ibid.; and Nelson M. Percy, "Partial Evisceration through Vagina during Attempted Abortion," *Surgical Clinics of Chicago* 1 (1917), 979. On abortifacients and advertising, see "Chicago Medical Society," 1891. The Children's Bureau study analyzed maternal deaths during 1927 and 1928 in fifteen states. Some abortion-related deaths could have been prevented, the study suggested, if physicians had provided better care. U.S. De-

partment of Labor, Children's Bureau, *Maternal Mortality in Fifteen States* (Washington, DC, 1934), 113, 115. In 1936, Dr. Frederick J. Taussig estimated that there were at least 681,000 abortions per year in the United States. Taussig revised his previous estimates of abortion mortality downward because he believed that the average abortionist's skills and equipment had improved. He estimated a mortality rate of 1.2 percent and 8,000 to 10,000 deaths due to abortions per year. Taussig, *Abortion*, 26–28.

8. On the number of working-class versus middle-class women having abortions, see Regine K. Stix and Dorothy G. Wiehl, "Abortion and the Public Health," *American Journal of Public Health* 28 (May 1938), 624; and Paul H. Gebhard et al., *Pregnancy, Birth, and Abortion* (New York, 1958), 109–10, 120, 139. Ibid., 194–95, 198; James C. Mohr, "Patterns of Abortion and the Response of American Physicians, 1790–1930," in *Women and Health in America*, ed. Leavitt, 122. On delay in seeking medical treatment, see James R. Reinberger and Percy B. Russell, "The Conservative Treatment of Abortion," *Journal of the American Medical Association*, November 7, 1936, p. 1530; and J. D. Dowling, "Points of Interest in a Survey of Maternal Mortality," *American Journal of Public Health* 27 (August 1937), 804. On the high level of complications and fatalities associated with self-induced abortions, see Regine K. Stix, "A Study of Pregnancy Wastage," *Milbank Memorial Fund Quarterly* 13 (October 1935), 362–63; Raymond E. Watkins, "A Five-Year Study of Abortion," *American Journal of Obstetrics and Gynecology* 26 (August 1933), 162; and Reinberger and Russell, "Conservative Treatment of Abortion," 1527. One doctor reported an abortion-related death as pneumonia. William J. Robinson, *The Law against Abortion: Its Perniciousness Demonstrated and Its Repeal Demanded* (New York, 1933), 38–39. See also Children's Bureau, *Maternal Mortality in Fifteen States*, 103–4; and Ransom S. Hooker, *Maternal Mortality in New York City: A Study of All Puerperal Deaths, 1930–1932* (New York, 1933), 52. I have not found an incident of families bribing officials, but on the corruption of police and coroners, see Mark H. Haller, "Historical Roots of Police Behavior: Chicago, 1890–1925," *Law and Society Review* 10 (Winter 1976), 306–7, 311, 316–17; and Julie Johnson, "The Politics of Death: The Philadelphia Coroner's Office, 1900–1956," paper delivered at the annual meeting of the American Association for the History of Medicine, Baltimore, May 1990, pp. 6, 7, 17 (in Leslie J. Reagan's possession).

9. I requested the Inquest on Flossie Emerson, who died February 28, 1916, but the Cook County Medical Examiner's Office has no record of her death. Emerson's abortion-related death was one of the cases for which Dr. Anna B. Schultz-Knighten was prosecuted, *People v. Schultz-Knighten*, 277 Ill. 238 (1917). Dr. Schultz-Knighten complained that the coroner's physician, Dr. Springer, had "sneered" at her and called her a "nigger." Abstract of Record, 117, *People v. Schultz-Knighten*, 277 Ill. 238 (1917), Case Files, Supreme Court of Illinois. Allan H. Spear, *Black Chicago: The Making of a Negro Ghetto* (Chicago, 1967), 140–46, 223.

10. "Symposium, Criminal Abortion. The Colorado Law on Abortion," *Journal of the American Medical Association*, April 18, 1903, p. 1099; James Foster Scott, "Criminal Abortion," *American Journal of Obstetrics and Diseases of Women and Children* 33 (January 1896), 77; Wilhelm Becker, "The Medical,

Ethical, and Forensic Aspects of Fatal Criminal Abortion," *Wisconsin Medical Journal* 7 (April 1909), 633; Taussig, *Abortion*, 402; Linda Gordon, *Woman's Body, Woman's Right: A Social History of Birth Control in America* (New York, 1977), 57; Mohr, "Patterns of Abortion and the Response of American Physicians," 120–21; Roger Lane, *Violent Death in the City: Suicide, Accident, and Murder in Nineteenth-Century Philadelphia* (Cambridge, Mass., 1979), 93.

11. [Thomas E. Harris], "A Functional Study of Existing Abortion Laws," *Columbia Law Review* 35 (January 1935), 91n.17.

12. William Durfor English, "Evidence—Dying Declaration—Preliminary Questions of Fact—Degree of Proof," *Boston University Law Review* 15 (April 1935), 382.

13. Ibid., 381–82; Inquest on Petrovitis, case 234-3-1916, Medical Records Department.

14. "Murder by abortion" was the standard phrase used in the coroner's jury's verdicts and grand jury indictments. See, for example, Inquest on Rosie Kawera, June 15, 1916, case 152-5-1916, Medical Records Department; Inquest on Augusta Bloom, March 4, 1916, case 176-3-1916, ibid.; *People v. Dennis*, 246 Ill. 559, 560–61 (1910); and *People v. Heisler*, 300 Ill. at 100. John H. Wigmore, ed., *Illinois Crime Survey* (Chicago, 1929), 195, 596. For examples of raids, see "Arrest Man as Quack Doctor," *Waukegan Sun*, November 14, 1932, Abortionists Files, Historical Health Fraud Collection; and "Troopers Smash 'Stork' Ring," *Bridgeport Herald*, August 23, 1936, ibid. For examples of cases in which women who had abortions testified, see *Baker v. People*, 105 Ill. 452 (1883); *People v. Patrick*, 277 Ill. 210 (1917); *People v. Pigatti*, 314 Ill. 626 (1924); *People v. Wyherk*, 347 Ill. 28 (1931). In 1904, Dr. C. S. Bacon remarked, "There are practically no accusations nor indictments for abortion unless the mother becomes seriously ill or dies." "Chicago Medical Society," 1889.

15. Chicago Medical Society, Council Minutes, [October 1905–July 1907], meetings of October 9, 1906 and May 14, 1907, Chicago Medical Society Records (Archives and Manuscripts Department, Chicago Historical Society, Chicago, Illinois). Chicago Medical Society, Council Minutes, [October 1911–June 1912], meeting of January 9, 1912, pp. 51, 55–56, ibid. On the Chicago Medical Society and midwives, see Rudolph W. Holmes et al., "The Midwives of Chicago," *Journal of the American Medical Association*, April 25, 1908, pp. 1346–50. "Abortion Lairs Facing Clean-up by Authorities," *Chicago Herald*, May 30, 1915, Abortionists Files, Historical Health Fraud Collection; Mohr, "Patterns of Abortion and the Response of American Physicians," 119–20; Arthur J. Cramp, "The Bureau of Investigation of the American Medical Association," *American Journal of Police Science* 2 (July–August 1931), 286–87.

16. R. W. Holmes, commenting on Walter B. Dorsett, "Criminal Abortion in Its Broadest Sense," *Journal of the American Medical Association*, September 19, 1908, p. 960. Chicago Medical Society, Council Minutes, [October 1911–June 1912], meeting of January 9, 1912, pp. 53, 57, 59, Chicago Medical Society Records.

17. Taussig reported that mortality reached 60 to 70 percent when septicemia or peritonitis had occurred. White House Conference on Child Health and Protection, *Fetal, Newborn, and Maternal Morbidity and Mortality* (New York, 1933),

466–67. Almuth C. Vandiver, "The Legal Status of Criminal Abortion, with Especial Reference to the Duty and Protection of the Consultant," *American Journal of Obstetrics and Diseases of Women and Children* 61 (March 1910), 434–35, esp. 497.

18. O. B. Will, "The Medico-Legal Status of Abortion," *Illinois Medical Journal* 2 (1900–1901), 506, 508; Edward W. Pinkham, "The Treatment of Septic Abortion, with a Few Remarks on the Ethics of Criminal Abortion," *American Journal of Obstetrics and Diseases of Women and Children* 61 (March 1910), 420.

19. Inquest on Mary L. Kissell, August 3, 1937, case 300-8-1937, Medical Records Department. See also Inquest on Edna M. Lamb, February 19, 1917, case 43-3-1917, ibid.; and Inquest on Anna P. Fazio, February 14, 1929, case 217-2-1929, ibid. Superintendent of Rhodes Avenue Hospital to Peter M. Hoffman, March 17, 1916, in Inquest on Annie Marie Dimford, September 30, 1915, case 75-11-1915, ibid. See also Inquest on Ellen Matson, November 19, 1917, case 330-11-1917, ibid.; D. S. J. Meyers and W. W. Richmond commenting on C. J. Aud, "In What Per Cent, Is the Regular Profession Responsible for Criminal Abortions, and What is the Remedy?" *Kentucky Medical Journal* 2 (September 1904), 98, 99.

20. This "agreement" is discussed in Inquest on Matson, case 330-11-1917, Medical Records Department. Transcript of *People v. Zwienczak*, 338 Ill. 237 (1929), Case Files, vault no. 44701, Supreme Court of Illinois.

21. Vandiver, "Legal Status of Criminal Abortion," 496–501, esp. 500; "Criminal Abortion from the Practitioner's Viewpoint," *American Journal of Obstetrics and Diseases of Women and Children* 63 (June 1911), 1094–96.

22. Chicago Medical Society, Council Minutes, [October 1911–June 1912], meeting of January 9, 1912, pp. 53–54, 56–57, Chicago Medical Society Records. The New Orleans Parish Medical Society published a letter to be sent to every physician in New Orleans, which included a model dying declaration. N. F. Thiberge, "Report of Committee on Criminal Abortion," *New Orleans Medical and Surgical Journal* 70 (1917–1918), 802, 807–8. See also "Criminal Abortion from the Practitioner's Viewpoint," 1093.

23. Chicago Medical Society, Council Minutes, [October 1911–June 1912], meeting of January 9, 1912, p. 57, Chicago Medical Society Records. For judicial discussions on the validity of dying declarations and examples of dying declarations, see *Hagenow v. People*, 188 Ill. 545, 550–51, 553 (1901); *People v. Buettner*, 233 Ill. at 274–77; *People v. Cheney*, 368 Ill. 131, 132–35 (1938).

24. "Criminal Abortion," *Journal of the American Medical Association*, September 20, 1902, p. 706; Palmer Findley, "The Slaughter of the Innocents," *American Journal of Obstetrics and Gynecology* 3 (January 1922), 37.

25. Inquest on Emily Projahn, October 10, 1916, case 26-12-1916, Medical Records Department. Abortion convictions appealed to higher courts in Texas and Wisconsin revealed that dying declarations were obtained from women under threats by physicians to refuse medical care. "Dying Declarations Obtained in Abortion Case as Condition to Rendering Aid," *Journal of the American Medical Association*, April 10, 1909, p. 1204; "Dying Declarations Made after Refusal of Physician to Treat Abortion Case without History," ibid., June 7, 1913,

pp. 1829–30. Inquest on Mathilde C. Kleinschmidt, September 22, 1930, case 255-9-30, Medical Records Department.

26. Vandiver, "Legal Status of Criminal Abortion," 435. Dr. Henry Dawson Furniss commenting on "Criminal Abortion from the Practitioner's Viewpoint," 1096.

27. H. Wellington Yates and B. Connelly, "Treatment of Abortion," *American Journal of Obstetrics and Gynecology* 3 (January 1922), 84–85. See also "Dying Girl Runaway Hides Name of Slayer," *Chicago Examiner*, March 8, 1918, Abortionists Files, Historical Health Fraud Collection; and "Slain Girl Dies Hiding Her Tragedy from Kin," *Chicago Examiner*, March 9, 1918, ibid.; Robinson, *Law against Abortion*, 106–7, 110; "Abortion 'Club' Exposed," *Birth Control Review* 4 (November 1936), 5.

28. "End Murders by Abortions," *Chicago Tribune*, June 2, 1915, Abortionists Files, Historical Health Fraud Collection; Transcript of *People v. Heissler*, 338 Ill. 596 (1929), Case Files, vault no. 44783, Supreme Court of Illinois. See also Robinson, *Law against Abortion*, 106.

29. "Symposium. Criminal Abortion," 1099. See also Will, "Medico-Legal Status of Abortion," 508; and "Criminal Abortion from the Practitioner's Viewpoint," 1095–96. Chicago Medical Society, Council Minutes, [October 1911–June 1912], meeting of January 9, 1912, p. 55, Chicago Medical Society Records. For similar complaints from the coroner, see Inquest on Fazio, case 217-2-1929, Medical Records Department; and Inquest on Kissell, case 300-8-1937, ibid. Robinson, *Law against Abortion*, 105–11. On Robinson, see Gordon, *Woman's Body, Woman's Right* (1977), 173–78.

30. Inquest on Lamb, case 43-3-1917, Medical Records Department; "Criminal Abortion from the Practitioner's Viewpoint," 1094.

31. Dr. Louis Frank commenting on Aud, "In What Per Cent," 100; "North Branch Philadelphia County Medical Society. Regular Meeting, held April 14, 1904," *Journal of the American Medical Association*, May 21, 1904, pp. 1375–76. Attorneys disagreed about whether or not physicians should act as informers in abortion cases. "Symposium. Criminal Abortion," 1097, 1098. Illinois law did not privilege communications between doctors and patients. "Chicago Medical Society," 1889.

32. "Girl's Letters Blame Dr. Mason in Death Case," *Chicago Tribune*, [April] 9, 1916, Abortionists Files, Historical Health Fraud Collection; "Voice from Grave Calls to Dr. Mason during Trial as His Fiancee's Betrayer," *Denver Post*, April 5, 1916, ibid. The death of Anna Johnson at the office of Dr. Eva Shaver, an abortionist, similarly filled Chicago's newspapers in late May and June 1915. Newspapers published photos of Johnson, her lover, and Dr. Shaver, as well as the couple's letters. For example, see "Who's Who in the 'Mystery House' Tragedy?" *Chicago Evening American*, May 31, 1915, ibid.; and "Death of Girl Perils Schools for Abortions," *Chicago Tribune*, May 28, 1915, ibid.; "Dying Girl Runaway Hides Name of Slayer," *Chicago Examiner*, March 8, 1918, ibid. See also "Girl Slain Here Gives Life to Hide Her Tragedy," *Chicago Examiner*, March 5, 1918, ibid.; "Slain Girl Dies Hiding Her Tragedy from Kin," *Chicago Examiner*, March 9, 1918, ibid.; and "Little Jane's Tragedy Typical of Hundreds Who Disappear Here," *Chicago Examiner*, [1918], ibid.

33. Inquest on Mary Shelley, October 30, 1915, case 352-10-1915, Medical Records Department; "Chicago Medical Society," 1889. Mamie Ethel Crowell's family tried to prevent an investigation into her abortion by lying to physicians and the coroner. Inquest on Mamie Ethel Crowell, April 16, 1930, case 305-4-30, ibid. For cases where family members wanted the state to investigate an abortion, see *People v. Hotz*, 261 Ill. 239 (1914); and Inquest on Frauciszka Gawlik, February 19, 1916, case 27-3-1916, Medical Records Department. "A Maryland Abortionist Gets No Pardon," *Journal of the American Medical Association*, November 12, 1904, p. 1476; Inquest on Frances Collins, May 7, 1920, case 161-5-20, Medical Records Department.

34. Comments of "Esther E.," *Birth Control Review* 4 (September 1920), 15.

35. Inquest on Petrovitis, case 234-3-1916, Medical Records Department. Transcript of *People v. Hobbs*, 297 Ill. 399 (1921), Case Files, vault no. 38773, Supreme Court of Illinois; Abstract of *People v. Heisler*, 300 Ill. 98 (1930), p. 38, Case Files, vault no. 44783, Supreme Court of Illinois.

36. Inquest on Eunice McElroy, November 14, 1928, case 486-11-28, Medical Records Department.

37. Inquest on Dimford, case 75-11-1915, ibid. Inquest on Kissell, case 300-8-1937, ibid.; Inquest on Esther Stark, June 12, 1917, case 65-6-1917, ibid.; *People v. Carrico*, 310 Ill. 543, 547 (1924). For an example of a woman who did not want to marry, see Inquest on Mary Colbert, March 25, 1933, case 7-4-1933, Medical Records Department. *People v. Rongetti*, 344 Ill. 278, 284 (1931).

38. Inquest on Anna Johnson, May 27, 1915, case 77790, Medical Records Department.

39. Inquest on Matson, case 330-11-1917, ibid.

40. "Death Threat to Hostetler," *Chicago Tribune*, June 5, 1915, Abortionists Files, Historical Health Fraud Collection. The police and press often called the man in such a case "the sweetheart." See "Doctor Faces Manslaughter Charge in Girl's Death," *Chicago Tribune*, April 18, 1930, ibid.; and "Woman Doctor Found Guilty in Death," *Chicago Tribune*, March 14, 1936, ibid. Inquest on Alma Bromps, April 27, 1931, case 35-5-1931, Medical Records Department; *People v. Ney*, 349 Ill. 172, 173–74 (1932). For similar cases, see *Cochran v. People*, 175 Ill. 28 (1898); and *People v. Hobbs*, 297 Ill. 399 (1921). Inquest on Rose Siebenmann, April 16, 1920, case 266-4-20, Medical Records Department. Transcript of *People v. Hobbs*; Transcript of *People v. Buettner*. For convictions of boyfriends, see *Dunn v. People*, 172 Ill. 582 (1898); and *People v. Patrick*, 277 Ill. 210 (1917).

41. I know of only one case where the husband was charged. Bertis Dougherty pled guilty to abortion and testified as a state witness against the abortionist in *People v. Schneider*, 370 Ill. 612, 613–14 (1939).

42. In the 163 cases studied by Louise DeKoven Bowen, 8 men were sent to jail for six months. It appears that 16 men were ordered to make a financial settlement. Juvenile Protective Association of Chicago, *A Study of Bastardy Cases, Taken from the Court of Domestic Relations in Chicago* (Chicago, 1914), 18, 19, 22. *Notable American Women: The Modern Period*, ed. Barbara Sicherman and Carol Hurd Green (Cambridge, MA, 1980), 99–100, s.v. "Bowen, Louise DeKoven."

43. On common perceptions of juvenile court proceedings regarding statutory rape, see Mary Ellen Odem, "Delinquent Daughters: The Sexual Regulation of Female Minors in the United States, 1880–1920" (Ph.D. diss., University of California, Berkeley, 1989), 75–136.

44. Transcript of *Dunn v. People*, 172 Ill. 582 (1898), Case Files, vault no. 7876, Supreme Court of Illinois. Women may have pursued cases against their lovers in *Scott v. People*, 141 Ill. 195 (1892); and *People v. Patrick*, 277 Ill. 210 (1917). On women's use of state regulation for their own ends and the need to analyze the state and social control with attention to women and gender, see Linda Gordon, *Heroes of Their Own Lives: The Politics and History of Family Violence, Boston, 1880–1960* (New York, 1988), 289–99.

45. *People v. Martin*, 382 Ill. 192 (1943); *People v. Stanko*, 402 Ill. 558 (1949); *People v. Smuk*, 12 Ill. 2d. 360 (1957).

46. Inquest on Fazio, case 217-2-1929, Medical Records Department. Dr. Edward W. Pinkham suggested reporting abortion cases to the "prosecuting authorities" for "complete protection." He noted, "Good legal authority has declared that if the physician does not do this, but maintains secrecy in the treatment, he becomes *particeps criminis*, and subjects himself to a possible prosecution." Pinkham, "Treatment of Septic Abortion," 420.

47. Jerome E. Bates and Edward Zawadzki, *Criminal Abortion: A Study in Medical Sociology* (Springfield, 1964), 61, 100, 103.

17   Connecticut's Statute on Abortionists

Between 1821 and 1841 ten states passed laws criminalizing abortion, making it a statutory offense for the first time in the nation's history. Generally, these early statutes sought to protect women from poisonous abortifacients and dangerous procedures performed by "unscrupulous" practitioners operating in the open medical market of the time. The laws punished individuals responsible for supplying abortifacients or performing mechanical procedures, not the women who had abortions. Because of widespread acceptance of the quickening doctrine (see Document 4), only a minority of the criminal codes written in this period made abortions before quickening a crime. Connecticut was the first state to enact abortion legislation. Its 1821 statute is printed here.

EVERY PERSON WHO SHALL, WILLFULLY and maliciously, administer to, or cause to be administered to, or taken by, any person or

From *The Public Statute Laws of the State of Connecticut, 1821* (Hartford, 1821), 152–53.

persons, any deadly poison, or other noxious and destructive substance, with an intention him, her, or them thereby to murder, or
thereby to cause or procure the miscarriage of any woman, then
being quick with child, and shall be thereof duly convicted, shall
suffer imprisonment, in Newgate Prison, during his natural life, or
for such other term as the Court having cognizance of the offence
shall determine.

18   Use of Poison to Induce an Abortion

Boston Medical and Surgical Journal

*By the 1860s the AMA had become the most vocal proponent of
abortion legislation. In keeping with its understanding of fetal
development as a continuous process that began at conception,
the AMA declared quickening, the bedrock of legal permissi-
bility, to be an unscientific measure of fetal life and an inappropriate gauge of criminality. The AMA not only demanded
that abortion measures be passed in every state but also that
the quickening distinction be struck from relevant codes. Physicians sought the legal regulation of abortion, not its complete elimination. They urged lawmakers to include "therapeutic
abortion" clauses that gave licensed physicians the power to
decide under which circumstances an abortion could be performed. Medical journals published accounts of abortion fatalities caused by lay health practitioners (including
pharmacists) in order to mobilize political support.*

*A*TTEMPT TO PRODUCE ABORTION WITH *Oil of Tansy, followed by
Death.*—Coroner Pratt was called last Wednesday, to hold an
inquest on the body of Elizabeth Sherman, 21 years of age, who
had been employed for some time past as seamstress in a family in
Kingston street, Boston, and who died, after an illness of three or
four hours. The jury returned a verdict that she came to her death in
consequence of taking two ounces of oil of tansy for the purpose of
procuring abortion.

From "Attempt to produce Abortion with Oil of Tansy, followed by Death"
and "Sale of Poisons by Apothecaries," *Boston Medical and Surgical Journal* 44,
no. 15 (May 14, 1851): 306.

The apothecary did wrong to sell that quantity, and especially to a child of 10 or 12 years of age, without a prescription from a physician.

Sale of Poisons by Apothecaries.—It is quite time for our Legislature to pass a law restraining apothecaries from selling poisonous substances without a physician's order. The necessity of such restriction has been repeatedly advocated in our pages, but we believe there never has been any definite action taken on the subject by our Legislature. If any thing would seem to demand immediate action by our law-makers, it is to prevent the frequent occurrence of such lamentable casualties as the one mentioned above.

19   The Comstock Act of 1873

In 1873 the first federal measure regulating abortion and birth control was passed. Named after its chief supporter, Anthony Comstock, head of the New York Society for the Suppression of Vice, the Comstock Act was an antiobscenity statute that classified as obscene all physical instruments, visual images, and written material pertaining to contraception or abortion. Comstock was appointed a special agent of the U.S. Post Office empowered to enforce the new law through mail inspection. Between 1873 and 1880 he arrested over fifty-five abortionists (more than any other inspector), including Madame Restell (see Document 14), who committed suicide the day before her trial.

*B*E IT ENACTED BY THE *Senate and House of Representatives of the United States of America in Congress assembled,* That whoever, within the District of Columbia or any of the Territories of the United States, or other place within the exclusive jurisdiction of the United States, shall sell, or lend, or give away, or in any manner exhibit, or shall offer to sell, or to lend, or to give away, or in any manner to exhibit, or shall otherwise publish or offer to pub-

From Public–No. 133, "An Act for the suppression of trade in and circulation of obscene literature and articles of immoral use," *Acts and Resolutions of the United States of America Passed at the Third Session of the Forty-Second Congress, December 2, 1872–March 3, 1873* (Washington, DC: Government Printing Office, 1873), 234–36.

lish in any manner, or shall have in his possession, for any such purpose or purposes, any obscene book, pamphlet, paper, writing, advertisement, circular, print, picture, drawing, or other representation, figure, or image on or of paper or other material, or any cast, instrument, or other article of an immoral nature, or any drug or medicine, or any article, whatever, for the prevention of conception, or for causing unlawful abortion, or shall advertise the same for sale, or shall write or print, or cause to be written or printed, any card, circular, book, pamphlet, advertisement, or notice of any kind, stating when, where, how, or of whom, or by what means, any of the articles in this section hereinbefore mentioned, can be purchased or obtained, or shall manufacture, draw, or print, or in any wise make any of such articles, shall be deemed guilty of a misdemeanor, and, on conviction thereof in any court of the United States having criminal jurisdiction in the District of Columbia, or in any Territory or place within the exclusive jurisdiction of the United States, where such misdemeanor shall have been committed; and on conviction thereof, he shall be imprisoned at hard labor in the penitentiary for not less than six months nor more than five years for each offense, or fined not less than one hundred dollars nor more than two thousand dollars, with costs of court.

SEC. 2. That section one hundred and forty-eight of the act to revise, consolidate, and amend the statutes relating to the Post-Office Department, approved June eighth, eighteen hundred and seventy-two, be amended to read as follows:

"SEC. 148. That no obscene, lewd, or lascivious book, pamphlet, picture, paper, print, or other publication of an indecent character, or any article or thing designed or intended for the prevention of conception or procuring of abortion, nor any article or thing intended or adapted for any indecent or immoral use or nature, nor any written or printed card, circular, book, pamphlet, advertisement or notice of any kind giving information, directly or indirectly, where, or how, or of whom, or by what means either of the things before mentioned may be obtained or made, nor any letter upon the envelope of which, or postal card upon which indecent or scurrilous epithets may be written or printed, shall be carried in the mail; and any person who shall knowingly deposit, or cause to be deposited, for mailing or delivery, any of the hereinbefore-mentioned articles or things, or any notice, or paper containing any advertisement relating to the aforesaid articles or things, and any person who, in pursuance of any plan or scheme for disposing of any of the hereinbefore-mentioned articles or things, shall take, or cause to be taken, from the mail any such letter or package, shall be deemed guilty of a misdemeanor, and, on conviction thereof, shall, for every offense, be fined not less than one hundred dollars nor more than five thousand dollars, or imprisoned at hard labor not less than one year nor more than ten years, or both, in the discretion of the judge."

Sec. 3. That all persons are prohibited from importing into the United States, from any foreign country, any of the hereinbefore-mentioned articles or things, except the drugs hereinbefore-mentioned when imported in bulk, and not put up for any of the purposes before mentioned; and all such prohibited articles in the course of importation shall be detained by the officer of customs, and proceedings taken against the same under section five of this act.

Sec. 4. That whoever, being an officer, agent, or employee of the government of the United States, shall knowingly aid or abet any person engaged in any violation of this act, shall be deemed guilty of a misdemeanor, and, on conviction thereof, shall, for every offense, be punished as provided in section two of this act.

Sec. 5. That any judge of any district or circuit court of the United States, within the proper district, before whom complaint in writing of any violation of this act shall be made, to the satisfaction of such judge, and founded on knowledge or belief, and, if upon belief, setting forth the grounds of such belief, and supported by oath or affirmation of the complainant, may issue, conformably to the Constitution, a warrant directed to the marshal, or any deputy marshal, in the proper district, directing him to search for, seize, and take possession of any such article or thing hereinbefore mentioned, and to make due and immediate return thereof, to the end that the same may be condemned and destroyed by proceedings, which shall be conducted in the same manner as other proceedings in case of municipal seizure, and with the same right of appeal or writ of error: *Provided*, That nothing in this section shall be construed as repealing the one hundred and forty-eighth section of the act of which this act is amendatory, or to affect any indictments heretofore found for offenses against the same, but the said indict-

ments may be prosecuted to judgment as if this section had not
been enacted.

Approved, March 3, 1873.

20 Georgia's Statute on Abortionists

*The passage of the Comstock Act in 1873 ushered in the second
major wave of abortion legislation. Unlike earlier measures,
late nineteenth-century restrictions criminalized abortions in
all stages of pregnancy, although, as the wording of the 1876
Georgia law reprinted here indicates, specified penalties often
distinguished between stages of gestation. These new restrictions
stood in marked contrast to earlier laws in two additional
ways: first, many made consenting women guilty of a crime;
and second, at regulars' urging, statutes often included therapeutic
abortion clauses. The Georgia statute reflects the shifting
legislative climate of the late nineteenth century.*

S ECTION I. *BE IT ENACTED, ETC.*, That from and after the passage of
this Act, the wilful killing of an unborn child, so far developed
as to be ordinarily called "quick," by any injury to the mother of
such child, which would be murder if it resulted in the death of
such mother, shall be guilty of a felony, and punishable by death or
imprisonment for life, as the jury trying the case may recommend.

SEC. II. *Be it further enacted*, That every person who shall administer
to any woman pregnant with a child, any medicine, drug,
or substance whatever, or shall use or employ any instrument or
other means, with intent thereby to destroy such child, unless the
same shall have been necessary to preserve the life of such mother,
or shall have been advised by two physicians to be necessary for
such purpose, shall, in case the death of such child or mother be
thereby produced, be declared guilty of an assault with intent to
murder.

SEC. III. *Be it further enacted*, That any person who shall wilfully
administer to any pregnant woman any medicine, drug or substance,
or anything whatever, or shall employ any instrument or

From "An Act to prevent and punish foeticide or criminal abortion in the
State of Georgia," *Acts and Resolutions of the General Assembly of the State of
Georgia, Passed at the Regular Session of January, 1876* (n.p.: H. G. Wright,
Public Printer, 1876), 113.

means whatever, with intent thereby to procure the miscarriage or abortion of any such woman, unless the same shall have been necessary to preserve the life of such woman, or shall have been advised by two physicians to be necessary for that purpose, shall, upon conviction, be punished as prescribed in section 4310 of the Revised Code of Georgia.

SEC. IV. Repeals conflicting laws.

Approved February 25, 1876.

V

Birth Control Revolution:
Reproductive Freedom
or Social Control?

21   The Struggle for Reproductive Freedom

Linda Gordon

In the first two decades of the twentieth century, a campaign for reproductive rights was waged under the joint banner of political and sexual radicalism. On speaking tours, at demonstrations, and in mass-circulated pamphlets and journals, female socialist and anarchist leaders denounced—often in open defiance of the law—restrictive birth control legislation. Pointing to working women's double burdens as laborers and mothers, they declared the availability of effective, inexpensive birth control to be a precondition of female emancipation. Linda Gordon, a historian at the University of Wisconsin at Madison, examines the changing ideology of birth control advocates from the mid-nineteenth century to the 1910s.

THE STRUGGLE FOR BIRTH CONTROL which emerged in the nineteenth century was not directed solely toward the legalization of certain information and technology. It was part of a feminist movement, challenging the subordination of women in sexuality particularly and in the family and society generally. From then on, the birth control movement, even when organizationally autonomous, has always reflected the historical strength and development of feminism.

In the last hundred years there have been [several] stages in the sexual ideology of the feminists, each of which strongly affected the struggle for reproductive freedom. First, from the mid-nineteenth century to the 1890s, the feminists of the suffrage movement adhered to a sexual ideal which I shall call domesticity; briefly, they believed that sexual activity belonged only within marriage and they were skeptical of its importance in women's lives. Second, in the period near World War I, a new group of feminists, including many men, rejected the antisexual attitudes of the suffragists and associated women's interests with sexual liberation—

From Linda Gordon, "The Struggle for Reproductive Freedom: Three Stages of Feminism," in *Capitalist Patriarchy and the Case for Socialist Feminism*, ed. Zillah R. Eisenstein (New York: Monthly Review Press, 1979), 110–19. © 1979 by Zillah R. Eisenstein. Reprinted by permission of the Monthly Review Foundation.

endorsing amarital sexual activity and, even more important, emphasizing and romanticizing the importance of sexual pleasure. . . .

In each of these stages the questions of reproductive freedom and sexual freedom were hardly separable. Since we cannot separate these issues nor divide reproductive goals from the process of their transformation, we must regard this as a history of conflict between social radicals and social conservatives, both sets of views historically specific.

1) Let us begin about the year 1870 and look at what I will call the Victorian sexual system. It is useful to think of it as a system because it was composed of many related parts; it had a fundamental coherence, although, like all such cultural systems, it contained dissidence and contradictions. The feminist reformers who took up the birth control issue shared many convictions with their conservative opponents.

Victorian conservative moralists agreed that the purpose of sexual activity for women should be reproduction, and many denied that women had a sex drive independent of a desire for motherhood. Those who recognized the existence of female sexuality assumed it to be entirely consonant with the satisfaction of men. The relationships that women had with other women, though often passionate, were virtually defined as asexual, making lesbianism practically invisible except as a rare aberration. Enjoying a sharply double standard, rationalized through a notion of separate spheres for the sexes, men simultaneously celebrated (and possibly resented) the chastity of their wives and indulged themselves with prostitutes and other low-status women.

By the mid-nineteenth century the same social changes that had created this system threatened its stability. The industrialization of production that had created the separation between men's and women's lives and work made women's traditional labor degraded, unrewarding, and unappreciated. But while the content of women's work changed, its form remained the same. The changes were not well understood, but were sharply felt. Even today few recognize that housework as we know it was born in advanced industrial society, reflecting the transformation of women who had been manufacturers, farmers, skilled teachers, and healers into small-scale janitors. At the same time, urban life increasingly detached men of all classes from their families and homes into other workplaces.

Responding to these changes, two directly antagonistic social movements developed around the issue of reproduction. On the conservative side, fears of underpopulation, the decline of the family, and the increasing independence of women coalesced into a series of pressures for more rigorous bans on birth control, sex education, and extra-domestic activities among women. In the United States these groups succeeded in enacting the "Comstock" law which prohibited the mailing of obscene material and in then classifying birth control information as obscene; they also secured federal prosecution of several cases under this law. They conducted a propaganda campaign, deliberately confounding contraception with abortion and branding as murder and licentiousness the whole project of birth control.

Contesting the conservative view of reproductive and sexual morality was a powerful feminist movement. It produced a birth control demand, "Voluntary Motherhood," which expressed its principles exactly. The main issue was a woman's right to dignity and autonomy, but it was also implied that willing mothers would be better parents, wanted children better people. The cult of motherhood was thus argued as passionately by feminists as by antifeminists: conservatives argued that motherhood was the basic reason women should stay at home; feminists argued that motherhood was the main reason women needed more power, independence, and respect. These feminists did not urge that women should desert the home, and certainly did not contemplate—as few feminists did until the 1930s—that men should share in domestic work.* Furthermore, by the explicitly sexual content of their birth control ideas, the feminists also endorsed a kind of domesticity. They believed that abstinence, not contraception, was the only proper form of birth control. They shared the general religious and moral view that sex should be only for reproduction and only within marriage. They were partly motivated by religious and antitechnological feelings, a response to the apparent degradation of women in industrial society. But they also understood contraception not as a tool for a woman's own self-assertion but as a weapon used by men against women: nonreproductive sex appeared to them to be a means for

---

*The popularity of matriarchy theory among nineteenth-century feminists suggests a longing for preexisting models of a good society rather than acceptance of the need to define and invent a good society anew. Their exclusive emphasis on suffrage (like the emphasis of later feminists on sexual liberation and birth control) suggests that they were mistaking symptoms and aspects of male supremacy for the whole, that they were unable to comprehend its systematic, coherent, and pervasive forms.

men to escape their responsibility to women.* They saw contraception as a tool of prostitutes and as a potential tool of men in turning women into prostitutes.

The feminists wanted not only voluntary motherhood but also voluntary sex. The nineteenth-century marital system rested, legally as well as in custom, on women's sexual submission to their husbands; refusal of sexual services was grounds for divorce in many states. Feminist insistence on women's right to say no and to justify this on birth control grounds was a fundamental rejection of male dominance in sex. They wanted to end the double standard by imposing chastity on men. Their strong emphasis on women's sisterhood had, at least for us today, sexual implications as well, for they created lasting bonds and passionate loves among women. Interestingly, it was often these voluntary motherhood advocates who simultaneously asserted the existence of female sexual drives. They understood, however, that the discovery of women's own sexual preferences and sensations could not even begin while women were subordinate to men's every sexual whim. Feminist ideas were thus at once antisex and prosex, and feminists were not able to resolve this tension because they did not (or perhaps did not dare) follow women's sexual feelings where they led—to woman-defined kinds of sexual activity not necessarily compatible with conventional heterosexual intercourse.

In their sexual attitudes the nineteenth-century feminists were mainly anti-male. In this respect they were the predecessors of today's radical feminists, not of socialist feminists or liberal feminists. Their critique of the family was a critique of male dominance within it. They did not analyze the family or the sexual division of labor as formations which had become assimilated to capitalism, nor did they perceive that men were not always free agents themselves in these formations. On the other hand, in other aspects of their feminism these activists were often pro-male. Seeing women as victims who had been deprived of the opportunity to realize their full human potential, they saw the male as the human type. This was explicit in the work of a few theorists, especially Charlotte Perkins Gilman, and was implicit in the demands of many other feminists for education and professional work. Feminist thought reflected rapid social changes which were sending women out of their homes into the man's world—into schools, offices, factories,

---

*The fact that contraception then was not a commodity but a "home-made" procedure or invention made it less fetishized, its social meaning clear.

restaurants, theaters, etc. The pro-male point of view made it seem inconceivable that men should do housework and parenting.

In their sexual attitudes, in short, the feminists were defending domesticity, yet their agitation on other questions was encouraging a rejection of domestic life. But celibacy was not a stable alternative for the thousands of single career women at the turn of the twentieth century.

Partly due to the large numbers of nonmarrying women, but also because of extensive use of birth control, by the turn of the century birth rate declines in the United States had become highly visible. Between 1905 and 1910 there arose a campaign against "race suicide," whose propagandists protested population decline (having been reared with the mercantilist notion that a healthy nation had to have a growing population), fearing the decline of WASP ruling-class hegemony due to the higher birth rate among Catholic working-class immigrants. Underlying it was an antifeminist backlash, an attack on women's "selfishness," or rejection of domesticity and mothering. (Ironically, the race suicide propaganda let a great many people know of the existence of birth control methods and probably promoted the use of contraception.)

2) Starting in the 1890s, a group of feminists, at first mainly European, began to espouse different sexual ideas critical of domesticity. Many were men, such as Havelock Ellis, Edward Carpenter, later Wilhelm Reich. Men and women alike tended to consider sexual repression as a problem of equal weight for both sexes, though different in nature; and they usually argued that women's liberation would be good for both sexes, that men as well as women suffered from the false sex-gender system, the polarization of sex roles.

In many ways this turn-of-the-century group of feminists took the focus off women and placed it on sex; they tended to view women's subordination as a function of sexual repression, whereas the suffrage movement by and large thought that the distortion of sexual needs and practices was a product of male supremacy.

Certain implications of this sexual liberation emphasis should be noticed. First, the concern with men's sexual repression tended to mask the fact that men remained the dominant sex, the beneficiaries of the exploitation* of women, and to present men and women as equal victims of a system so abstract that its persistence was

---

*I am purposefully using this word not only in its Marxist sense, referring to the production of surplus value, but also in the common sense usage of being

inexplicable. In this respect the sexual liberation theorists did not encourage a women's movement. Second, the attack on sexual repression tended inevitably to spotlight the family as the central structure for the perpetuation of repression and to endorse nonmarital sex. Inasmuch as the family was undoubtedly still the main prop of male supremacy in the early twentieth century (and possibly still is), sexual liberation theory was extremely encouraging to the development of a more fundamental challenge to the sex-gender system from a feminist perspective.

Birth control was a very important issue for the sexual liberation feminists because without it sex could not be separated from the family. They therefore enthusiastically supported and built the birth control movement when it revived in the World War I era. Its reemergence was a response both to the publicity of the race suicide proponents and partly because of the new demographic and sexual situation of women. The urban economy was making smaller families economically possible for professional, business, and working-class women; women were more in the world—working-class women often in the labor force, more privileged women in higher education, the professions, and volunteerism; the requirements of female chastity were weakening for all classes. These developments were all part of the decline of patriarchal power, which had been founded not only on control of women but also on control of families. The entire family structure was being altered by industrial capitalism. The employment of sons and daughters weakened fatherly authority, while the wage labor of the fathers removed them from the home, where they had traditionally exercised authority, and deprived them of the economic and psychic ability to enjoy large families. The uprooting experience of immigration and the impact of individualist liberal ideology also weakened the legitimacy of the patriarchal organization of society. And feminism was itself a product of the frustrations and opportunities presented to women, middle-class women first and most prominently, by the decline of patriarchy.

The organizational impetus for the revived birth control movement came primarily from feminists in the Socialist Party. Their energy was available because so many women were repelled by the

---

used, ripped off. I do this because I think feminists are correct in perceiving a fundamental similarity between the two forms of exploitation and the alienation from one's labor and one's self that they produce.

conservatism of the suffrage organizations and because socialism was not dealing energetically with any women's issues. They learned the political importance of the birth control issue from the masses, and I use that word advisedly. The experiences of Margaret Sanger and many other birth control organizers show that enormous popular demand virtually forced the issue upon them. Once they began to organize around it, birth control information reached thousands of women previously unexcited by suffrage or other women's rights issues; birth control seemed to them more immediate, more personal, and more tied to class struggle.

The birth control movement of 1914–1920 was a mass movement with leagues in all big cities and many towns. It was a grassroots movement: a few speakers toured nationally, and in the 1920s national organizations arose, but most leagues sprang up locally and autonomously, often initiated by women socialists. People distributed illegal birth control leaflets on the streets, opened illegal clinics, courted arrest in order to use their trials as political forums, and even served time in jail.

This movement should not be seen as some kind of spontaneous revolt of pre-political women. Underlying it was a new radicalism in sexual behavior among many young urban women, influenced by and participating in the feminist sexual liberation ideology. Their work in birth control was part of an attempt to resolve the contradictions of nineteenth-century feminism which had criticized the family but remained faithful to ideas of permanent monogamy, sex only for reproduction and within marriage.

World War I-era feminist socialists began a critique of the family itself, calling it a prop of bourgeois, male supremacist society, morality, and character structure. In differing degrees these feminists accepted the "sexual revolution"—the normality of divorce; sexual relations before marriage, without ruining a woman's reputation; numerous sexual partners; contraception; and a host of activities previously considered improper, including dating. They thought that enjoyment was a good enough reason for sex and most other activities. They despised so-called bourgeois hypocrisy and paid at least lip service to a single standard of sexual freedom.

In this rejection of domesticity and family-centered sex these early twentieth-century feminists became, despite their intentions, more pro-male than their predecessors. Their characteristic solution to problems of child care and housework was to propose that women be hired to do those tasks. They were socialists but their proposals, like those of most socialists of their era, were in line with the development of capitalism. And the male was still for them the human type, male culture in most respects human culture. This group of radicals did not fully challenge the sex-gender system either. Redefining the possibilities of the feminine somewhat, they continued to accept a certain view of male gender as permanent.

No feminism prior to the mid-twentieth century analyzed the full complexities of women's reproductive and sexual imprisonment. But, without bemoaning the loss of something doomed by historical change, we should recognize that nineteenth-century feminist ideas had certain important realizations about women that were lost in the early twentieth century. Feminist thinkers like Elizabeth Cady Stanton, Elizabeth Blackwell, and Charlotte Perkins Gilman understood that women needed a space—physical, psychological, and intellectual—where they were separated from men and insulated from men's demands before they could develop their own sexual feelings, hopes, and theories. Their emphasis on sisterhood and women's solidarity put them in a position of greater fidelity to the masses of women and gave them a strategic sense of the power of women as a collectivity. By contrast, many early twentieth-century feminists, including birth control leaders like Margaret Sanger and Emma Goldman, had uncritically bought a "sexual" revolution that was really a heterosexual revolution. It drew women out of protected areas, out of women's spaces, into a man's world. It ignored the fact that it is dangerous—physically, emotionally, socially, and economically—for women to indulge in nonmarital sex. Although their sex manuals contributed to sex education and to breaking the chains of prudish ignorance, they steadfastly encouraged women to get sexual pleasure and orgasms from male-oriented intercourse and, by implication, blamed them for frigidity if they could not. Most of them did not believe in the need for an autonomous women's movement. In sexual relations, education, and work they accepted a set-up that placed women *individually* in a man's world, isolated in their danger. Although it was progressive that they urged women to dare, to find the confidence—they didn't say where—to take on men's burdens, their strategy in effect denied women solidarity with other women. Nor did they offer a way to reject women's traditional burdens while assuming men's.

Nevertheless, the birth control movement of the World War I period was a big advance for women. It promoted and finally legalized contraception, and it encouraged partial emergence from sexual constriction. But as part of the heterosexual "sexual revolution," it also created pain, confusion, and loneliness for many women; the transformation out of millennia of subordination cannot be expected to be easy.

22   The Prevention of Conception

Margaret Sanger

Margaret Sanger, the founder of the Planned Parenthood Federation of America, was one of the most outspoken and important birth control advocates of this century. Born in 1879 as Margaret Higgins, she studied nursing for two years in White Plains, New York, stopping her studies to marry artist, architect, and socialist William Sanger. In 1911 the family, which now included three children, moved to Manhattan. After serving briefly as an organizer for the Industrial Workers of the World and the Socialist Party, Sanger worked as an obstetrical nurse for a Lower East Side settlement house. By 1912 she had made a name for herself as a sex education lecturer and the author of "What Every Girl Should Know," published weekly in the Socialist organ, The Call. *In 1914 she established* The Woman Rebel, *a journal in which she demanded legal birth control and full women's rights. After the* Rebel, *which appeared seven times before being deemed unmailable by the U.S. Post Office, she flaunted the law again by writing the pamphlet "Family Limitation," a practical home guide to contraception. It was Sanger who first coined the term "birth control" in 1915.*

I S THERE ANY REASON WHY women should not receive clean, harmless, scientific knowledge on how to prevent conception? Everybody is aware that the old, stupid fallacy that such knowledge will cause a girl to enter into prostitution has long been shattered. Seldom does a prostitute become pregnant. Seldom does the girl practicing promiscuity become pregnant. The woman of the upper middle class has all available knowledge and implements to prevent conception. The woman of the lower middle class is struggling for this knowledge. She tries various methods of prevention,

From Margaret Sanger, "The Prevention of Conception," *The Woman Rebel*, no. 1 (March 1914): 8.

and after a few years of experience plus medical advice succeeds in discovering some method suitable to her individual self. The woman of the people is the only one left in ignorance of this information. Her neighbors, relatives and friends tell her stories of special devices and the success of them all. They tell her also of the blood-sucking men with M.D. after their names who perform operations for the price of so-and-so. But the working woman's purse is thin. It's far cheaper to have a baby, "though God knows what it will do after it gets here." Then, too, all other classes of women live in places where there is at least a semblance of privacy and sanitation. It is easier for them to care for themselves whereas the large majority of the women of the people have no bathing or sanitary conveniences. This accounts too for the fact that the higher the standard of living, the more care can be taken and fewer children result. No plagues, famines or wars could ever frighten the capitalist class so much as the universal practice of the prevention of conception. On the other hand no better method could be utilized for increasing the wages of the workers.

As is well known, a law exists forbidding the imparting of information on this subject, the penalty being several years' imprisonment. Is it not time to defy this law? And what fitter place could be found than in the pages of the WOMAN REBEL?

23   Prevention or Abortion—Which?

Margaret Sanger

By the early 1920s the determination and perseverance of women such as Margaret Sanger had made it legal in some states for married women to obtain information on birth control from physicians. Unfortunately, however, many of them could not afford the services of a physician, and those who could often found doctors reluctant to prescribe birth control. Desperate for information on how to prevent pregnancy, many women wrote for help directly to the acknowledged leader of the birth control movement, Margaret Sanger.

From Margaret Sanger, "Prevention or Abortion—Which? Letters Showing the Dilemma Faced by Many Mothers," *Birth Control Review* 7, no. 7 (July 1923): 181–82.

THERE IS NO COMMONER MISAPPREHENSION concerning Birth Control than that which identifies it with abortion. In the case of many of the opponents of Birth Control this misapprehension is deliberately made use of to discredit the cause. In other cases it arises out of ignorance. . . . The following letters are only a few samples of the many that come to Mrs. Sanger from women who have practically been forced into abortion. Can it be imagined that any woman would resort to these painful and dangerous means of checking the increase of her family if she had access to scientific medical information that would enable her, without the slightest danger of injury to herself, to prevent conception? Without Birth Control the mother is given the choice of two crimes—to injure herself and to destroy her unborn child by abortion, or to bring into the world children for whom she cannot care, and who are doomed from birth to misery, ill health, deficiency or physical defect. The mother conscience often prevails over the individual conscience, and even when she feels that she is running the risk of eternal damnation, the mother resorts to abortion rather than bring children into the world to suffer, and to cause suffering to the whole family. But ought there to be any such hard choice for a woman, when science has discovered harmless means of prevention? What right has any government to inflict such tyranny on women as to keep this knowledge from them by law?

Which Is the Greater Sin?

Pennsylvania

Dear Mrs. Sanger:

I am now just past 26 years; am married about 5 years and 5 months. I was married about 13 months when our first child was born, a little baby girl, and never was a child more wished for, or welcomed than she was, but little did we know the heart aches we would have to raise her past a year. She was a bottle baby. About 15 months later a baby boy was born to us and we had the same trouble raising him past a year. One year and eight months later a pair of twins boys I gave birth to. That made our oldest child less than 2 years and 4 months old. I had four children in less than two years and four months. Doctors looked at me in horror and asked me, "Woman, what are you, a machine?" But I thought it was the only thing for me to do, go on having them, because I was brought up to believe it was a crime to do away with them or even prevent conception.

Having the children so close kept us down financially and we could not afford to hire any one to assist me. Oh! How much happier I would be if they were farther apart and we were longing for another as we did the first. . . .

How much better it would be to give birth to children you were longing and looking for and not their coming being mere accidents. I have often been puzzled which was the greatest sin, bringing children into the world to keep them in poverty for life or preventing their conception. God alone knows how I have studied over this very thing and now that I have read your book [*Woman and the New Race*, published in 1920] I see your way of putting it, and I firmly believe that this world would be a heaven below if such would be the universal belief.

I always did have a horror of a large family brought up in poverty and dirt as is the result of crushed and broken women. Yet I have often said I will have fifteen before I will do murder and so I will. But I believe now your book is surely the truth and it is a crime to bring dear sickly little babies into the world and for them to suffer.

Fifteen Abortions

Oklahoma

Dear Mrs. Sanger:

I am the mother of two lovely little girls. I have been married fifteen years. I married at the age of fifteen to escape a home that was overcrowded with unloved and unwanted children, where there was never clothing or food enough to divide among the eight of us. When I married, I was as ignorant of sex life or of my own body as any six-year-old child. My husband's salary was $12 a week and we did well to live on that and did not want babies. I took all kinds of drugs each month to bring on my menses. After two years, my husband made more money and we each wanted a child. I was never so happy in my life as when I was carrying my first baby, knowing I could keep it.

When my little girl was 4 1/2 years old, I had my second little girl. I had three miscarriages between the two, going to a mid-wife each time and begging her to help me. Since my last little girl was born, I can safely say I have been pregnant 15 times, most of the time doing things myself to get out of it and no one knows how I have suffered from the effect of it, but I would rather die than bring as many children into the world as my mother did and have nothing to offer them.

Living in constant fear of getting pregnant makes me hate my husband who is a good man and a loving father. I hate married life and would rather see my little girls dead than to go through the suffering I have.

Distasteful and Repugnant

Iowa

Dear Mrs. Sanger:

We have one child and my husband's salary does not permit us to have any more. It is all we can do to make a living just for us and I think it a greater crime to bring children into the world when you are unable to support them and care for them properly than it is to practice abortion.

I have been practicing abortion for a number of years, because it was the only way I could do, but it is very distasteful and repugnant to me and I would give anything in the world to learn of birth control as you describe it in your book. Won't you please help me?

24   On Race Decay and Wilful Sterility

Theodore Roosevelt

Falling birth rates among the native born and middle class along with the widespread emigration of foreigners from southern and eastern Europe (over twenty-three million arrived on America's shores between 1880 and 1920) prompted many Progressives to condemn the use of birth control by "selfish" middle-class and upper-class women as "race suicide." Influenced by the tenets of social Darwinism, advocates of race suicide argued that native-born middle-class women who practiced fertility control were forsaking their natural duties as women and as citizens. Leading the race suicide charge in 1911 was the voluble and outspoken political leader and former president, Theodore Roosevelt.

From Theodore Roosevelt, "Race Decadence," *The Outlook*, April 8, 1911.

THE UNITED STATES SHARES WITH the other English-speaking countries the melancholy and discreditable position of coming next
to the people of France, among great civilized countries, in that
rapid decline of the birth-rate which inevitably signalizes race de-
cay, and which, if unchecked, means racial death. . . .

The American stock is being cursed with the curse of sterility,
and it is earning the curse, because the sterility is wilful. It is due to
moral, and not physiological, shortcomings. It is due to coldness,
to selfishness, to love of ease, to shrinking from risk, to an utter
and pitiful failure in sense of perspective and in power of weighing
what really makes the highest joy, and to a rooting out of the sense
of duty or a twisting of that sense into improper channels. . . .

During the last decade the increase in population of the United
States was almost two-thirds by immigration, the increase by birth-
rate showing a far lower percentage than ever before. . . .

Again, to quiet their uneasy consciences, cheap and shallow
men and women, when confronted with these facts, answer that
"quality is better than quantity," and that decrease of numbers will
mean increase in individual prosperity. It is false. When quantity
falls off, thanks to wilful sterility, the quality will go down too. We
can say that, if the processes now at work for a generation continue
to work in the same manner and at the same rate of increase during
the present century, by its end France will not carry the weight in
the civilized world that Belgium now does, and the English-
speaking peoples will not carry anything like the weight that the
Spanish-speaking peoples now do, and the future of the white race
will rest in the hands of the German and the Slav. Are Americans
really content that this land of promise, this land of the future, this
abounding and vigorous nation, shall become decrepit in what
ought to be the flower of its early manhood? Our forefathers were
the heroes of the tremendous epic that tells of the conquest of a
continent. The conquerors, the men who dared and did, with hearts
of steel and thews [sinews] of iron, looked fearlessly into the eyes
of the future, and quailed before no task and no danger; are their
sons and daughters, in love of effortless ease and fear of all work
and risk, to let the blood of the pioneers die out of the land because
they shrink from the most elemental duties of manhood and
womanhood? . . .

Many wilfully sterile people actually regard themselves as good
citizens, and even look down on what they stigmatize as "vice."
But in reality wilful sterility inevitably produces and accentuates

every hideous form of vice. Nor is this all. It is itself worse, more debasing, more destructive, than ordinary vice. Every decent citizen must abhor vice; I rank celibate profligacy as not one whit better than polygamy; yet, after all, such vice may be compatible with a nation's continuing to live; and while there is life, even a life marred by wrong practices, there is chance of reform. But the cardinal sin of wilful sterility in marriage means death; and for the dead there is no reform. . . .

In the partnership of man and woman the woman risks most, and for that reason we should hold in peculiar abhorrence the man who fails to realize this and to be gentle and tender and loyal in his dealings with her. The birth pangs make all men the debtors of all women; and those men have indeed touched the lowest abyss of brutality and depravity who do not recognize something holy in the names of wife and mother. No man, not even the soldier who does his duty, stands quite on the level with the wife and mother who has done her duty.

I do not believe that there is identity of duties as between man and woman, and I do believe that it is far more important for both to dwell upon their duties than their rights. But I also believe in a full equality of rights; if women wish to vote, I favor it (although I do not think it anything like as important for them or for the state as are many other things that they can and should do); but the extent of my reverence for and belief in a woman who does her duty measures also the depth of my contempt for the woman who shirks her primal and most essential duty. . . . Exactly as the measure of our regard for the soldier who does his full duty in battle is the measure of our scorn for the coward who flees, so the measure of our respect for the true wife and mother is the measure of our scorn and contemptuous abhorrence for the wife who refuses to be a mother. . . .

I hope I shall not be misunderstood, unless wilfully. I no more mean that a man and a woman are good citizens merely because they have children than I mean that a man is a good soldier merely because he can fight. In each case the possession of one essential quality does not atone for the lack of other qualities which are only less essential. Criminals should not have children. Shiftless and worthless people should not marry and have families which they are unable to bring up properly. Such marriages are a curse to the community. But this is only the negative side of the matter; and the positive is always more important than the negative. In our civilization to-day the great danger is that there will be failure to have enough children of the marriages that ought to take place.

25 Voices from within the Veil

W. E. B. Du Bois

A frequent and forceful critic of race suicide theory was W. E. B. Du Bois, an African-American historian, sociologist, and civil rights activist. A founding officer of the National Association for the Advancement of Colored People, Du Bois distanced himself from other black leaders, such as Booker T. Washington, by advocating racial integration and full legal and economic rights for blacks. In Darkwater *(1920), Du Bois criticizes the classist and racist dimensions of the birth control struggle and demands respect for and appreciation of African-American women's unique hardships.*

THE WORLD WANTS HEALTHY BABIES and intelligent workers. Today we refuse to allow the combination and force thousands of intelligent workers to go childless at a horrible expenditure of moral force, or we damn them if they break our idiotic conventions. Only at the sacrifice of intelligence and the chance to do their best work can the majority of modern women bear children. This is the damnation of women.

All womanhood is hampered today because the world on which it is emerging is a world that tries to worship both virgins and mothers and in the end despises motherhood and despoils virgins.

The future woman must have a life work and economic independence. She must have knowledge. She must have the right of motherhood at her own discretion. The present mincing horror at free womanhood must pass if we are ever to be rid of the bestiality of free manhood; not by guarding the weak in weakness do we gain strength, but by making weakness free and strong. . . .

The uplift of women is, next to the problem of the color line and the peace movement, our greatest modern cause. When, now, two of these movements—woman and color—combine in one, the combination has deep meaning.

From W. E. B. Du Bois, *Darkwater: Voices from within the Veil* (New York: Harcourt, Brace and Howe, 1920), 164–65, 181–82, 184–85.

In other years women's way was clear: to be beautiful, to be petted, to bear children. Such has been their theoretic destiny, and if perchance they have been ugly, hurt, and barren, that has been forgotten with studied silence. In partial compensation for this narrowed destiny the white world has lavished its politeness on its womankind—its chivalry and bows, its uncoverings and courtesies—all the accumulated homage disused for courts and kings and craving exercise. The revolt of white women against this preordained destiny has in these latter days reached splendid proportions, but it is the revolt of an aristocracy of brains and ability—the middle class and rank and file still plod on in the appointed path, paid by the homage, the almost mocking homage, of men. . . .

God send us a world with woman's freedom and married motherhood inextricably wed, but until He sends it, I see more of future promise in the betrayed girl-mothers of the black belt than in the childless wives of the white North, and I have more respect for the colored servant who yields to her frank longing for motherhood than for her white sister who offers up children for clothes. Out of a sex freedom that today makes us shudder will come in time a day when we will no longer pay men for work they do not do, for the sake of their harem; we will pay women what they earn and insist on their working and earning it; we will allow those persons to vote who know enough to vote, whether they be black or female, white or male; and we will ward [off] race suicide, not by further burdening the over-burdened, but by honoring motherhood, even when the sneaking father shirks his duty.

26   The Program of Eugenics and the Negro Race

Paul Popenoe and Roswell Johnson

Eugenics, the supposition that behavioral, physical, and intellectual traits are inherited, framed arguments for and against birth control in the late nineteenth and early twentieth centuries. When Theodore Roosevelt demanded more children from "old stock" Americans (Document 24), he placed himself firmly

From Paul Popenoe and Roswell Johnson, *Applied Eugenics* (New York: Macmillan Company, 1926), 156–59, 284–85, 292, 297.

in the positive eugenics camp. In the 1920s and 1930s support for negative eugenics, or fewer births from the unfit, surpassed the popularity of positive eugenics. Advocates of negative eugenics cited glaringly racist studies such as the one in 1926 by popular author Paul Popenoe and professor and scientist (of oil and gas production) Roswell Johnson to "prove" that undesirable traits—indolence, indigence, criminality, and excessive sexual desire, to name a few—were inherited.

T HE PROGRAM OF EUGENICS NATURALLY divides itself in two parts:
1) Reducing the racial contribution of the least desirable part of the population.
2) Increasing the racial contribution of the superior part of the population.

The first part of this program is the most pressing and the most easily dealt with; it is no cause for surprise, then, that to many people it has seemed to be the predominant aim of eugenics. Certainly the problem is great enough to stagger anyone who looks it full in the face; although for a variety of reasons, satisfactory statistical evidence of racial degeneracy is hard to get.

Considering only the "institutional population" of the United States, one gets the following figures:

BLIND: Total, 64,763 according to census of 1900. Of these, 35,645 were totally blind and 29,118 partly blind. The affection [*sic*] is stated to have been congenital in 4,730 cases. . . .

DEAF: Total, 86,515, according to the census of 1900. More than 50,000 of them were deaf from childhood (under 20), 12,609 being deaf from birth. At least 4.5 percent of the deaf were stated to be offspring of cousin marriages, and 32.1 percent to have deaf relatives. . . .

INSANE: The census of 1910 enumerated only the insane who were in institutions; they numbered 187,791. The number outside of institutions is doubtless considerable but can not be computed. The institutional population is not a permanent, but mainly a transient one, the number of persons discharged from institutions in 1910 being 29,304. As the number and size of institutions does not increase very rapidly, it would appear probable that 25,000 insane persons pass through and out of institutions, and back into the general population, each year. From this one can get some idea of the amount of neurotic weakness in the population of the United States—much of it congenital and heritable in character.

FEEBLE-MINDED: The census (1910) lists only those in institutions, who totaled about 40,000. The census experts believe that 200,000 would be a conservative estimate of the total number of feeble-minded in the country, and many psychologists think that 300,000 would be more nearly accurate. . . .

PAUPERS: There were 84,198 paupers enumerated in almshouses on January 1, 1910, and 88,313 admitted during the year, which indicates that the almshouse paupers are a rapidly shifting group. This population, probably of several hundred thousand persons, who drift into and out of almshouses, can hardly be characterized accurately, but in large part it must be considered at least inefficient and probably of mentally low grade.

CRIMINALS: The inmates of prisons, penitentiaries, reformatories, and similar places of detention numbered 111,609 in 1910; this does not include 25,000 juvenile delinquents. The jail population is nearly all transient; one must be very cautious in inferring that conviction for an offense against the law indicates lack of eugenic value; but it is worth noting that the number of offenders who are feeble-minded is probably not less than one-fourth or one-third. If the number of inebriates could be added, it would greatly increase the total; and inebriacy or chronic alcoholism is generally recognized now as indicating in a majority of cases either feeble-mindedness or some other defect of the nervous system. The number of criminals who are in some way neurotically tainted is placed by some psychologists at 50 percent or more of the total prison population.

Add to these a number of epileptics, tramps, prostitutes, beggars, and others whom the census enumerator finds it difficult to catch, and the total number of possible undesirable parents becomes very large. It is in fact much larger than appears in these figures, because of the fact that many people carry defects that are latent and only appear in the offspring of a marriage representing two tainted strains. Thus the feeble-minded child usually if not always has feeble-mindedness in both his father's and mother's ancestry, and for every one of the patent feeble-minded above enumerated, there may be several dozen latent ones, who are themselves probably normal in every way and yet carry the dangerously tainted germ-plasm.

The estimate has frequently been made that the United States would be much better off eugenically if it were deprived of the future racial contributions of at least 10 percent of its citizens. While literally true, this estimate is too high for the group which could be considered for attempts to directly control in a practical eugenics program.

Natural selection, in the early days of man's history, would have killed off many of these people early in life. They would have been unable to compete with their physically and mentally more vigorous fellows and would have died miserably by starvation or violence. Natural selection's use of the death-rate was a brutal one, but at least it prevented such traits as these people show from increasing in each generation. Eugenists hope to arrive at the same result, not by the death-rate but by the birth-rate. If germinally antisocial persons are kept humanely segregated during their lifetime, instead of being turned out after a few years of institutional life and allowed to marry, they will leave no descendants, and the number of congenital defectives in the community will be notably diminished. If the same policy is followed through succeeding generations, the number of defectives, of those incapable of taking a useful part in society, will become smaller and smaller. One who does not believe that these people hand on their traits to their descendants may profitably consider the famous history of the so-called Juke family, a strain originating among the "finger lakes" of New York, whose history was published by R. L. Dugdale as far back as 1877 and lately restudied by A. H. Estabrook.

"From one lazy vagabond nicknamed 'Juke,' born in 1720, whose two sons married five degenerate sisters, six generations numbering about 1,200 persons of every grade of idleness, viciousness, lewdness, pauperism, disease, idiocy, insanity and criminality were traced. Of the total seven generations, 300 died in infancy; 310 were professional paupers, kept in almshouses a total of 2,300 years; 440 were physically wrecked by their own 'diseased wickedness'; more than half the women fell into prostitution; 130 were convicted criminals; 60 were thieves; 7 were murderers; only 20 learned a trade, 10 of these in state prison, and all at a state cost of over $1,250,000.". . .

~

If the number of original contributions which it has made to the world's civilization is any fair criterion of the relative value of a race, then the Negro race must be placed very near zero on the scale.*

The following historical considerations suggest that in comparison with some other races the Negro race is germinally lacking in the higher developments of intelligence:

1) That the Negro race in Africa has never, by its own initiative, risen much above barbarism, although it has been exposed to a considerable range of environments and has had abundant time in which to bring to expression any inherited traits it may possess.

2) That when transplanted to a new environment—say, Haiti—and left to its own resources, the Negro race has shown the same inability to rise; it has there, indeed, lost most of what it had acquired from the superior civilization of the French.

3) That when placed side by side with the white race, the Negro race again fails to come up to their standard, or indeed to come anywhere near it. It is often alleged that this third test is an unfair one; that the social heritage of slavery must be eliminated before the Negro can be expected to show his true worth. But contrast his career in and after slavery with that of the Mamelukes of Egypt, who were slaves, but slaves of good stock. They quickly rose to be the real rulers of the country. Again, compare the record of the Greek slaves in the Roman republic and empire or that of the Jews under Islam. Without pushing these analogies too far, is not one forced to conclude that the Negro lacks in his germ-plasm excellence of some qualities which the white races possess, and which are essential for success in competition with the civilizations of the white races at the present day?

If so, it must be admitted not only that the Negro is *different* from the white, but that he is in the large eugenically *inferior* to the white. . . .

There is some evidence from life insurance and medical sources, that the mulatto stands above the Negro but below the white in respect to his health. There is considerable evidence that he occupies the same relation in the intellectual world; it is a matter of general observation that nearly all the leaders of the Negro race in the United States are not Negroes but mulattoes.

---

*The Negro's contribution has perhaps been most noteworthy in music. This does not necessarily show advanced evolution; August Weismann long ago pointed out that music is a primitive accomplishment. For an outline of what the Negro race has achieved, particularly in America, see the *Negro Year Book,* Tuskegee Institute, Ala.

Without going into detail, we feel perfectly safe in drawing this conclusion: that in general the white race loses and the Negro gains from miscegenation.

This applies, of course, only to the germinal nature. Taking into consideration the present social conditions in America, it is doubtful whether either race gains. But if social conditions be eliminated for the moment, biologists may believe that intermarriage between the white and Negro races represents, on the whole, an advance for the Negro; and that it represents for the white race a distinct loss. . . .

We favor, therefore, the support of the taboo which society has placed on these mixed marriages, as well as any legal action which can practicably be taken to make miscegenation between white and black impossible. Justice requires that the Negro race be treated as kindly and considerately as possible, with every economic and political concession that is consistent with the continued welfare of the nation. Such social equality and intercourse as might lead to marriage are not compatible with this welfare.

27   *Buck v. Bell* (1927)

The growing popularity of negative eugenics marshaled support for the passage of sexual sterilization laws. In its 1927 ruling in Buck v. Bell, *the Supreme Court upheld the constitutionality of a 1924 Virginia eugenics statute that legalized the coerced sterilization of "socially inadequate person[s]." Carrie Buck, the plaintiff, was single, white, pregnant, and seventeen when she was brought to the Virginia Colony for Epileptics and Feeble Minded in Lynchburg. Although she insisted that her pregnancy was the result of rape, her "condition" and her status as the "daughter of an imbecile" supplied the primary evidence substantiating the charge of mental ineptitude. She was sterilized on October 19, 1927, a few months after the Supreme Court's ruling.*

The Court's decision gave free license to other states to pass similar eugenics legislation. By 1932 at least twenty-six states had laws permitting the forced sterilization of individuals considered feebleminded, retarded, delinquent, or otherwise

From *Buck v. Bell* 274 U.S. 200 (1927).

"unfit." The Virginia act served as the model for the drafting of Germany's Hereditary Health Law in 1933. During the Nuremberg trials following World War II, Nazi war criminals cited Buck v. Bell *to justify the forced sterilization of two million Germans.*

Argument for Plaintiff

THE OBJECT OF THE ACT is to prevent the reproduction of mentally defective people. . . . If this Act be a valid enactment, then the limits of the power of the State (which in the end is nothing more than the faction in control of the government) to rid itself of those citizens deemed undesirable according to its standards, by means of surgical sterilization, have not been set. We will have "established in the State the science of medicine and a corresponding system of judicature." A reign of doctors will be inaugurated, and in the name of science new classes will be added, even races may be brought within the scope of such regulation, and the worst forms of tyranny practiced. . . .

Argument for Defendant

An exercise of the police power analogous to that of the statute here in question may be found in the compulsory vaccination statutes; for there, as here, a surgical operation is required for the protection of the individual and of society. . . . The State may and does confine the feeble minded, thus depriving them of their liberty. When so confined they are by segregation prohibited from procreation— a further deprivation of liberty that goes unquestioned. The appellant is under the Virginia statutes already by law prohibited from procreation. The precise question therefore is whether the State, in its judgment of what is best for appellant and for society, may through the medium of the operation provided for by the sterilization statute restore her to the liberty, freedom and happiness which thereafter she might safely be allowed to find outside of institutional walls. . . .

Opinion of the Court, delivered by MR. JUSTICE HOLMES

The case comes here upon the contention that the statute authorizing the judgment [Buck's sterilization] is void under the Fourteenth

Amendment as denying to the plaintiff . . . due process of law and the equal protection of the laws.

Carrie Buck is a feeble minded white woman who was committed to the State Colony. . . . in due form. She is the daughter of a feeble minded mother in the same institution, and the mother of an illegitimate feeble minded child. . . . An Act of Virginia, approved March 20, 1924, recites that the health of the patient and the welfare of society may be promoted in certain cases by the sterilization of mental defectives, under careful safeguard, &c.; that the sterilization may be effected in males by vasectomy and in females by salpingectomy [cutting the Fallopian tubes], without serious pain or substantial danger to life; that the Commonwealth is supporting in various institutions many defective persons who if now discharged would become a menace but if incapable of procreating might be discharged with safety and become self-supporting with benefit to themselves and to society; and that experience has shown that heredity plays an important part in the transmission of insanity, imbecility, &c. The statute then enacts that whenever the superintendent of certain institutions including the above named State Colony shall be of opinion that it is for the best interests of the patients and of society that an inmate under his care should be sexually sterilized, he may have the operation performed upon any patient afflicted with hereditary forms of insanity, imbecility, &c. . . .

We have seen more than once that the public welfare may call upon the best citizens for their lives. It would be strange if it could not call upon those who already sap the strength of the State for these lesser sacrifices, often not felt to be such by those concerned, in order to prevent our being swamped with incompetence. It is better for all the world, if instead of waiting to execute degenerate offspring for crime, or to let them starve for their imbecility, society can prevent those who are manifestly unfit from continuing their kind. The principle that sustains compulsory vaccination is broad enough to cover cutting the Fallopian tubes. . . . Three generations of imbeciles are enough.

VI

Reproductive Rights

28   The Role of Popular Organizing:
Feminists and Libertarians

Rosalind Pollack Petchesky

In 1973, exactly one century after the passage of the Comstock Act, the Supreme Court decriminalized abortion. The Court accepted the legal argument—supported by many feminists—that a woman's right to individual reproductive privacy (her "right to choose") had been unconstitutionally abridged by state abortion statutes. As political scientist Rosalind Pollack Petchesky points out, however, the continued feminist categorization of abortion as an individual *right affirms a laissez-faire view of the state's obligations to women that, ironically, may work against the realization of other feminist goals. Petchesky assesses the degree to which the abortion victory was also a feminist victory.*

B IRTH CONTROL POLITICS THROUGHOUT MOST of the twentieth century in America have been laced with a tension between the ideas and methods of popular organizers and mass movements on the one hand and those of liberal reformers and sympathetic medical and legal professionals on the other. "Abortion on demand" and "a woman's right to control over her body" were never ideas that carried much weight in family planning conferences and AMA [American Medical Association] committees, in the legislative hearings and courtrooms where abortion policy was made, even though those ideas created important pressures on clinicians and policymakers to find more "moderate" principles to accommodate women's demands. Among such accommodationist principles the most important was the legitimacy of "therapeutic" abortion. This is the concept that the conditions justifying abortion are those that involve a woman's health, though "health" may be broadly defined to include a woman's mental or emotional health as well as fetal health. Those exclusively qualified to determine when such

From Rosalind Pollack Petchesky, *Abortion and Woman's Choice: The State, Sexuality, and Reproductive Freedom*, rev. ed. (Boston: Northeastern University Press, 1990), 125–32, 135–38. © 1984 and 1990 by Rosalind Pollack Petchesky. Reprinted by permission of Northeastern University Press.

conditions, or "medical indications," exist, and to administer the procedures, are certified physicians.

Feminists have strongly opposed the distinction between therapeutic ("necessary") and elective ("unnecessary"?) abortions. Ellen Willis recalls this debate during the campaign for legalization in the late 1960s:

> When the radical feminist campaign for repeal of the abortion laws began in 1969, our first target was the "reformers" who sat around splitting hairs over how sick or poor or multiparous a pregnant woman had to be to deserve exemption from reproductive duty. It was the feminist demand for the *unconditional right to abortion* that galvanized women *and created effective pressure for legalization.* Now the idea that abortions without some special justification are not necessary but merely "convenient"—as if unwanted pregnancy were an annoyance comparable to, say, standing in a long line at the supermarket—has been revived with a vengeance.[1]

Radical and socialist feminists, working through organizations such as the Chicago Women's Liberation Union, NOW [National Organization for Women], Redstockings, and women's health activist groups, consciously rejected both the medical model of reproductive health and (though not always) populationist goals as the basis of birth control. In contrast to family planners and public health practitioners, feminists put forward a libertarian view of "abortion on demand" as a necessary condition of women's right to control their bodies and pregnancy:

> All the excellent supporting reasons—improved health, lower birth and death rates, freer medical practice, the separation of church and state, happier families, sexual privacy, lower welfare expenditures—are only embroidery on the basic fabric: *woman's right to limit her own reproduction.* It is *this* rationale that the new woman's movement has done so much to bring to the fore. Those who caution us to play down the women's rights argument are only trying to put off the inevitable day when the society must face and eradicate the misogynistic roots of the present situation. And anyone who has spoken publicly about abortion from the feminist point of view knows all too well that it is *feminism*—not abortion—that is the really disturbing idea.[2]

Contrasting "reform" to the more radical demand for repeal, feminists argued that the former was steeped in conditions that denied women's capacity and right to make reproductive decisions.

Medical and legalistic models of abortion, they pointed out, focused on "hardship" situations—rubella, rape, mental illness—and thus "always pictured women as victims, . . . never as possible shapers of their own destinies."[3] And these models implicitly suggested that women were incompetent to act as moral agents on their own behalf. Repeal, on the other hand, would simply abolish any restrictive, discriminatory conditions impeding abortion so that medical authorities could no longer be moral gatekeepers.

Legal abortions had always been possible in some states to save a woman's life or spare her "serious" health problems, or for the other classic "hard" reasons: the fetus was known to be defective or the pregnancy resulted from rape or incest. But to obtain an abortion even under these conditions involved going through hospital committees and private networks that were penetrable only to privileged women. When the laws of some states underwent reform in the late 1960s, these restrictive conditions continued and, if anything, became more apparent under the rubric of (now legal) "therapeutic" abortions. Punitive therapeutic abortion committees put women through intense and often moralizing inquiries to determine whether their abortion request was truly justified on "health" grounds. Physicians and hospital authorities in California and Colorado, for example, imposed enormous red tape, requiring written consent from at least two physicians as well as the hospital committee and insisting on inpatient (hence much costlier) procedures. Many hospitals, particularly smaller ones, feared the label "abortion mill" or had chiefs of service opposed to abortion; thus they refused to perform abortions or imposed strict residency requirements.[4] These restrictions effectively excluded poor women, who lacked the personal connections to private doctors and the funds necessary to obtain a safe hospital abortion.

In the radical political context that existed from 1968 through the early 1970s, however, feminists and other proabortion activists sometimes found it possible to use "health" and "mental health" provisions expansively, to push them to their limits. Abortion referral groups in California, for example, were able to use "psychiatric indications" to sidestep much of the red tape that encumbered hospital abortions—evidently finding cooperative physicians with less difficulty—and thus to process most abortion cases.[5] Along with abortion activists in progressive church groups and radical health groups, civil libertarians, and some sympathetic doctors, organized feminists functioned as shock troops in the struggle to

break through legal barriers. By pushing at the soft spots in existing laws (utilizing "health" and "mental health" provisions, testing
hospital rules), they were able to open a wedge through which the
growing need of women for access to abortion services could make
itself felt even among the most resistant physicians.[6]

These tactics affected only a small number of women and were
really test cases. The most important action feminists took to expand women's access to abortion and change the medical
profession's position was through providing information and a network of alternative—and in at least one case, underground—services. Popular feminist pamphlets published from 1969 to 1971,
especially *The Birth Control Handbook* and the now classic *Our
Bodies, Ourselves*, circulated in the many thousands of copies, giving practical information about abortion procedures, risks, and
sources of information and service.[7] As in the early twentieth century, alternative clinics and a network of cooperating private doctors were set up in the vacuum created by the institutionalized
medical profession's refusal to provide care even after liberal abortion laws were passed. . . .

Politically, the impact of confronting the medical profession
and the state with a rival set of institutions that could clearly meet
people's needs, and do so at a lower cost, was powerful. More than
anything else, it illustrated that the criminal statutes could not be
enforced. Feminists believed—and they were not altogether
wrong—that new abortion techniques, when used early in a pregnancy and under safe conditions, were so simple they could be
"seized" from medical control.[8] Indeed, it is ironic to speculate that
the fact of abortion's technical simplicity and lack of "heroic" surgical challenge is one reason why many doctors disdain it. Acting
on this belief, at least one group of feminists set up an underground
abortion clinic in Chicago that operated over a four-year period
(1969–73) practically under the eyes of the police, providing eleven
thousand illegal abortions.

Known as Jane and originating out of the Chicago Women's
Liberation Union, the clinic delivered services to women of all ages
and stages of pregnancy. At first it contracted with illegal abortionists, trying to bargain down their fees, but then Jane volunteers
learned to perform the operation themselves, using the aspiration
technique, which made it possible to reduce fees to an average of
$50, although "no one was turned away for lack of funds."[9] In this

way, the theory and practice of self-help became an essential part of the struggle for legal abortion, proving "that abortions could be performed safely, humanely and very inexpensively by non-professional paramedics working in apartments." Jane maintained a safety record that compared "favorably with that of licensed medical facilities in New York and California" in the early years of legal abortion, and it was able to provide its services primarily to low-income women. It not only monitored clients' reproductive health (through Pap smears, taking blood pressure, referrals for complications) but focused on counseling as "the heart of the procedure"—a form of counseling that attempted to give the woman sisterly support and to demystify the abortion experience.[10]

In part, the threat posed by Jane and the freestanding (legal) clinics that succeeded it was economic. Low fees made "the bottom fall out of the abortion black market," hence undercutting what had long been a boondoggle for some doctors.[11] Even more important, the fact that these clinics provided (and continue to provide) a vital service that thousands of women desperately need, under safe conditions, has been the major determinant of their "unstoppability." It is interesting that in four years of illegal operation involving dozens of activists, only seven members of Jane were arrested; the charges were dropped in 1973. "The police were not interested in stopping them, . . . the police had known what they were doing and had not intervened . . . since they were providing a necessary service for policemen's wives, mistresses and daughters and for all policewomen," and did so in a manner that left women healthy and well rather than bloody or dying.[12]

From 1968 to 1973 the organized feminist movement used a variety of direct-action methods to put pressure on the medical profession, state legislatures, and popular consciousness to repeal abortion laws. The 1969 AMA Convention in New York was surrounded by picketers from the women's movement wielding signs and leaflets "demanding that doctors sign a petition for repeal."[13] Feminists from NOW and other women's liberation groups invaded the AMA meeting, as well as courtrooms, legislative hearing rooms, district attorneys' offices, and the streets—no bastion of patriarchy was sacrosanct—and provided the most visible external pressure for change in the abortion laws. Joined by radical health and welfare rights groups, they sat in at public hospitals and health agencies to demand that abortion services be provided to poor women.

Redstockings (a New York women's liberation group) sponsored a "speakout on abortion" at which dozens of women testified publicly about the horrors of their illegal abortions.[14]

The shift in medical and family planning policy from 1969 to 1971 was a response to this political pressure, as well as to the threatened growth of alternative abortion services outside the control of the medical hierarchy. These two factors—the militant organizing of feminists and the threat of "alternative services"—were crucial political influences toward loosening population establishment and medical abortion policy. The role of feminist activists as "shock troops"—doing underground abortion referrals and counseling, conducting speakouts, sit-ins, and demonstrations—was critical for the timing of the Supreme Court decision and earlier decriminalization statutes in several states.

Unfortunately, the impact of feminist *ideas* about abortion and birth control was less clear. Part of this confusion was the failure of women's liberationists of the pre-*Roe* period—unlike the present reproductive rights movement—to distinguish sharply between the demand for birth control and abortion services on behalf of women's choice and the aims of population control. As in the late nineteenth and early twentieth centuries, some feminists of the "second wave" conflated their values about abortion as a social need and right of all women with arguments about "overpopulation," echoing the dominant ideology and state policy.[15] The result was, in the late 1960s, a deepening of divisions between the mainly white women's liberation movement and the black liberation movement, whose predominantly male leadership, from its most militant to its most conservative wings, had long been suspicious of any government-sponsored family planning program as a weapon of racial "genocide." Given the racist policies of government-funded clinics and family planners—targeting minority neighborhoods for family planning services; providing birth control devices and "follow-up" in abundance, but not jobs, decent housing, basic health care, maternity care or child care; sterilizing poor black, Hispanic, and Native American women without their informed consent—these suspicions grew out of a stark reality.

But the polemic about genocide has usually overlooked the distinction between birth control and population control. It has ignored the question of *who* controls, and the very real need of black and other ethnic minority women to control their fertility, which necessarily requires government funding and services. Occasionally it has carried a populationist-misogynist message of its own, such as the statement of one Florida NAACP official that "our women need to produce more babies, not less . . . ; until we comprise 30 to 35 percent of the population we won't really be able to affect the power structure in this country."[16] Black women, speaking out of their identity within the black movement but with a feminist voice, responded forcefully to such statements and the male supremacy they implied. Acknowledging the racism of population control policies, Toni Cade Bambara, Shirley Chisholm, and others argued that the "male rhetoric" of genocide went against the needs and feelings of black and Puerto Rican women growing out of their own responsibilities for children and could not be heeded at the expense of those women's lives or the well-being of their children.[17] Opposition to population control and support for birth control and abortion *as paired feminist values* originated here, in the political thinking and experience of black women.

Another ambiguity in the white feminist movement's ideas about abortion arose from its emphasis on the practical rather than the theoretical or broadly social aspects of abortion. During the New York State campaign, radical feminists made clear the differences between their approach, which emphasized concrete access to abortion for all women, and that of more liberally oriented groups (e.g., the National Association for Repeal of Abortion Laws, which became the National Abortion Rights Action League, or NARAL), which emphasized the legal "right to choose." Feminists consistently opposed legislative proposals that restricted legal abortion to licensed physicians, therapeutic criteria, and so forth, insisting on the importance of paramedicals and nonhierarchical forms of reproductive health care if all women were to have access to services.[18] This was a practical way to critique the elitism of the medical care system and the abstract idea of abortion as a private matter between "a woman and her doctor." For the majority of women did not and do not have access to a cozy, confidential relationship with a private physician, traditionally the ticket to a safe abortion. Thus the feminist position implicitly called for substantive changes in the quality and conditions of reproductive health care. But this practical approach was not developed into an analysis and an ideology that could communicate to popular understanding the sexual and social as well as the health reasons why women of all classes and age groups, married and unmarried, ought to have access to abortion; why legal abortion is a positive benefit and not a "necessary evil."

The philosophy of removing the state from abortion decisions altogether, of repeal pure and simple (implied in the slogan "Get the State's laws off our bodies") is at bottom one of laissez-faire. It contains an implicit presumption that the "right to choose," or the relegation of abortion to the private sphere, will in itself guarantee that good, safe abortions will be provided. Many feminists have understood that this is not a reasonable presumption; the existing medical-care system, like other capitalist markets, does not adequately meet people's needs; how and by whom abortions (or other health services) are provided is a critical dimension of whether real needs will be met. This deeper understanding was often implicit in how radical feminists conducted the abortion struggle, but it failed to be translated either into a popular feminist discourse or into public policy. More seriously, the powerful idea that restricting abortion means compelling motherhood, that motherhood is a social relationship and not a punishment or a destiny, remained—remains still—far removed from the consciousness of most people. As a result, feminists in the campaign for legal abortion won the battle but not the war. On the level of public discourse—policy, law, media representation—the feminist voice on the abortion question was and remains barely audible. More disturbing, within popular consciousness, it would seem that medical and neo-Malthusian, not feminist, justifications for abortion prevail.

Yet, in a vague and diffuse way, on some deeper cultural level, articulated in a negative sense by the antifeminist right wing, the women's liberation movement of the 1960s and 1970s brought to light the taboo sexual meanings of fertility control politics that the family planning and population control establishment had tried so methodically to conceal. More than anything else, the fight for "abortion on demand," as a demand of and by women, asserted these meanings even when some feminists were not eager to, or when their ideas about abortion remained rhetorical and confused. When a large and clamoring body of women—single, lesbian, and divorced, as well as married with kids, or grandmothers—began marching by the thousands for legal abortion, it created a political context that by definition exposed the connections between fertility control and women's sexuality. As a reaction to this feminist movement, the conservative forces now in power and the sexual/ family ideology they represent are a challenge not only to feminism but to the hegemony and contradictions in the previous thirty years of population control and family planning policy. For the former policy hoped to make birth control (and, later, abortion) available but without any radical sexual or gender-related consequences.

In the late 1970s the pendulum began to swing back again, and the preoccupation of policymakers, public and private, with population control receded before their growing concern to refortify the boundaries of sexual control. This was apparent in the first Hyde Amendment, passed in 1977, to cut off most federal finds for abortion services. There the impulse of legislators to curb "promiscuous sex" among poor young women seemed to take priority over their more recent urge (since the 1940s) to reduce the fertility of the poor. The past two decades of liberalized policies around fertility control, including abortion, are perceived as having unleashed a wave of "illicit" sexual activity, especially among young unmarried middle-class women but also among welfare recipients. Thus the policies must be revised; the connection between fertility control and sexual freedom must be contained. But it should be clear that this readjustment of policy has little to do with political parties, nor is it the invention of the New Right. Antiabortion policies have been a constant under every president since Eisenhower, and the constitutionality of abortion was declared in spite of verbal presidential opposition. These shifts reflect, not partisan leanings, but the tensions embedded in the patriarchal state between population control and sexual control, and the persistent view of abortion as uniquely subversive.

There is a lesson to be learned from *Roe v. Wade*, a lesson that could have a bearing on its sequel in the 1980s. If, after a century of medical and eugenicist domination of reproductive politics, abortion became legal in the first place, it was because at a particular historical moment social need, feminist activism, and populationist ideology came together. This was sufficient to change state policy, but in order for that change to have been radical—a liberating force for masses of women, and lasting—social need and feminist activism would have had to merge with a popular *feminist* ideology, one that turned the accepted meanings of abortion upside down. And this did not happen.

Notes

1. Ellen Willis, *Village Voice*, 3 March 1980, p. 8.

2. Lucinda Cisler, "Unfinished Business: Birth Control and Women's Liberation," in *Sisterhood Is Powerful*, ed. Robin Morgan (New York: Vintage, 1970), p. 276.

3. Ibid., p. 275

4. Lawrence Lader, *Abortion Two: Making the Revolution* (Boston: Beacon Press, 1973), pp. 22, 114; and Daniel Callahan, *Abortion: Law, Choice and Morality* (New York: Macmillan, 1970), pp. 137–42.

5. Lader, p. 111.

6. Failure to grant a hospital abortion in cases of rubella or severe emotional distress might be grounds for a malpractice suit.

7. The Boston Women's Health Book Collective, *Our Bodies, Ourselves* (New York: Simon and Schuster, 1971); there were two subsequent printings and two later editions. Donna Cherniak and Shirley Gardiner, *Birth Control Handbook* (Montreal: Montreal Health Press, 1973).

8. Cisler, p. 265; and Pauline Bart, "Seizing the Means of Reproduction: An Illegal Feminist Abortion Collective, How and Why It Worked" (unpublished ms., n.d.).

9. Bart, pp. 4, 10. This unpublished manuscript is the only written source available documenting the story of Jane.

10. Ibid., pp. 4, 7.

11. Ibid., p. 5.

12. Ibid., p. 6 and note 2.

13. Lader, p. 82.

14. Cisler, pp. 271, 278; and Florynce Kennedy and Diane Schulder, *Abortion Rap* (New York: McGraw-Hill, 1971).

15. See, for example, Cisler, p. 287.

16. Quoted in Thomas B. Littlewood, *The Politics of Population Control* (Notre Dame: University of Notre Dame Press, 1977), p. 75.

17. See Shirley Chisholm, "Facing the Abortion Question," in *Black Women in White America: A Documentary History*, ed. Gerda Lerner (New York: Vintage, 1973), pp. 602–7; and Toni Cade (Bambara), "The Pill: Genocide or Liberation," in *The Black Woman*, ed. Toni Cade Bambara (New York: New American Library, 1970).

18. Lader, pp. 126, 130.

29   *Griswold v. Connecticut* (1965)

On November 10, 1961, Estelle Griswold, executive director of the Planned Parenthood League of Connecticut, and D. Led Buxton, chair of the Department of Obstetrics at the Yale Uni-

From *Griswold v. Connecticut* 381 U.S. 479 (1965).

versity School of Medicine, were arrested for operating a birth control clinic for married women in New Haven. Griswold and Buxton had opened the clinic on November 1 to challenge the constitutionality of Connecticut's anticontraceptive statute. The 1879 measure proscribed the use of any "drug, medicinal article or instrument for the purpose of preventing conception" and imposed a comparable sentence on "any person who assists, abets, counsels, causes, hires or commands another to commit [this] offense." The effect of the Supreme Court's landmark decision, handed down on June 7, 1965, was twofold. First, it invalidated the Connecticut law. Second, by determining that a constitutional right to privacy for married couples fell within the "penumbra" of the Bill of Rights—understood in this context to be the right to matrimonial privacy in the bedroom—it established a precedent crucial to the outcome of subsequent reproductive rights cases.

Opinion of the Court, delivered by Mr. Justice Douglas

THE PRESENT CASE . . . CONCERNS A relationship lying within the zone of privacy created by several fundamental constitutional guarantees. And it concerns a law which, in forbidding the *use* of contraceptives rather than regulating their manufacture or sale, seeks to achieve its goals by means having a maximum destructive impact upon that relationship. Such a law cannot stand in light of the familiar principle, so often applied by this Court, that a "governmental purpose to control or prevent activities constitutionally subject to state regulation may not be achieved by means which sweep unnecessarily broadly and thereby invade the area of protected freedoms.". . . Would we allow the police to search the sacred precincts of marital bedrooms for telltale signs of the use of contraceptives? The very idea is repulsive to the notions of privacy surrounding the marriage relationship.

We deal with a right of privacy older than the Bill of Rights— older than our political parties, older than our school system. Marriage is a coming together for better or for worse, hopefully enduring, and intimate to the degree of being sacred. It is an association that promotes a way of life, not causes; a harmony in living, not political faiths; a bilateral loyalty, not commercial or social projects. Yet it is an association for as noble a purpose as any involved in our prior decisions.

MR. JUSTICE GOLDBERG, whom THE CHIEF JUSTICE and MR. JUSTICE BRENNAN join, concurring.

I agree with the Court that Connecticut's birth-control law unconstitutionally intrudes upon the right of marital privacy, and I join in its opinion and judgment. . . . In reaching the conclusion that the right of marital privacy is protected [by the U.S. Constitution], as being within the protected penumbra of specific guarantees of the Bill of Rights, the Court refers to the Ninth Amendment. . . . I add these words to emphasize the relevance of that Amendment to the Court's holding. . . .

The Ninth Amendment to the Constitution may be regarded by some as a recent discovery and may be forgotten by others, but since 1791 it has been a basic part of the Constitution which we are sworn to uphold. To hold that a right so basic and fundamental and so deep-rooted in our society as the right of privacy in marriage may be infringed because that right is not guaranteed in so many words by the first eight amendments to the Constitution is to ignore the Ninth Amendment and to give it no effect whatsoever. Moreover, a judicial construction that this fundamental right is not protected by the Constitution because it is not mentioned in explicit terms by one of the first eight amendments or elsewhere in the Constitution would violate the Ninth Amendment, which specifically states that "[t]he enumeration in the Constitution, of certain rights, shall not be *construed* to deny or disparage others retained by the people." (Emphasis added.) . . .

The entire fabric of the Constitution and the purposes that clearly underlie its specific guarantees demonstrate that the rights to marital privacy and to marry and raise a family are of similar order and magnitude as the fundamental rights specifically protected.

Although the Constitution does not speak in so many words of the right of privacy in marriage, I cannot believe that it offers these fundamental rights no protection. The fact that no particular provision of the Constitution explicitly forbids the State from disrupting the traditional relation of the family—a relation as old and as fundamental as our entire civilization—surely does not show that the Government was meant to have the power to do so. Rather, as the Ninth Amendment expressly recognizes, there are fundamental personal rights such as this one, which are protected from abridgment by the Government though not specifically mentioned in the Constitution.

30   *Eisenstadt v. Baird* (1972)

What Griswold v. Connecticut *did for married couples,*
Eisenstadt v. Baird *did for contracepting singles. The case challenged the constitutionality of Massachusetts's "crimes against
chastity" law that prohibited the distribution of birth control
information or supplies to unmarried persons. On April 6, 1967,
at a public lecture at Boston University, reproductive rights
activist Bill Baird offered containers of free contraceptive foam
to a crowd of fifteen hundred. When twelve unmarried women
attempted to take him up on his offer, he was arrested. The Supreme Court's 1972 decision upheld the appellant's claim by
articulating freedom from government intervention in matters
pertaining to sexuality and reproduction as a quintessentially*
individual *right. In this extract from* Eisenstadt v. Baird, *Justice William Brennan delivers the opinion of the Court.*

APPELLEE WILLIAM BAIRD WAS CONVICTED at a bench trial in the
Massachusetts Superior Court under Massachusetts General
Laws Ann., c. 272, § 21, first, for exhibiting contraceptive articles
in the course of delivering a lecture on contraception to a group of
students at Boston University and, second, for giving a young
woman a package of Emko vaginal foam at the close of his
address. . . .

Massachusetts General Laws Ann., c. 272, § 21, under which
Baird was convicted, provides a maximum five-year term of imprisonment for "whoever . . . gives away . . . any drug, medicine,
instrument or article whatever for the prevention of conception,"
except as authorized in § 21A. Under § 21A, "[a] registered physician may administer to or prescribe for any married person drugs
or articles intended for the prevention of pregnancy or conception.
[And a] registered pharmacist actually engaged in the business of
pharmacy may furnish such drugs or articles to any married person
presenting a prescription from a registered physician." . . .

If under *Griswold* the distribution of contraceptives to married
persons cannot be prohibited, a ban on distribution to unmarried
persons would be equally impermissible. It is true that in *Griswold*
the right of privacy in question inhered in the marital relationship.
Yet the marital couple is not an independent entity with a mind and

From *Eisenstadt v. Baird* 405 U.S. 438 (1972).

heart of its own, but an association of two individuals each with a separate intellectual and emotional makeup. If the right of privacy means anything, it is the right of the *individual*, married or single, to be free from unwarranted governmental intrusion into matters so fundamentally affecting a person as the decision whether to bear or beget a child. . . . We hold that by providing dissimilar treatment for married and unmarried persons who are similarly situated, Massachusetts General Laws Ann., c. 272, §§ 21 and 21A, violate the Equal Protection Clause.

31   A Back-Alley Abortion

Although the criminalization of abortions in the nineteenth century did not eliminate them, it made them more difficult to obtain, more costly, and more dangerous. In the 1950s almost one million illegal (so-called back alley) abortions were performed annually in the United States; each year close to one thousand women died from botched procedures and unhygienic conditions. Women of color were most at risk; in 1969 they constituted 75 percent of those who died. In 1972 an estimated twenty-five hundred American women were having abortions daily, many traveling to New York and California, states that had recently legalized abortion. In this selection, "Janet," now a thirty-seven-year-old single parent and computer consultant, recalls what it was like to have an illegal abortion in the days before Roe v. Wade.

MY FIRST ABORTION WAS WHEN I was a freshman in college. So I was about 18, which means it was about 1968. I was going to school in Cleveland. I'd grown up in a small town outside of Boston. It was an upper-middle-class suburb. My father had a degree in physics. My mother stayed home with us for most of my growing-up life.

Abortions were not legal at that time. I had been sexually active for many years—actually, for about four years—and had used and not used various methods of birth control. Sometimes my boyfriend and I would use condoms, sometimes we'd use foam. Some-

From Sumi Hoshiko, ed., *Our Choices: Women's Personal Decisions about Abortions* (New York: Haworth Press, 1993), 31–36. Reprinted by permission of Haworth Press.

times we'd sort of use rhythm. Hope and prayer is what my friends used to call it.

I got pregnant on a visit to my boyfriend in California. We'd broken up for a while and then we'd just basically gotten back together again at the end of the summer. It was part of a reconciliation that I had gone to California to visit him. My initial reaction upon hearing I was pregnant was joy, because I really love kids and I always wanted to have kids. I always wanted to have a family. And I actually kind of thought that, Well, it might not be the best aspiration, but I'll probably be a suburban housewife, which is very far from what I am.

I remember my friends and roommates convincing me that this was really not practical. It was sort of like: Oh, come on—I don't really have to, do I? But I already kind of knew that I really did.

My boyfriend wanted me to quit school and move to California, and I didn't have to marry him but he wanted to support me and the baby. I was afraid of what it would do to my life; and what it would do to me to be dependent upon him in that way. Because I would have had to be completely dependent on him for my financial stuff, and I just didn't want to put myself in that position. I mean, it would definitely have been an end to my college career, at least temporarily and perhaps forever. There's no way of knowing. It's funny, I don't remember crying over that one. I really don't. I was very sort of: Say, come on, I'm 18, I'm going to do a lot of growing and changing, and I'm really not ready to have a kid. So I wanted the abortion, which he agreed to pay for. I suspect that he was sad that I wasn't willing to make that kind of a move for him. But I was pretty strong about it. I was enjoying my independence, and I really did not want to give it up.

My oldest sister lived in Washington, D.C., at the time. I have three sisters; I'm number three out of four. She had known a woman there who had gotten an abortion from a doctor in his office. So my sister lent me a hundred dollars and arranged for me to stay with a friend in Washington.

So I flew to Washington, D.C. This was a very, very frightening experience for me. So frightening I threw up the night before I went to see the guy. I was staying with friends of my sisters, but they were people I didn't know. I was very, very nervous. So I did feel quite isolated. Although, you know, people were very good to me. They took me—this woman took me—to the doctor's office and he examined me and said I wasn't pregnant. I have never figured it out. Because I was quite obviously pregnant. I don't know what he thought he was doing for me. I really don't. But he massaged my uterus. I don't know if he thought he was going to induce an abortion. And then I think he gave me those pills that sometimes bring on a late period, or something. I just don't know. It's completely confusing to me, and I can get angry at him for his deception. Better he should have said to me, "You are pregnant, and I can't help you." Maybe he thought that I'd come back to him and then perhaps, you know, at the next stage, he'd do something else. I really don't know, but I didn't live in Washington, and I had to get back to go to classes, and I couldn't hang out and see what was going to happen. I'm as mystified as you are.

He sent me home and charged me $5, which was his office fee. Well, I was pregnant. But I didn't know that at the time. I got on a plane and went back to Cleveland. It was just a waste of my money.

This was in the autumn. By the time Christmas vacation rolled around, which was another couple of weeks, three weeks later, I realized I was still very pregnant. I went home to Massachusetts, and my Number Two sister in Washington found me an abortionist. This was for me really shocking. First of all, because she was always the most conservative member of the family, I was really surprised that she was able to locate a doctor—and somewhat surprised that she was so supportive. My sisters are great.

First I went to see my sister's gynecologist, just to verify I was still pregnant. Her gynecologist was Catholic, and would only give diaphragms to married women. But he examined me and he was very, very reasonable. And he told me that he knew that I had to make a decision and that he wanted me to know that whatever decision I made, that I should feel comfortable coming back to see him again.

We contacted the doctor, and he said it was going to cost $600. My boyfriend was able to get that $600 from his parents without telling them what it was for. He came from a wealthy background. And we arranged an evening. The doctor said on the evening that it was to be, that we should go to these hotels. He gave us the name of three hotels we could go to that were on Route 128, which is a circular route that goes around the circumference of Boston—about twelve miles out of the city—and call him at a special number when we had checked into a hotel.

My boyfriend was home from college, so he and myself and my sister said we were going out to the movies, and drove up to these hotels and checked into one of them and gave him a call, and he said he would be there.

I was totally freaked out about checking into a hotel. It was probably the first time I'd checked into a hotel my *entire life*. I was incredibly nervous and scared. Giddy. We didn't do that. Oh, maybe once or twice on vacations with my parents, but I mean, it was just—it was just a foreign situation. I think my sister went and checked in. She was all of two years older than me. Because it just didn't seem like—why would a bunch of teenagers go and check into a hotel? That was kind of frightening. And it did feel kind of seedy. I mean, if the doctor had not been the kind of guy he was— he was kind of a grandfatherly type; he was very reasonable—I don't know if I could have gone through with it. I was pretty clear that I didn't want to go to anybody who wasn't a doctor.

But I think also that the three of us were in a way—well, we were scared and my boyfriend was sad—I think that we were kind of afraid to really acknowledge what was going on, because I think it would have been too hard to deal with. You know, if we'd really said: We're here to have an abortion, that's what we're doing. So on one level we were keeping up a really brave front, and I think that it must have been a real stretch for my sister, to do that for me. Because it was really not the sort of thing that she would do, that she would choose to do, that she would have felt comfortable with in her own life. She did it because she loved me. She's my sister. You help your sisters; it's family, I guess.

The guy came and he was an elderly physician, and really kindly. He explained that the money was not all his. I don't know if you know very much about New England or Massachusetts, but it is *very* conservative. Until very recently, you couldn't even buy alcohol on Sundays. It's Catholic, and abortions were not very legal there at all. But this guy I think had some kind of sense of purpose about why he was performing abortions. He was just not a greedy guy.

I didn't ask him, but I assume he must have been paying protection. The instruments used to perform a D & C* were kept under lock and key in hospitals, and I presume he had to pay somebody off to get them out of the hospital. But I presume he was paying the Mafia. I do remember seeing many years later that he was busted

---

*D & C: dilation and curettage, or enlarging the opening to the uterus and removing the contents with a long narrow instrument inserted into the uterine cavity.

for performing abortions. And I think that was not the first time that he had been busted; I think that he had been busted before he had performed my abortion.

It was really very surreal. He asked me what kind of medication I wanted. And he offered me a shot of morphine, but I had to go home afterwards, so I took a Darvon and two Seconal, or a Seconal and two Darvon, I don't know what it was—I took a bunch of pills. He gave me the pills, and then he sort of hung out with us for a while for them to take effect, while they were setting everything up. He spread out all this rubber stuff and everything and unwrapped his instruments. He had us turn up the TV in case I screamed.

He took the drawers out of the dresser. We lifted the bed and put them under the end of the bed so that the edge of the bed was raised up. The he took one of the chairs and laid it on the bed. It's hard to describe, but I would be leaning back on the seat, but it would be the underside of the seat, with the legs of the chair coming out to the side of me, so that I could hold on to the legs of the chair. My sister was on one side, and my boyfriend was on the other. I can remember that when I was in the bed, my sister was on my right, my boyfriend was on the left. He sat down, he was smart. My sister stayed up, but she got woozy and went to the bathroom and fainted and cracked a tooth, which my parents had to pay for!

After the procedure was over, he sat down and talked to me for quite a while. I guess he wanted to make sure I was okay. I'm pretty much of a trooper. I didn't scream or anything. It did hurt, and I was biting on a rolled-up piece of a matchbook. He explained to me the entire procedure and he showed me all of the instruments. He had the whole thing worked out as to how it had to be. The instruments were wrapped up in towels that were soaked in alcohol. Thank goodness, you know, I could tell he'd been careful. He explained to me what would happen to me over the next few days, and said I should not hesitate to call him. And gave me some pain pills. And I went home.

32   *Roe v. Wade* (1973)

Roe v. Wade *challenged the legality of an 1857 Texas statute that criminalized abortion at any stage of pregnancy except*

From *Roe v. Wade* 410 U.S. 113 (1973).

when necessary to save the life of the mother. Norma McCorvey (using the alias "Jane Roe" to protect her anonymity) was single and pregnant when she agreed in 1969 to serve as plaintiff in a test case. (Ironically, she gave birth long before the Court's decision in January 1973.) McCorvey's lawyers, Linda Coffee and Sarah Weddington, recent graduates of the University of Texas Law School, argued that the state law violated the Constitution's implied right to privacy derived from the Ninth and Fourteenth Amendments, as articulated in Griswold v. Connecticut. *This implied right, they maintained, protected a woman's freedom to choose when and under what circumstances she became a mother. Coffee and Weddington also argued that the Texas law gave the unborn rights of personhood that both the Constitution and historical practice furnished only to born citizens. In finding for the plaintiff, the Court declared unconstitutional the Texas law and others like it. Furthermore, the Court divided pregnancy into trimesters, thereby delineating specific rights to the state and to women according to the stage of pregnancy. In this extract from* Roe v. Wade, *Justice Harry Blackmun delivers the opinion of the Court.*

THE PRINCIPAL THRUST OF APPELLANT's attack on the Texas statutes is that they improperly invade a right, said to be possessed by the pregnant woman, to choose to terminate her pregnancy. Appellant would discover this right in the concept of personal "liberty" embodied in the Fourteenth Amendment's Due Process Clause; or in personal, marital, familial, and sexual privacy said to be protected by the Bill of Rights or its penumbras, see *Griswold v. Connecticut*, 381 U.S. 479 (1965); *Eisenstadt v. Baird*, 405 U.S. 438 (1972); . . . or among those rights reserved to the people by the Ninth Amendment. . . . Before addressing this claim, we feel it desirable briefly to survey, in several aspects, the history of abortion, for such insight as that history may afford us, and then to examine the state purposes and interests behind the criminal abortion laws.

It perhaps is not generally appreciated that the restrictive criminal abortion laws in effect in a majority of States today are of relatively recent vintage. Those laws, generally proscribing abortion or its attempt at any time during pregnancy except when necessary to preserve the pregnant woman's life, are not of ancient or even of common-law origin. Instead, they derive from statutory changes effected, for the most part, in the latter half of the 19th century. . . .

Three reasons have been advanced to explain historically the enactment of criminal abortion laws in the 19th century and to justify their continued existence.

It has been argued occasionally that these laws were the product of a Victorian social concern to discourage illicit sexual conduct. Texas, however, does not advance this justification in the present case, and it appears that no court or commentator has taken the argument seriously. The appellants and *amici* contend, moreover, that this is not a proper state purpose at all and suggest that, if it were, the Texas statutes are overbroad in protecting it since the law fails to distinguish between married and unwed mothers.

A second reason is concerned with abortion as a medical procedure. When most criminal abortion laws were first enacted, the procedure was a hazardous one for the woman. This was particularly true prior to the development of antisepsis. Antiseptic techniques, of course, were based on discoveries by Lister, Pasteur, and others first announced in 1867, but were not generally accepted and employed until about the turn of the century. Abortion mortality was high. Even after 1900, and perhaps until as late as the development of antibiotics in the 1940's, standard modern techniques such as dilation and curettage were not nearly so safe as they are today. Thus, it has been argued that a State's real concern in enacting a criminal abortion law was to protect the pregnant woman, that is, to restrain her from submitting to a procedure that placed her life in serious jeopardy.

Modern medical techniques have altered this situation. Appellants and various *amici* refer to medical data indicating that abortion in early pregnancy, that is, prior to the end of the first trimester, although not without its risk, is now relatively safe. Mortality rates for women undergoing early abortions, where the procedure is legal, appear to be as low as or lower than the rates for normal childbirth. Consequently, any interest of the State in protecting the woman from an inherently hazardous procedure, except when it would be equally dangerous for her to forgo it, has largely disappeared. Of course, important state interests in the areas of health and medical standards do remain. The State has a legitimate interest in seeing to it that abortion, like any other medical procedure, is performed under circumstances that insure maximum safety for the patient. This interest obviously extends at least to the performing physician and his staff, to the facilities involved, to the availability of after-care, and to adequate provision for any complication or emergency that might arise. The prevalence of high mortality rates at illegal "abortion mills" strengthens, rather than weakens, the State's interest in regulating the conditions under which abortions are performed. Moreover, the risk to the woman increases as her pregnancy continues. Thus, the State retains a definite interest in protecting the woman's own health and safety when an abortion is proposed at a late stage of pregnancy.

The third reason is the State's interest—some phrase it in terms of duty—in protecting prenatal life. Some of the argument for this justification rests on the theory that a new human life is present from the moment of conception. The State's interest and general obligation to protect life then extends, it is argued, to prenatal life. Only when the life of the pregnant mother herself is at stake, balanced against the life she carries within her, should the interest of the embryo or fetus not prevail. Logically, of course, a legitimate state interest in this area need not stand or fall on acceptance of the belief that life begins at conception or at some other point prior to live birth. In assessing the State's interest, recognition may be given to the less rigid claim that as long as at least *potential* life is involved, the State may assert interests beyond the protection of the pregnant woman alone.

Parties challenging state abortion laws have sharply disputed in some courts the contention that a purpose of these laws, when enacted, was to protect prenatal life. Pointing to the absence of legislative history to support the contention, they claim that most state laws were designed solely to protect the woman. Because medical advances have lessened this concern, at least with respect to abortion in early pregnancy, they argue that with respect to such abortions the laws can no longer be justified by any state interest. There is some scholarly support for this view of original purpose. The few state courts called upon to interpret their laws in the late 19th and early 20th centuries did focus on the State's interest in protecting the woman's health rather than in preserving the embryo and fetus. Proponents of this view point out that in many States, including Texas, by statute or judicial interpretation, the pregnant woman herself could not be prosecuted for self-abortion or for co-operating in an abortion performed upon her by another. They claim that adoption of the "quickening" distinction through received common law and state statutes tacitly recognizes the greater health hazards inherent in late abortion and impliedly repudiates the theory that life begins at conception.

It is with these interests, and the weight to be attached to them, that this case is concerned.

The Constitution does not explicitly mention any right of privacy. In a line of decisions, however, . . . the Court has recognized that a right of personal privacy, or a guarantee of certain areas or zones of privacy, does exist under the Constitution. . . .

The right of privacy, whether it be founded in the Fourteenth Amendment's concept of personal liberty and restrictions upon state action, as we feel it is, or, as the District Court determined, in the Ninth Amendment's reservation of rights to the people, is broad enough to encompass a woman's decision whether or not to terminate her pregnancy. The detriment that the State would impose upon the pregnant woman by denying this choice altogether is apparent. Specific and direct harm medically diagnosable even in early pregnancy may be involved. Maternity, or additional offspring, may force upon the woman a distressful life and future. Psychological harm may be imminent. Mental and physical health may be taxed by child care. There is also the distress, for all concerned, associated with the unwanted child, and there is the problem of bringing a child into a family already unable, psychologically and otherwise, to care for it. In other cases, as in this one, the additional difficulties and continuing stigma of unwed motherhood may be involved. All these are factors the woman and her responsible physician necessarily will consider in consultation.

On the basis of elements such as these, appellant and some *amici* argue that the woman's right is absolute and that she is entitled to terminate her pregnancy at whatever time, in whatever way, and for whatever reason she alone chooses. With this we do not agree. Appellant's arguments that Texas either has no valid interest at all in regulating the abortion decision, or no interest strong enough to support any limitation upon the woman's sole determination, are unpersuasive. The Court's decisions recognizing a right of privacy also acknowledge that some state regulation in areas protected by that right is appropriate. As noted above, a State may properly assert important interests in safeguarding health, in maintaining medical standards, and in protecting potential life. At some point in pregnancy, these respective interests become sufficiently compelling to sustain regulation of the factors that govern the abortion decision. The privacy right involved, therefore, cannot be said to be absolute. . . .

We, therefore, conclude that the right of personal privacy includes the abortion decision, but that this right is not unqualified and must be considered against important state interests in regulation. . . .

The appellee and certain *amici* argue that the fetus is a "person" within the language and meaning of the Fourteenth Amendment. In support of this, they outline at length and in detail the well-known facts of fetal development. If this suggestion of personhood is established, the appellant's case, of course, collapses, for the fetus's right to life would then be guaranteed specifically by the Amendment. The appellant conceded as much on reargument. On the other hand, the appellee conceded on reargument that no case could be cited that holds that a fetus is a person within the meaning of the Fourteenth Amendment.

The Constitution does not define "person" in so many words. Section 1 of the Fourteenth Amendment contains three references to "person." The first, in defining "citizens," speaks of "persons born or naturalized in the United States." The word also appears both in the Due Process Clause and in the Equal Protection Clause. "Person" is used in other places in the Constitution. . . . But in nearly all these instances, the use of the word is such that it has application only postnatally. None indicates, with any assurance, that it has any possible prenatal application.

All this, together with our observation, *supra*, that throughout the major portion of the 19th century prevailing legal abortion practices were far freer than they are today, persuades us that the word "person," as used in the Fourteenth Amendment, does not include the unborn. . . .

Texas urges that, apart from the Fourteenth Amendment, life begins at conception and is present throughout pregnancy, and that, therefore, the State has a compelling interest in protecting that life from and after conception. We need not resolve the difficult question of when life begins. When those trained in the respective disciplines of medicine, philosophy, and theology are unable to arrive at any consensus, the judiciary, at this point in the development of man's knowledge, is not in a position to speculate as to the answer. . . .

In view of all this, we do not agree that, by adopting one theory of life, Texas may override the rights of the pregnant woman that are at stake. We repeat, however, that the State does have an important and legitimate interest in preserving and protecting the health of the pregnant woman, whether she be a resident of the State or a nonresident who seeks medical consultation and treatment there, and that it has still *another* important and legitimate interest in protecting the potentiality of human life. These interests are separate and distinct. Each grows in substantiality as the woman approaches term and, at a point during pregnancy, each becomes "compelling."

With respect to the State's important and legitimate interest in the health of the mother, the "compelling" point, in the light of present medical knowledge, is at approximately the end of the first trimester. This is so because of the now-established medical fact . . . that until the end of the first trimester mortality in abortion may be less than mortality in normal childbirth. It follows that, from and after this point, a State may regulate the abortion procedure to the extent that the regulation reasonably relates to the preservation and protection of maternal health. Examples of permissible state regulation in this area are requirements as to the qualifications of the person who is to perform the abortion; as to the licensure of that person; as to the facility in which the procedure is to be performed, that is, whether it must be a hospital or may be a clinic or some other place of less-than-hospital status; as to the licensing of the facility; and the like.

This means, on the other hand, that, for the period of pregnancy prior to this "compelling" point, the attending physician, in consultation with his patient, is free to determine, without regulation by the State, that, in his medical judgment, the patient's pregnancy should be terminated. If that decision is reached, the judgment may be effectuated by an abortion free of interference by the State.

With respect to the State's important and legitimate interest in potential life, the "compelling" point is at viability. This is so because the fetus then presumably has the capability of meaningful life outside the mother's womb. State regulation protective of fetal life after viability thus has both logical and biological justifications. If the State is interested in protecting fetal life after viability, it may go so far as to proscribe abortion during that period, except when it is necessary to preserve the life or health of the mother. . . .

To summarize and to repeat:

1. A state criminal abortion statute of the current Texas type, that excepts from criminality only a *life-saving* procedure on be-

half of the mother, without regard to pregnancy stage and without recognition of the other interests involved, is violative of the Due Process Clause of the Fourteenth Amendment.

(a) For the stage prior to approximately the end of the first trimester, the abortion decision and its effectuation must be left to the medical judgment of the pregnant woman's attending physician.

(b) For the stage subsequent to approximately the end of the first trimester, the State, in promoting its interest in the health of the mother, may, if it chooses, regulate the abortion procedure in ways that are reasonably related to maternal health.

(c) For the stage subsequent to viability, the State in promoting its interest in the potentiality of human life may, if it chooses, regulate, and even proscribe, abortion except where it is necessary, in appropriate medical judgment, for the preservation of the life or health of the mother.

2. The State may define the term "physician". . . to mean only a physician currently licensed by the State, and may proscribe any abortion by a person who is not a physician as so defined. . . .

In *Doe v. Bolton*, . . . procedural requirements contained in one of the modern abortion statutes are considered. That opinion and this one, of course, are to be read together.

This holding, we feel, is consistent with the relative weights of the respective interests involved, with the lessons and examples of medical and legal history, with the lenity of the common law, and with the demands of the profound problems of the present day. The decision leaves the State free to place increasing restrictions on abortion as the period of pregnancy lengthens, so long as those restrictions are tailored to the recognized state interests. The decision vindicates the right of the physician to administer medical treatment according to his professional judgment up to the points where important state interests provide compelling justifications for intervention. Up to those points, the abortion decision in all its aspects is inherently, and primarily, a medical decision, and basic responsibility for it must rest with the physician.

33 *Doe v. Bolton* (1973)

The companion to Roe v. Wade, *the case of* Doe v. Bolton *challenged the constitutionality of a Georgia statute that permitted*

From *Doe v. Bolton* 410 U.S. 179 (1973).

abortions under certain conditions. By 1972, Georgia was one of fourteen states (the others were Arkansas, California, Colorado, Delaware, Florida, Kansas, Maryland, Mississippi, New Mexico, North Carolina, Oregon, South Carolina, and Virginia) that had recently revised its laws to allow abortions in cases where pregnancy threatened the mother's physical or mental health, pregnancy was the result of rape or incest, or where the child was likely to be born with severe birth defects. The difficulty with these newly instituted reform provisions was access. Under the Georgia code the termination of pregnancies meeting these criteria—criteria often empirically difficult and personally painful to document—could be performed only in accredited hospitals after a majority vote of a hospital committee and the recommendation of two physicians, in addition to that of the woman's own doctor. A final requirement was that abortions could be performed only on established Georgia residents. Lawyers for the American Civil Liberties Union, representing Planned Parenthood, doctors, clergy, and social workers, successfully argued that the elaborate bureaucratic requirements of the Georgia law infringed upon personal and marital privacy. In this extract from Doe v. Bolton, *Justice Harry Blackmun delivers the opinion of the Court.*

IN THIS APPEAL, THE CRIMINAL abortion statutes recently enacted in Georgia are challenged on constitutional grounds. . . . In *Roe v. Wade,* . . . we today have struck down, as constitutionally defective, the Texas criminal abortion statutes that are representative of provisions long in effect in a majority of our States. The Georgia legislation, however, is different and merits separate consideration. . . .

The appellants . . . argue that the District Court should have declared unconstitutional three procedural demands of the Georgia statute: (1) that the abortion be performed in a hospital accredited by the Joint Commission on Accreditation of Hospitals; (2) that the procedure be approved by the hospital staff abortion committee; and (3) that the performing physician's judgment be confirmed by the independent examinations of the patient by two other licensed physicians. The appellants attack these provisions not only on the ground that they unduly restrict the woman's right of privacy, but also on procedural due process and equal protection grounds. The physician-appellants also argue that, by subjecting a doctor's individual medical judgment to committee approval and to confirming consultations, the statute impermissibly restricts the physician's right to practice his profession and deprives him of due process.

1. *JCAH accreditation.* The Joint Commission on Accreditation of Hospitals is an organization without governmental sponsorship or overtones. No question whatever is raised concerning the integrity of the organization or the high purpose of the accreditation process. That process, however, has to do with hospital standards generally and has no present particularized concern with abortion as a medical or surgical procedure. In Georgia, there is no restriction on the performance of nonabortion surgery in a hospital not yet accredited by the JCAH so long as other requirements imposed by the State, such as licensing of the hospital and of the operating surgeon, are met. . . . We hold that the JCAH-accreditation requirement does not withstand constitutional scrutiny in the present context. . . .

Appellants and various *amici* have presented us with a mass of data purporting to demonstrate that some facilities other than hospitals are entirely adequate to perform abortions if they possess [the appropriate] qualifications. The State, on the other hand, has not presented persuasive data to show that only hospitals meet its acknowledged interest in insuring the quality of the operation and the full protection of the patient. We feel compelled to agree with appellants that the State must show more than it has in order to prove that only the full resources of a licensed hospital, rather than those of some other appropriately licensed institution, satisfy these health interests. . . .

2. *Committee approval.* The second aspect of the appellants' procedural attack relates to the hospital abortion committee and to the pregnant woman's asserted lack of access to that committee. . . . Doe first argues that she was denied due process because she could not make a presentation to the committee. It is not clear from the record, however, whether Doe's own consulting physician was or was not a member of the committee or did or did not present her case, or, indeed, whether she herself was or was not there. We see nothing in the Georgia statute that explicitly denies access to the committee by or on behalf of the woman. If the access point alone were involved, we would not be persuaded to strike down the committee provision on the unsupported assumption that access is not provided.

Appellants attack the discretion the statute leaves to the committee. The most concrete argument they advance is their suggestion that it is still a badge of infamy "in many minds" to bear an illegitimate child, and that the Georgia system enables the committee members' personal views as to extramarital sex relations, and punishment therefor, to govern their decisions. This approach obviously is one founded on suspicion and one that discloses a lack of confidence in the integrity of physicians. To say that physicians will be guided in their hospital committee decisions by their predilections on extramarital sex unduly narrows the issue to pregnancy outside marriage. (Doe's own situation did not involve extramarital sex and its product.). . .

Viewing the Georgia statute as a whole, we see no constitutionally justifiable pertinence in the structure for the advance approval by the abortion committee. With regard to the protection of potential life, the medical judgment is already completed prior to the committee stage, and review by a committee once removed from diagnosis is basically redundant. We are not cited to any other surgical procedure made subject to committee approval as a matter of state criminal law. The woman's right to receive medical care in accordance with her licensed physician's best judgment and the physician's right to administer it are substantially limited by this statutorily imposed overview. . . .

We conclude that the interposition of the hospital abortion committee is unduly restrictive of the patient's rights and needs that, at this point, have already been medically delineated and substantiated by her personal physician. To ask more serves neither the hospital nor the state.

3. *Two-doctor concurrence.* The third aspect of the appellants' attack centers on the "time and availability of adequate medical facilities and personnel." It is said that the system imposes substantial and irrational roadblocks and "is patently unsuited" to prompt determination of the abortion decision. Time, of course, is critical in abortion. Risks during the first trimester of pregnancy are admittedly lower than during later months. . . .

It should be manifest that our rejection of the accredited-hospital requirement and, more important, of the abortion committee's advance approval eliminates the major grounds of the attack based on the system's delay and the lack of facilities. There remains, however, the required confirmation by two Georgia-licensed physicians in addition to the recommendation of the pregnant woman's own consultant (making under the statute, a total of six physicians involved, including the three on the hospital's abortion committee). We conclude that this provision, too, must fall.

The statute's emphasis, as has been repetitively noted, is on the attending physician's "best clinical judgment that an abortion is necessary." That should be sufficient. The reasons for the presence of the confirmation step in the statute are perhaps apparent, but they are insufficient to withstand constitutional challenge. Again, no other voluntary medical or surgical procedure for which Georgia requires confirmation by two other physicians has been cited to us. If a physician is licensed by the State, he is recognized by the State as capable of exercising acceptable clinical judgment. If he fails in this, professional censure and deprivation of his license are available remedies. Required acquiescence by co-practitioners has no rational connection with a patient's needs and unduly infringes on the physician's right to practice. . . .

The appellants attack the residency requirement of the Georgia law . . . as violative of the right to travel. . . . We do not uphold the constitutionality of the residence requirement. It is not based on any policy of preserving state-supported facilities for Georgia residents, for the bar also applies to private hospitals and to privately retained physicians. There is no intimation, either, that Georgia facilities are utilized to capacity in caring for Georgia residents. . . . A contrary holding would mean that a State could limit to its own residents the general medical care available within its borders. This we could not approve.

34 Testimony on Behalf of the Human Life Amendment

Mildred F. Jefferson

The Roe *and* Doe *decisions intensified the commitment and broadened the support of the pro-life movement. In 1973 the*

From the statement of Mildred F. Jefferson, M.D., U.S. Congress, House, Subcommittee on Civil and Constitutional Rights of the Committee on the Judiciary, *Hearings on Proposed Constitutional Amendment on Abortion*, 94th Cong., 2d sess. (Washington, DC: Government Printing Office, 1976), 452–54.

Pro-Life Affairs Committee of the National Conference of Catholic Bishops (NCCB) announced its intention to wage a legal and educational war against abortion. The National Right to Life Committee, initially affiliated with the NCCB, was organized in the same year and supported a similar agenda: antiabortion education, political support for antiabortion candidates, and a constitutional ban on abortion. In June 1973, Senator James Buckley (R-NY) and six other senators introduced a bill for a constitutional amendment, popularly referred to as the "Human Life Amendment," to bestow legal rights of personhood on "all human beings, including their unborn offspring at every stage of their biological development, irrespective of age, health, function or condition of dependency." By September 1973, eighteen bills sponsoring constitutional amendments against abortion had been introduced in Congress. In 1974 subcommittees of the House and Senate Judiciary Committees conducted hearings on proposed amendments. Dr. Mildred F. Jefferson, assistant clinical professor of surgery at the Boston University School of Medicine and president of the National Right to Life Committee, testified on behalf of the Human Life Amendment.

THE SURPASSING VALUE OF THE Hippocratic tradition in medicine is that it represents an ethical system where killing and curing functions of the doctor are separated and the society is obliged not to ask the doctor to kill. The assignment of killing functions to the doctor even with the permission of the highest court in the land jeopardizes the entire foundation of an organized society.

A society must indulge in considerable subterfuge to avoid realizing the consequences of such an action. One way of avoiding such realization is to assume a notion that pregnancy is a condition that somehow only affects a woman. This notion disregards the fact that a woman cannot be pregnant without the young of her own kind growing within her body.

It ignores the biological reality that no matter how she may claim to control her own fertility, she cannot reliably become pregnant without the help of the male of her own species even though it may be without his consent by artificial means. As long as the human family has only woman naturally equipped to bring forth its own kind, it must not grant her the privilege of throwing the offspring away.

Why is there an unwillingness to see the consequences of asking the doctor to kill for social and economic reasons? Why are there no Ob-Gyn specialists with the experience of a Dr. Jasper F. Williams, now president of the National Medical Association, to show the women with complications that do not go back to the abortionists? Where are the women who have started the organizations WHA—Women Who Have Had Abortions—and WE—Women Exploited—who would tell from their personal experiences the aftermath of this perversion of surgical practice?

Where are the parents who have had their rights to protect the lives and health of their pregnant minor daughters canceled on order of Federal courts? Where are the fathers who now have no defined rights to protect the lives of their children before birth? Where are the representatives of hospitals which have been forced under court orders to provide abortion on their premises against the voted will of their staffs?

Where are the attorneys for the women who have been irreparably damaged or who have lost their lives after the abortion sold as "clean, safe and legal"? Where are the members of the State legislatures that are defending against passive and active euthanasia bills in at least 20 States across the land?

Leaving the final decision on abortion up to a doctor's medical judgment has been too great a burden for some doctors who are suspending all medical judgment and are using the Supreme Court's decisions as an excuse for doing abortion. Others have thought the abortion permission dissolved the network of moral, civil, and criminal laws that border a doctor's every action in treating a patient. Some who have so willingly accepted the direction from outside the experience of their own profession and historical tradition are considered social technicians by their colleagues who no longer consider them worthy of the designation "professionals."

The most cruel effect of the abortion decisions is to legitimatize the requirement of "viability" in evaluating an immature, premature infant. The ability to survive outside the mother, albeit with artificial means, does not depend solely on the child. Aside from the child's biological capability, there is the sophistication and availability of necessary support equipment, the skill of the staff and their willingness to use it in saving the life of a particular premature child. Enforcing the viability concept requires that the struggling child prove that it can survive before being provided with the equipment that would help it survive.

There are some very good pro-abortion emotional appeals and they work on a very wide range of people.

First, of course, is the appeal to the kind gullibility of men who generally have been closed away from the mysterious reproductive business conducted by women. Because they are kind, they are easily intimidated and will believe anything about pregnancy and will do almost anything to spare their pregnant wives or girlfriends any discomfort that they can be blamed for. They never understand that they are only half responsible for the pregnancy.

Second, proposing to defend a "right to choose" without finishing the sentence, which regarding pregnancy means demanding the private right to choose to kill an unborn child.

Three, restoring the protection of the law would drive women back to the "backroom abortionist." In the first 12 weeks now, the "backroom abortionist," if a licensed doctor, may be in the front room and advertising in the local papers under protection of the U.S. Supreme Court's decisions.

Four, "Every child should be a wanted child." "Wantedness" is a changing thing and has never been proved as necessary to success, fame or fortune. The attitude makes the poor child responsible for the social crime against it and demands that it pay the capital penalty of its life. As one of a group of people that has been variously unwanted in various times and places, I do not care very much for the philosophy.

Five, attempting to relate the defense of the traditional respect for life against abortion as a "Catholic position." The great religions based on the Judaeo-Christian tradition have had a shared heritage of the sanctity-of-life ethic.

We do have an amendment preference. Our objective is to reestablish the protection of life as the principle that we assumed under the Constitution until the U.S. Supreme Court canceled the right to life of the unborn child.

The States rights' proposals seek an accommodation for abortion. The human life amendment establishes human life as a priority of this society. We will not compromise. We will not accept anything less.

35   Statement against the Human Life Bill

Bob Packwood

The failure of the constitutional campaign did not deter the pro-life movement; pro-lifers pursued other strategies to realize their goal. In 1981, Senator Jesse Helms (R-NC) began an eighteen-month campaign to annul Supreme Court abortion rights through congressional legislation. Helm's Human Life Bill, S. 158, declared it a finding of Congress "that human life shall be deemed to exist from conception." On September 15, 1982, the measure was defeated after a filibuster, followed by a 47-to-46 vote to table the bill. Several Republicans, including Senator Bob Packwood of Oregon, testified against it.

I THINK IT IS ESSENTIAL TO make it perfectly clear from the outset of my testimony that this bill is about abortion. While the testimony on when life starts may have been intellectually invigorating, it begged the true purpose of this bill and the true motivation of its supporters.

Congressman Mazzoli, a chairman of the pro-life caucus, says it very well in his testimony which will soon follow when he says: "In essence, the caucus supports the enactment of the Right to Life Act as an interim step until a Human Life Amendment is adopted."

Congressman Hyde has said essentially the same thing: S. 158 will ban abortions.

Stephen Galebach, in the pamphlet he authored entitled "A Human Life Statute," reiterates the same thing. S. 158 is a means to outlaw abortion in lieu of a constitutional amendment.

Therefore, the issue, Mr. Chairman, is not when does life start. The issue, stated clearly, is when does society deem an abortion to be a homicide?

S. 158, and these hearings, in my mind, are designed to conclude that abortion from the moment of conception is murder.

From the statement of Senator Bob Packwood, U.S. Congress, Senate, Subcommittee on the Separation of Powers of the Committee on the Judiciary, *Hearings on the Human Life Bill*, 97th Cong., 1st sess. (Washington, DC: Government Printing Office, 1982), 155–58.

Now, having established the true purpose of these hearings, two key questions must be answered: One, should abortions be banned in this country; two, is S. 158 a legal and proper method to achieve that goal?

Let me address myself to the second issue first: Is S. 158 a proper vehicle to achieve that end, that is, to reverse the Supreme Court decision legalizing abortion?

In its decision legalizing abortion, the Supreme Court clearly said that at least during the first trimester of pregnancy, a woman has a constitutional right to decide for herself without hindrance or help from anyone, including the Government, whether or not she wants to have an abortion.

If S. 158 passes, it would allow not only the States to declare abortion from the moment of conception murder, but it would allow the Federal Government to do the same thing if we wanted to make abortion a Federal crime. The Court would then be faced with the constitutional issue of whether or not the constitutional right of a woman to have an abortion can be overridden by a statute making abortion murder. . . .

There is a growing force in this country, fueled by a Cotton Mather mentality, that wishes to impose on this country a Cotton Mather morality. From the perspective of one who is a practicing politician, I hope that we will always remember that passion can obscure judgment.

We should remember that governing officials in dictatorships and democracies find it easy and convenient to bend to transitory public opinion and popular prejudices which would subjugate individual liberties.

Those of us in public office should always remember that we can never err enough on the side of protecting individual liberty and freedom. We who have been elected to a position of public trust should be willing at all costs to withstand the buffets of a temporary storm that would trammel or even extinguish our freedom for the alleged common good.

Mr. Chairman, the danger to the liberties of all Americans is most threatened by those who want to compel conformity of thought and deed. Conversely, our liberties are most secured by a decent respect for diversity, and most especially on those subjects upon which there is no consensus.

God did not speak to any one of us and say, "You are right and those who disagree with you are wrong." If any one of us thinks that God had ordained us to speak for him, we are wrong. Worse, if we are in a position of power and we believe we speak for God, we become dangerous.

For, indeed, if I am right and you are wrong, then it is just a short step to the end justifies the means. I do not need to tell you, Mr. Chairman, who has taught political science, what that philosophy means to your liberties, and mine, and all Americans.

36 The Hyde Amendment of 1977

In June 1976, Representative Henry Hyde (R-IL) proposed an amendment to the Department of Health, Education, and Welfare's (HEW) appropriations bill to ban the use of Medicaid funds for abortions. On December 7, 1977, a compromise measure was passed in the House and Senate as an amendment to the 1978 HEW-Department of Labor appropriations bill. The Hyde Amendment banned federal funding for abortions in all cases except where rape or incest had been promptly reported to police or to a public health agency, or where the mother's life was in danger. President Jimmy Carter signed H. J. Res. 662 into law on December 9. The 20,000-member National Abortion Rights Action League immediately denounced the restrictive measure as "inhumane and quite possibly unconstitutional," although the Supreme Court subsequently upheld the law's constitutionality in Harris v. McRae *448 U.S. 297 (1981). The Hyde Amendment created a two-tier system of abortion care in the United States. From this point forward, only women with adequate financial resources could afford to exercise their legal "right to choose."*

*R*ESOLVED BY THE SENATE AND *House of Representatives of the United States of America in Congress assembled,* That the following sums are appropriated out of any money in the Treasury not otherwise appropriated, and out of applicable corporate or other revenues, receipts, and funds, for the several departments, agencies, corporations, and other organizational units of the Government for the fiscal year 1978, namely:

From Public Law 95–205, 95th Cong., 1st sess., December 9, 1977.

SEC. 101. . . . Such amounts as may be necessary for projects or activities provided for in the Departments of Labor, and Health, Education, and Welfare, and Related Agencies Appropriation Act, 1978 (H.R. 7555), at a rate of operations, and to the extent and in the manner, provided for in such Act, notwithstanding the provisions of Sec. 106 of this joint resolution: *Provided,* That none of the funds provided for in this paragraph shall be used to perform abortions except where the life of the mother would be endangered if the fetus were carried to term; or except for such medical procedures necessary for the victims of rape or incest, when such rape or incest has been reported promptly to a law enforcement agency or public health service; or except in those instances where severe and long-lasting physical health damage to the mother would result if the pregnancy were carried to term when so determined by two physicians.

Nor are payments prohibited for drugs or devices to prevent implantation of the fertilized ovum, or for medical procedures necessary for the termination of an ectopic pregnancy.

The Secretary shall promptly issue regulations and establish procedures to ensure that the provisions of this section are rigorously enforced.

VII

The Political Economy
of Birth Control

37   Contraceptive Consumers: Gender and the Political Economy of Birth Control in the 1930s

Andrea Tone

Although birth control has always been an important part of the female experience, widespread use of commercial female contraceptives is a recent development. The majority of American women in the 1870s used home-made remedies or natural methods such as coitus interruptus *to prevent pregnancy. One hundred years later, most contracepting women had come to depend on mass-manufactured products—the pill, the IUD (intrauterine device), the diaphragm, and the ineffective antiseptic douche—for birth control. The availability and popularity of these products transformed the contraceptive behavior of American women, making birth control not only a personal decision but also a market transaction. Today, over ninety percent of American women of or beyond child-bearing age have used commercially devised female birth control. Historian Andrea Tone of the Georgia Institute of Technology examines the impact that the construction of the first contraceptive mass market had on women's health and well-being in the 1930s, when birth control was still illegal.*

IN 1933, READERS OF *McCALL'S* probably noticed the following advertisement for Lysol feminine hygiene in the magazine's July issue:

The most frequent eternal triangle:
A HUSBAND. . . A WIFE. . . and her FEARS
Fewer marriages would flounder around in a maze of misunderstanding and unhappiness if more wives knew and practiced regular marriage hygiene. Without it, some minor physical irregularity plants in a woman's mind the fear of a major crisis. Let so devastating a fear recur again and again, and the most gracious wife turns into a nerve-ridden, irritable travesty of herself.[1]

From Andrea Tone, "Contraceptive Consumers: Gender and the Political Economy of Birth Control in the 1930s," *Journal of Social History* 29 (March 1996): 485–506. Reprinted by permission of the *Journal of Social History.*

Hope for the vexed woman was at hand, however. In fact, it was as close as the neighborhood store. Women who invested their faith and dollars in Lysol, the ad promised, would find in its use the perfect panacea for their marital woes. Feminine hygiene would contribute to "a woman's sense of fastidiousness" while freeing her from habitual fears of pregnancy. Used regularly, Lysol would ensure "health and harmony . . . throughout her married life."[2]

The *McCall's* ad, one of hundreds of birth-control ads published in women's magazines in the 1930s, reflects the rapid growth of the contraceptive industry in the United States during the Depression. Birth control has always been a matter of practical interest to women and men. By the early 1930s, despite long-standing legal restrictions and an overall decline in consumer purchasing power, it had also become a profitable industry. Capitalizing on Americans' desire to limit family size in an era of economic hardship, pharmaceutical firms, rubber manufacturers, mail-order houses, and fly-by-night peddlers launched a successful campaign to persuade women and men to eschew natural methods for commercial devices whose efficacy could be "scientifically proven." In 1938, with the industry's annual sales exceeding $250 million, *Fortune* pronounced birth control one of the most prosperous new businesses of the decade.[3] . . .

Depression-era manufacturers were the first to create a mass market for contraceptives in the United States. Through successful advertising they heightened demand for commercial birth control while building a permanent consumer base that facilitated the industry's subsequent expansion. Significantly, this consumer constituency was almost exclusively female. Condoms, the most popular commercial contraceptive before the Depression, generated record sales in the 1930s. But it was profits from female contraceptives—sales of which outnumbered those of condoms five to one by the late 1930s—that fuelled the industry's prodigious growth.[4] Then, as now, women were the nation's leading contraceptive consumers.

An important feature distinguished the birth-control market of the 1930s from that of today, however: its illegality. Federal and state laws dating from the 1870s proscribed the interstate distribution and sale of contraceptives. Although by the 1920s the scope of these restrictions had been modified by court interpretations permitting physicians to supply contraceptive information and devices in several states, the American Medical Association's ban on medically dispensed contraceptive advice remained intact. Neither legal restrictions nor medical disapproval thwarted the industry's ascent, however. Instead, they merely pushed the industry underground, beyond regulatory reach.

Contraceptive manufacturers in the 1930s exploited this vacuum to their advantage, retailing devices that were often useless and/or dangerous in a manner that kept the birth-control business on the right side of the law. The industry thrived within a grey market characterized by the sale of contraceptives under legal euphemisms. Manufacturers sold a wide array of items, including vaginal jellies, douche powders and liquids, suppositories, and foaming tablets as "feminine hygiene," an innocuous-sounding term coined by advertisers in the 1920s. Publicly, manufacturers claimed that feminine hygiene products were sold solely to enhance vaginal cleanliness. Consumers, literally deconstructing advertising text, knew better. Obliquely encoded in feminine hygiene ads and product packaging were indicators of the product's *real* purpose; references to "protection," "security," or "dependability" earmarked purported contraceptive properties.[5]

Tragically, linguistic clues could not protect individuals from product adulteration or marketing fraud. Because neither the government nor the medical establishment condoned lay use of commercial contraceptives, consumers possessed no reliable information with which to evaluate the veracity of a product's claim. The bootleg status of the birth-control racket left contraceptive consumers in a legal lurch. If an advertised product's implied claims to contraceptive attributes failed, they had no acceptable means of recourse.

Within this highly profitable and unfettered trade, women became the market's most reliable and, by extension, most exploited customers. The rise of the birth-control industry was an important episode in the advance of consumer society in interwar America. Mass production, a predominantly urban population, and innovations in consumer credit supplied the structural underpinning for the expansion of the consumer economy. The advertising industry, manufacturers, retailers, and political leaders provided a concomitant cultural ethos that celebrated the emancipating properties of consumption; the power to purchase was lauded as a desirable, deserved, and quintessentially American freedom. Women became favored recipients of this self-congratulatory encomium. . . . In the 1920s, when advertising consultants agreed that purchases by women accounted for eighty percent of consumer spending (this, in an economy increasingly dependent on consumer sales), the gendered dimensions of consumption were readily apparent. Hoping to influence women's buying behavior, advertisers shrewdly cast women's time-worn role as consumers in a flattering light. Universally endorsing among themselves a psychological profile of the female shopper as mercurial and easily swayed by emotional appeals, advertisers attempted to convince women that consumption was an inherently empowering task. Advertising copy and images accentuated a common theme: that the freedom to choose between Maybelline and Elizabeth Arden lipsticks hallmarked women's newfound authority and liberation in the postsuffrage age.[6]

Depression-era manufacturers and retailers of birth control adopted the same consumption/liberation formula used to sell women lipstick, Hoover vacuum cleaners, and Chrysler cars to construct the first contraceptive mass market in the United States. Just as consumption was trumpeted as a characteristically female freedom, so, too, was reproduction portrayed as a distinctively female task. On this latter point, women needed little convincing. By virtue of biology, pregnancy was an exclusively female experience; by virtue of convention, raising children in the 1930s was principally a female responsibility. Drawing upon and simultaneously reinforcing the prevailing gender system, the birth-control industry reified the naturalness of women's twin roles as consumers and reproducers. Conjoining these functions, manufacturers and retailers urged women to use their purchasing "power" to assume full responsibility for pregnancy prevention. The industry's sales pitch struck a resonant chord with American women in the 1930s. At a time when the cost of raising children was rising and an unprecedented and increasing proportion of the laboring population was officially unemployed, controlling fertility assumed added urgency. With public birth-control clinics few in number and privately prescribed diaphragms financially and medically out of reach to most women, access to easily acquired, affordable, and effective birth control became a widely shared goal. With advertisers' prodding, millions of women turned to the contraceptive market to achieve it.[7] . . .

When Congress enacted the Comstock Act in 1873, a new nadir in reproductive rights had arrived. . . . Passed after minimal debate, the Comstock Act had long-term repercussions. Following

Congress's lead, most states enacted so-called "mini" Comstock acts which criminalized the circulation of contraceptive devices and information within state lines. . . .

By the time state and federal legislatures had begun to abandon their laissez-faire attitude toward birth control, a fledging contraceptive industry had already surfaced in the United States. Indeed, the two developments were integrally yoked: the initiative to regulate contraceptives arose out of the realization that there was a growing number to regulate. The nineteenth century witnessed the emergence of a contraceptive trade that sold for profit goods that had traditionally been prepared within the home. Douching powders and astringents, dissolving suppositories, and vaginal pessaries had supplemented male withdrawal and abstinence as mainstays of birth-control practice in preindustrial America.[8] As the nineteenth century progressed, these conventional contraceptives became increasingly available from commercial vendors. Technologically upgraded versions of other standard contraceptives also entered the birth-control trade. The vulcanization of rubber in the 1840s figured prominently in contraceptive commercialization, expanding birth-control options even as it increased individuals' dependence on the market to acquire them. Vulcanization spurred the domestic manufacture of condoms, yielding American-made condoms that were cheaper than imported European condoms made from fish bladders or animal intestines.[9] The subsequent development of seamless condoms made of thinner latex, more appealing to users than earlier models, heightened condom demand. Vulcanization also facilitated the development of female contraceptives by supplying the requisite technology for the manufacture of rubber cervical caps and diaphragms. By the 1870s, condoms, douching syringes, douching solutions, vaginal sponges, and cervical caps could be purchased from mail-order houses, wholesale drug-supply houses, and pharmacies. Pessaries—traditionally used to support prolapsed uteruses but sold since the 1860s in closed-ring form as "womb veils"— could be obtained from sympathetic physicians. Thus, when supporters of the Comstock Act decried the "nefarious and diabolical traffic" of "vile and immoral goods," they were identifying the inroads commercialized contraception had already made.[10]

After the Comstock restrictions were passed, birth control continued to be sold, marketed for its therapeutic or cosmetic, rather than its contraceptive, value. Significantly, however, commercial contraceptive use became more closely associated with economic privilege. The clandestine nature of the market prompted many reputable firms—especially rubber manufacturers—to cease production altogether. Those that remained charged exorbitant prices for what was now illegal merchandise. For many wage-earning and immigrant families, the high price of contraceptives made them unaffordable. In addition, the suppression of birth-control information reduced the availability of published material on commercial and noncommercial techniques, as descriptions previously featured openly in pamphlets, books, journals, broadsides, and newspaper medical columns became harder to find. In effect, contraceptive information, like contraceptives themselves, became a privileged luxury.

Only in the 1930s were birth-control manufacturers able to create a mass market characterized by widespread access to commercial contraceptives. This market developed in response to a combination of important events. The birth-control movement of the 1910s and 1920s, spearheaded by Margaret Sanger, made birth control a household word (indeed, it was Sanger who introduced the term) and a topic of protracted debate and heated public discussion. Sanger insisted that women's sexual liberation and economic autonomy depended upon the availability of safe, inexpensive, and effective birth control. Sanger conducted speaking tours extolling the need for female contraception and published piercing indictments of "Comstockery" in her short-lived feminist newspaper *The Woman Rebel*, the *International Socialist Review*, and privately published pamphlets. In October 1916, she opened in Brooklyn the first birth-control clinic in the United States where she instructed neighborhood women on contraceptive techniques. The clinic's closure and Sanger's subsequent jail sentence only increased her notoriety. Sanger was not alone in her efforts to legitimize contraception, of course. The birth-control movement was a collective struggle waged by hundreds of individuals and organizations, including IWW [Industrial Workers of the World] locals, women's Socialist groups, independent birth-control leagues, and the liberal-minded National Birth Control League. But Sanger's single-minded devotion to the birth-control cause and her casual and frequent defiance of the law captured the media spotlight. In the 1910s it was Sanger, more than anyone else, who pushed contraception into the public arena and who, quite unintentionally, set the stage for the commercial exploitation that followed. . . .

The popularization of the idea of birth control supplied the cultural backdrop to the economic birth-control boom of the 1930s. In the absence of government approval and regulation, the rising desire for contraceptives provided the perfect environment in which a bootleg trade could thrive. As journalist Elizabeth Garrett explained in a 1932 article in *The New Republic*, "so long as contraception was wholly unknown and tabu [*sic*], saleswomen could not get very far with their prospects. But when 'birth control' became a familiar and at least partially respectable term, all that was needed to induce a woman to order contraceptive wares by mail, or to buy them from peddlers . . . was skilful advertising."[11]

As the demand for birth control accelerated, the inability of institutions to satisfy it became apparent. By 1932, only 145 public clinics operated to service the contraceptive needs of the nation; twenty-seven states had no clinics at all. Each year in New York City, birth-control organizations received over 10,000 letters requesting contraceptive information; because of chronic understaffing, most went unanswered.[12] Many women, spurred on by public attention to birth control but unable to secure the assistance needed to make informed contraceptive choices, took contraception—and their lives—into their own hands. A Chicago physician noted in 1930 with alarm the growing number of doctors reporting the discovery of chewing gum, hairpins, needles, tallow candles, and pencils lodged in female patients' urinary bladders. The doctor blamed these desperate attempts to restrict fertility on the "wave of publicity concerning contraceptive methods that has spread over the country." Equally eager to control reproduction through self-administered means, other women turned to the burgeoning birth-control market to purchase what they believed were safe and reliable contraceptives.[13]

That there was a commercial market to which to turn was the result of liberalized legal restrictions that encouraged manufacturers to enter the birth-control trade. The structure of the birth-control industry of the early 1930s was markedly different from that which preceded it only a few years earlier. From 1925 to 1928, Holland-Rantos had enjoyed a monopoly on the manufacture of diaphragms and contraceptive jellies in the United States; other manufacturers expressed little interest in producing articles that might invoke government prosecution and whose market was confined to a handful of nonprofit clinics. A 1930 decision, *Youngs*

Rubber Corporation, Inc., v. C. I. Lee & Co., et al., lifted legal impediments to market entry. The *Youngs* case, in which the makers of Trojan condoms successfully sued a rival company for trademark infringement, forced the court to decide whether the contraceptive business was legal, and thus legitimately entitled to trademark protection. The court ruled that insofar as birth control had "other lawful purposes" besides contraception, it could be legally advertised, distributed, and sold as a noncontraceptive device. The outcome of a dispute between rival condom manufacturers, the *Youngs* decision left its most critical mark on the female contraceptive market. Companies that had previously avoided the birth-control business quickly grasped the commercial opportunities afforded by the court's ruling. Provided that no reference to a product's contraceptive features appeared in product advertising or on product packaging, female contraceptives could now be legally sold—not only to the small number of birth-control clinics in states where physician-prescribed birth control was legal, but to the consuming public nationwide. Manufacturers realized that the court's legal latitude would not affect the diaphragm market, monopolized, as it was, by the medical profession. Because diaphragms required a physician's fitting, the number of buyers, given financial and regional obstacles to this type of medical consultation, would remain proportionately small. Jellies, suppositories, and foaming tablets, on the other hand, possessed untapped mass-market potential. They could be used without prior medical screening. And because chemical compounds were cheaper to mass produce than rubber diaphragms, they could be sold at a price more women could afford.[14]

By 1938, only twelve years after Holland-Rantos had launched the female contraceptive industry in the United States, at least four hundred other firms were competing in the lucrative market.[15] The $212 million industry acquired most of its profits from the sale of jellies, suppositories, tablets, and antiseptic douching solutions retailed over the counter as feminine hygiene and bought principally by women. Historians of birth control, attentive to the findings of medical studies in the 1930s, have rightly emphasized the rising popularity of diaphragms at this time, especially among urban, middle-class women. Progressive physicians and public clinics consistently endorsed combined diaphragm and jelly use as the safest and most effective female-controlled contraception available. But as important as increased diaphragm use was to the medicalization of birth control, its surging popularity was incidental to the escalating profitability of the industry itself. The contraceptive industry thrived in the 1930s precisely because, while capitalizing on public discussions of birth control to which the medical community contributed, it operated outside customary medical channels. Manufacturers supplied women with something that clinics and private physicians did not: birth control that was conveniently located, discreetly obtained, and, most importantly, affordably priced. While the going rate for a diaphragm and a companion tube of jelly ranged from four to six dollars, a dollar purchased a dozen suppositories, ten foaming tablets, or, most alluring of all, up to three douching units, depending on the brand. Contraceptive manufacturers pledged, furthermore, that customer satisfaction would not be sacrificed on the altar of frugality. They reassured buyers that bargain-priced contraceptives were just as reliable as other methods. Without lay guides to help them identify the disjunction between advertising hyperbole and reality, women could hardly be faulted for taking the cheaper path. By the late 1930s, purchases of diaphragms accounted for less than one percent of total contraceptive sales.[16]

Manufacturers' grandiose claims aside, not all contraceptives were created alike. The dangers and deficiencies of birth-control products were well known in the health and hygiene community. Concerned pharmacists, physicians, and birth-control advocates routinely reviewed and condemned commercial preparations. . . .

Critics reserved their harshest comments for the most popular, affordable, and least reliable contraceptive of the day, the antiseptic douche. Noting the method's alarming failure rate—reported at the time to be as high as seventy percent—they condemned the technique as mechanically unsound and pharmacologically ineffectual. For one thing, the method's technique weakened its potential for success: by the time the solution was introduced, seminal fluid that had already penetrated the cervix and surrounding tissues was difficult to reach and negate. In addition, the method's ineffectiveness was compounded by the benignity or toxicity of the solutions themselves. Scores of douching preparations, while advertised as modern medical miracles, contained nothing more than water, cosmetic plant extracts, and table salt. On the other hand, many others, including the most popular brand, Lysol disinfectant, contained cresol (a distillate of coal and wood) or mercury chloride, either of which, when used in too high a concentration, caused severe inflammation, burning, and even death. Advertising downplayed the importance of dilution by drawing attention to antiseptics' gentleness and versatility; single ads praising Lysol's safety on "delicate female tissues" also encouraged the money-wise consumer to use the antiseptic as a gargle, nasal spray, or household cleaner. By the same token, the makers of PX, a less-known brand, sold a liquid disinfectant that ads claimed could be used interchangeably for "successful womanhood" or athlete's foot.[17]

This strategy won sales, but it did so only by jeopardizing women's health. With even one-time douching a potentially deleterious act, women guided by the logical assumption that "more was better" strove to beat the pregnancy odds by increasing the frequency of their douching and the concentration of the solution used. In one case, a nineteen-year-old married woman relied on regular douching with dissolved mercury chloride tablets for birth control. Eager to avoid pregnancy, she doubled the dose and douched "several times daily." Her determination landed her in a doctor's office where she was diagnosed with acute vaginal and cervical burns. In what must have seemed to her like a grave injustice, she also learned she was pregnant.[18]

Reports on douche-related deaths and injuries and the general ineffectiveness of popular commercial contraceptives were widely discussed among concerned constituents of the health community. Sadly, however, these findings failed to prod the medical establishment as a united profession to take a resolute stand against the contraceptive scandal. Nor, regrettably, did blistering indictments of manufacturing fraud trickle down to the lay press where they might have enabled women to make informed contraceptive choices. The numerous women's magazines that published feminine hygiene ads—from *McCall's* to *Screen Romances* to the *Ladies' Home Journal*—were conspicuously silent about the safety and efficacy of the products they tacitly endorsed. The paucity of information impeded the development of informed consumerism. In advertising text and in many women's minds, the euphemism "feminine hygiene" continued to signify reliable contraception. For unscrupulous manufacturers eager to profit from this identification, feminine hygiene continued to be a convenient term invoked to sell products devoid of contraceptive value.

Manufacturers absolved themselves of responsibility by reminding critics that by the letter of the law, their products were not being sold as contraceptives. If women incurred injuries or became pregnant while using feminine hygiene for birth control, that was their fault, not manufacturers'. Thus contraceptive firms whose profits depended on consumers' loose and liberal deconstruction of advertising text duplicitously clung to a rigid, literalist construction of language when defending their own integrity. . . .

Added to the growing list of groups unwilling to expose the hucksterism of the birth-control bonanza was the federal government. Neither the Food and Drug Administration (FDA) nor the Federal Trade Commission (FTC) was in a strong position to rally to consumers' aid. The FDA, authorized to take action only against product mislabeling, was powerless to suppress birth-control manufacturers' rhetorically veiled claims. The FTC, in turn, regulated advertising, but only when one company's claims were so egregious as to constitute an unfair business practice. The subterfuge prevalent in all feminine hygiene marketing campaigns, as well as a unanimous desire on manufacturers' part to eschew protracted scrutiny, kept the FTC at bay. Sadly for the growing pool of female contraceptive consumers, without regulation and reliable standards for discriminating among products, the only way to discern a product's safety and efficacy was through trial and error.[19]

Clamoring for a larger share of the hygiene market, manufacturers did their utmost to ensure that their product would be one women would want to try. Aggressive advertising was instrumental to the industry's success. Appealing to women in the privacy of their homes, feminine hygiene companies blanketed middle-class women's magazines in the 1930s with advertisements, many of full-page size. Targeting the magazines' predominantly married readership, advertisements were headlined by captions designed to inculcate and inflate apprehensions in readers' minds. Ads entitled "Calendar Fear," "Can a Married Woman Ever Feel Safe?," "Young Wives Are Often Secretly Terrified," and "The Fear That 'Blights' Romance and Ages Women Prematurely" relied on standard negative advertising techniques to heighten the stakes of pregnancy prevention.[20]

Ads conveyed the message that ineffective contraception led not only to unwanted pregnancies, but also to illness, despair, and marital discord. Married women who ignored modern contraceptive methods were courting lifelong misery. "Almost before the honeymoon ends," one ad warned, "many a young bride is plagued by foreboding. She pictures the early departure of youth and charm . . . sacrificed on the altar of marriage responsibilities." Engulfed by fear, the newlywed's life only got worse—fear itself, women were told, engendered irreparable physical ailments. According to one douche advertisement, fear was a "dangerous toxin." "[It] dries up valuable secretions, increases the acidity of the stomach, and sometimes disturbs the bodily functions generally. So it is that FEAR greys the hair . . . etches lines in the face, and hastens the toll of old age."[21]

As if these physical penalties were not disconcerting enough, feminine hygiene ads insisted that a woman's apprehensions and their attendant woes could ruin the marriage itself. On this point, the transcendent parable of ads was clear: the longevity of a marriage depended upon the right commercial contraceptive. "She was a lovely creature before she married," one ad began, "beautiful, healthy, and happy. But since her marriage she seems forever worried, nervous and irritable . . . always dreading what seems inevitable. Her husband, too, seems to share her secret worry. Frankly, they are no longer happy. Poor girl, she doesn't know that she's headed for the divorce court."[22] And as ads—whose sole purpose was to convince women, not men, to buy contraceptives—hastened to remind readers, women alone shouldered the blame for divorce. After all, why should a man be held accountable for distancing himself from a wife made ugly and cantankerous by her own anxieties? "Many marriage failures," one advertisement asserted authoritatively, "can be traced directly to disquieting wifely fears." "Recurring again and again," marriage anxieties were "capable of changing the most angelic nature, of making it nervous, suspicious, irritable." "I leave it to you," the ad concluded, "is it easy for even the kindliest husband to live with a wife like that?"[23]

Having divulged the ugly and myriad hazards of unwanted pregnancy while saddling women with the burden of its prevention, advertisements emphasized that peace of mind and marital happiness were conditions only the market could bestow. Readers of feminine hygiene ads, newly enlightened, returned to the world with the knowledge necessary to "remove many of their health anxieties, and give them that sense of well being, personal daintiness and mental poise so essential to wifely security." In the modern age, the personal tragedies accompanying a woman's existence were easily avoided. "Days of depressing anxiety, a wedded life in which happiness is marred by fear and uncertainty—these need be yours no longer," one douche ad reassured. In the imagined world of contraceptive advertising, feminine hygiene was the commodity no modern woman could afford to be without. Fortunately, none had to. The path to unbridled happiness was only a store away.[24]

As advertisements reminded prospective customers, however, not all feminine hygiene products were the same. The contraceptive consumer had to be discriminating. Hoping both to increase general demand for hygiene products and to inculcate brand loyalty, manufacturers presented their product as the one most frequently endorsed for its efficacy and safety by medical professionals. Dispelling consumer doubts by invoking the approval of the scientific community was not an advertising technique unique to contraceptive merchandising—the same strategy was used in the 1930s to sell women laxatives, breakfast cereal, and mouthwash. What was exceptional about contraceptive advertising, however, was that the experts endorsing feminine hygiene were not men. Rather, they were female physicians whose innate understanding of the female condition permitted them to share their birth-control expertise "woman to woman."[25]

The Lehn & Fink Corporation used this technique to make Lysol disinfectant douche the leading feminine hygiene product in the country.[26] In a series of full-page advertisements entitled "Frank Talks by Eminent Women Physicians," stern-looking European female gynecologists urged "smart-thinking" women to entrust their health only to doctor-recommended Lysol disinfectant douches. "It amazes me," wrote Dr. Madeleine Lion, "a widely recognized gynecologist of Paris,"

> in these modern days, to hear women confess their carelessness, their lack of positive information, in the so vital matter of feminine hygiene. They take almost anybody's word . . . a neighbor's, an afternoon bridge partner's . . . for the correct technique. . . . Surely in this question of correct marriage hygiene, the modern woman should accept only the facts of scientific research and medical experience. The woman who does demand such facts uses "Lysol" faithfully in her ritual of personal antisepsis.[27]

Another ad, part of the same series, underscored the point. "It is not safe to accept the counsels of the tea table," explained Dr. Auguste Popper, a female gynecologist from Vienna, "or the advice of a well-meaning, but uninformed friend." Only the advice of scientific experts could be trusted. While feminine hygiene "has alleviated woman's oldest fear," an Italian gynecologist advised readers in yet another Lysol douche ad, the greatest obstacle to

Advertisement, *McCall's* 40 (August 1993).

realizing health and happiness lay in selecting the right hygiene merchandise: "Some are good, some are not. My own preference is for 'Lysol,' " the gynecologist concluded, "in common with almost every other doctor I know."[28]

    While insisting that women defer to medical opinion when choosing birth control, contraceptive ads simultaneously celebrated the tremendous "power" women wielded in the consumer market. The two claims were not antithetical; advertisements contended that women who heeded physicians' advice and purchased "scientific" birth control were intelligently harnessing the advances of modern medicine to promote their own liberation. Consistent with the consumer ethic of the day, birth-control advertising successfully equated contraceptive consumption with female emancipation. An ad by the Zonite Products Corporation claimed that birth control was not only a matter of pragmatism, but also a "protest against those burdens of life which are wholly woman's." When it came to as important an issue as birth control, Zonite explained, the modern woman was not interested in the "timid thoughts of a past generation"; her goal was "to find out and be sure." It was no surprise, the company boasted, that Zonite hygiene products were favored by "women of the independent, enlightened type all over the world."[29]

Contraceptive manufacturers' creation of a mass market in the 1930s depended not only upon effective advertising, but also on the availability of advertised goods. Prospective customers needed quick, convenient, and multiple access to contraceptives. Manufacturers made sure that they had it. Flooding a wide array of commercial outlets with their merchandise, companies guaranteed that contraceptives became a commodity within everyone's reach. Here, again, gender was the crucial variable, determining product availability and sales venue. Condoms were sold in pharmacies, but also in newsstands, barbershops, cigar stores, and gas stations—locations where men were most likely to congregate. Women, on the other hand, were targeted in more conventional female settings: in stores and in the home.[30]

The department store became the leading distributor of female contraceptives in the 1930s. By the mid-1930s women could purchase feminine hygiene products at a number of national chains, including Woolworth, Kresge, McLellan, and W. T. Grant.[31] Already fashioned as a feminized space, department stores established sequestered "personal hygiene" departments where women could shop in a dignified and discreet manner for contraceptives and other products related to female reproduction such as sanitary napkins and tampons. Stores emphasized the exclusively female environment of the personal hygiene department as the department's finest feature. The self-contained department was not only separated from the rest of the store, where "uncontrollable factors . . . might make for . . . embarrassment," but it was staffed solely by saleswomen trained in the "delicate matter of giving confidential and intimate personal advice to their clients." As one store assured female readers in the local newspaper: "Our Personal Hygiene Department [has] Lady Attendants on Duty at all Times." Female clerks, furthermore, were instructed to respect the private nature of the department's transactions; sensitive, knowledgeable, and tactful, they were "understanding wom[en] with whom you may discuss your most personal and intimate problems."[32] . . .

Manufacturers reasoned that many prospective female customers would not buy feminine hygiene in a store. Many did not live close enough to one, while others, notwithstanding the store's discretion, might remain uncomfortable with the public nature of the exchange. To eliminate regional and psychological obstacles to birth-control buying, companies sold feminine hygiene to women directly in their homes. Selling contraceptives by mail was one such method. Mail-order catalogues, including those distributed by Sears, Roebuck and Montgomery Ward, offered a full line of female contraceptives; each catalogue contained legally censored ads supplied by manufacturers. As a reward for bulk sales, mail-order houses received a discount from the companies whose products they sold. Other manufacturers bypassed jobbers and encouraged women to send their orders directly to the company. To eliminate the possibility of embarrassment, ads typically promised that the order would be delivered in a "plain wrapper."[33]

To create urban and working-class markets, dozens of firms hired door-to-door sales representatives to canvass urban districts. All representatives were women, a deliberate attempt on manufacturers' part to profit from the prudish marketing scheme that tried to convince women that, as one company put it, "There are some problems so intimate that it is embarrassing to talk them over with a doctor."[34] At the Dilex Institute of Feminine Hygiene, for example, five separate female crews, each headed by a female crew manager, combed the streets of New York. The cornerstone of the company's marketing scheme was an aggressive sales pitch delivered by saleswomen dressed as nurses. As *Fortune* discovered in an undercover investigation, however, the Dilex canvassers had no medical background. In fact, the only qualification required for employment was previous door-to-door sales experience. Despite their lack of credentials, newly hired saleswomen were instructed to assume the role of the medical professional, a tactic the Institute reasoned would gain customers' trust, respect, and dollars. "You say you're a nurse, see?" one new recruit was told. "That always gets you in." Canvassers walked from house to house delivering by memory the standard Dilex sales speech:

> Good morning. I am the Dilex Nurse, giving short talks on feminine hygiene. It will take only three minutes. Thank you—I will step in.
>
> Undoubtedly you have heard of many different methods of feminine hygiene, but I have come to tell you of THE DILEX METHOD, which is so much more simple and absolutely sure and harmless, and which EVERY woman is so eager to learn about and have without delay.
>
> At one time this was a very delicate subject to discuss, but today with all our modern ideas, we look at this vital subject as one of the most important of all time, and for that reason, we call to acquaint you with THIS GREAT SECRET, a most practical, convenient way.
>
> The Dilex Method meets every protective and hygienic requirement. It is positive and safe and may be used with the utmost confidence. Each item has been given the most careful thought to fit the increasing strides in feminine hygiene. . . . ABSOLUTE FEMININE PROTECTION is assured.[35]

The saleswoman then attempted to peddle the company's top-of-the-line contraceptive kit. For seven dollars, a woman could purchase jelly, a douching outfit, an antiseptic douche capsule, and—most alarming of all—a universal "one-size-fits-all" diaphragm. Poverty, women were told, was not an impediment to the personal happiness the company was selling: "luckily" for them, the Dilex kit was available on the installment plan.[36]

Contraceptive companies' tactics paid off. By 1940, the size of the female contraceptive market was three times that of the 1935 market.[37] The industry's unabated growth continued despite important changes in legal interpretation and medical attitudes in the late 1930s that might have reduced the industry's hold over American women. In 1936, the Supreme Court's *One Package* decision allowed physicians in every state to send and receive contraceptive devices and information. The following year, the American

Medical Association reversed its long-standing ban on contraception, endorsing the right of a physician to prescribe birth control.
The court's decision and the AMA's liberalized policy did not foster the immediate medicalization of birth control, a process that
might have encouraged women to turn to the medical profession
instead of the market for contraception. Indeed, in the short term,
these sweeping changes proved remarkably inconsequential to the
state of the industry. Many Americans could not afford the luxury
of a personal physician, and only a minority lived close enough to
the 357 public birth-control clinics operating in 1937 to avail themselves of clinic services. But of even more significance than medical barriers was manufacturers' enticing sales message. Companies'
pledges to supply birth control that was affordable, immediate, and
discreetly sold—either anonymously or in a completely feminized
setting—continued to strike a responsive chord with American
women. In addition, manufacturers promised what no lay guide
could dispute: that what was bought from the market was as effective as doctor-prescribed methods. Out of pragmatic necessity and
personal preference, most women worried about pregnancy prevention continued to obtain birth control from the contraceptive
market.[38] . . .

In a 1936 letter to Harrison Reeves, a New York journalist study-
ing the commercial aspects of contraception for the *American Mercury*, Margaret Sanger reflected on the state of the birth-control
business in America. Sanger was no stranger to the commercial
scene. Since the early 1930s she had instructed her secretary to clip
all commercial advertisements for birth control for Sanger's personal review. Sanger corresponded frequently with manufacturers
eager to obtain her endorsement of new products. From direct involvement in the daily operation of public clinics that she had
founded, to the multiple tests on birth-control products conducted
at her request by doctors at the Birth Control Clinical Research
Bureau, Sanger was keenly aware of the perils and pitfalls of commercial contraception.[39]

And yet, in what amounted to more than a loyal defense of her
husband's business activities, Sanger refused to vilify manufacturers for the commercial hucksterism, fraud, and misinformation that
so many of them had spawned. As she explained to Reeves, "I do
not feel as many do about manufacturing concerns. . . . They have

not lagged behind like the medical profession but have gone ahead and answered [a] growing and urgent need."[40]

Sanger's observation, although anchored in what in hindsight appears to be misplaced charity, perspicaciously speaks to the expanding role of manufacturers in shaping contraceptive practices in the 1930s. The strictures and liberties of the law, the inertia of the medical profession, and the determination of American women to find affordable and effective female-controlled birth control, provided new economic opportunities that manufacturers eagerly seized. By the end of the 1930s, manufacturers had created a lively and vigorous market that could be easily accessed in stores, by mail, and within the home. Drawing on a gendered culture that designated consumption and reproduction female roles, manufacturers implored women to "purchase" their happiness and security from the contraceptive market. Reinforcing Victorian sensibilities about female sexuality that self-servingly bolstered their marketing scheme, they feminized sites of birth-control buying. Instead of visiting a male doctor or druggist, women were encouraged to acquire birth control in sex-segregated departments staffed by "discreet" female attendants, from visiting saleswomen, or through the mail upon the advertised recommendation of female physicians "who know."

The escalation of industry profits followed closely on the heels of the construction of the female contraceptive consumer; by World War II, not only did sales of feminine hygiene products surpass those of condoms, but more women depended on feminine hygiene for birth control than on any other method. Tragically, the very legal climate that permitted the birth-control business to flourish in a bootleg state also encouraged it to peddle inferior goods. For too many women, the freedom, pleasure, and security pledged by contraceptive manufacturers amounted to nothing more than empty promises.

The commercialization of birth control in the 1930s illuminates the important but overlooked role of industry in shaping birth-control developments in the United States. Historians have typically framed birth-control history as a tale of doctors, lawmakers, and women's rights activists. The events of the 1930s suggest that we need to recast this story to include the agency of a new set of actors, birth-control manufacturers. The commercialization that manufacturers engendered at this time left an indelible imprint on the lives of ordinary women and men. It also revealed a world in which industry, gender, and reproduction were frequently and intimately intertwined.

Notes

1. *McCall's* LX (July 1933): 85.

2. *McCall's* LX (July 1933): 85.

3. "The Accident of Birth," *Fortune* (February 1938): 84.

4. According to *Fortune*, sales from condoms accounted for $38 million of the industry's annual $250 million sales. See "The Accident of Birth," p. 84.

5. Elizabeth H. Garrett, "Birth Control's Business Baby," *New Republic* (January 17, 1934): 270; Dorothy Dunbar Bromley, "Birth Control and the Depression," *Harper's* (October 1934): 563; "The Accident of Birth," pp. 110, 112.

6. Christine Frederick, *Selling Mrs. Consumer* (New York, 1929), pp. 43–44.

7. A poll published in *Ladies' Home Journal* in 1938 found that seventy-nine percent of American women surveyed favored birth control. The most frequent argument given in its favor was economic considerations. See Henry F. Pringle, "About Birth Control," *Ladies' Home Journal* 55 (March 1938): 15.

8. Linda Gordon, *Woman's Body, Woman's Right: A Social History of Birth Control in America* (New York, 1977), pp. 48–49, 64–71; James Reed, *From Private Vice to Public Virtue: The Birth Control Movement and American Society since 1830* (New York, 1978), pp. 4–13; Norman Himes, *Medical History of Contraception* (Baltimore, 1936), chapter 11.

9. See Himes, *Medical History of Contraception*, pp. 201–4; Vern L. Bullough, "A Brief Note on Rubber Technology and Contraception: The Diaphragm and the Condom," *Technology and Culture* 22 (January 1981): 104, 107–11; Reed, *From Private Vice to Public Virtue*, pp. 13–15. According to Carl Degler, the price of condoms dropped by approximately forty percent between 1847 and 1865. See Degler, *At Odds: Women and the Family in America from the Revolution to the Present* (New York, 1980), pp. 219–20.

10. Michael A. La Sorte, "Nineteenth-Century Family Planning Practices," *Journal of Psychohistory* 4 (Fall 1976): 175–76; Bullough, "A Brief Note on Rubber Technology and Contraception: The Diaphragm and the Condom," pp. 105–6; Reed, *From Private Vice to Public Virtue*, pp. 15–17; Gordon, *Woman's Body, Woman's Right*, pp. 67–70.

11. Garrett, "Birth Control's Business Baby," p. 269.

12. Bromley, "Birth Control and the Depression," p. 566; James Rorty, "What's Stopping Birth Control," *New Republic* (February 3, 1932): 313.

13. Dorrin F. Rudnick, "A New Type of Foreign Body in the Urinary Bladder," *Journal of the American Medical Association* 94 (May 17, 1930): 1565.

14. "*Youngs Rubber Corporation, Inc., v. C. I. Lee & Co., et al.,*" 45 *Federal Reporter*, 2nd Series 103; Morris L. Ernst, "How We Nullify," *The Nation* (Janu-

ary 27, 1932): 114; Garrett, "Birth Control's Business Baby," p. 270. The effectiveness of contraceptive jellies when used alone was well documented. See "The Accident of Birth," p. 85.

15. "The Accident of Birth," p. 108.

16. Reed, *From Private Vice to Public Virtue*, pp. 244–46; J. M. Ray and F. G. Gosling, "American Physicians and Birth Control, 1936–1947," *Journal of Social History* 18 (1985): 399–408 passim; John Winchell Riley and Matilda White, "The Use of Various Methods of Contraception," *American Sociological Review* 5 (December 1940): 896–900; "The Accident of Birth," p. 84; "Feminine Hygiene Products Face a New Marketing Era," *The Drug and Cosmetic Industry* 37 (December 1935): 745; Harrison Reeves, "The Birth Control Industry," *American Mercury* 155 (November 1936): 287; "Birth Control Industry," *The Drug and Cosmetic Industry* 46 (January 1940): 58; "Building Acceptances for Feminine Hygiene Products," *The Drug and Cosmetic Industry* 38 (February 1936): 177.

17. Robert L. Dickinson and Louise Stevens Bryant, *Control of Conception: An Illustrated Medical Manual* (Baltimore, 1931), pp. 39–44, 69–74; Dorothy Dunbar Bromley, *Birth Control: Its Use and Misuse* (New York, 1934), pp. 92–98; Rachel Lynn Palmer and Sara K. Greenberg, *Facts and Frauds in Woman's Hygiene: A Medical Guide Against Misleading Claims and Dangerous Products* (New York, 1938), pp. 12–15, 142–51; Lysol ad from pamphlet by Dr. Emil Klarmann, *Formula L-F: A New Antiseptic and Germicide* (Lehn & Fink Inc.) appended to letter from Lehn & Fink to Margaret Sanger, November 24, 1931, reel 29, Margaret Sanger Papers, Library of Congress; PX ad from Margaret Sanger Papers, Box 232, folder "Commercial Advertisements, 1932–34," Library of Congress.

18. "Effects of Corrosive Mercuric Chloride ('Bichloride') Douches," *Journal of the American Medical Association* 99 (August 6, 1932): 497.

19. Garrett, "Birth Control's Business Baby," pp. 270–71; "The Accident of Birth," pp. 110, 112; "Birth Control and the Depression," p. 572; Reed, *From Private Vice to Public Virtue*, p. 114; David M. Kennedy, *Birth Control in America: The Career of Margaret Sanger* (New Haven, 1970), p. 183; Palmer and Greenberg, *Facts and Frauds in Woman's Hygiene*, pp. 21–24.

20. For sample captions see Bromley, "Birth Control and the Depression"; the advertisement captioned "The Fear That 'Blights' Romance and Ages Women Prematurely" is from *McCall's* LX (October 1932): 102.

21. "The Incompatible Marriage: Is it a Case for Doctor or Lawyer?" *McCall's* LX (May 1933): 107; "The Fear That 'Blights' Romance and Ages Women Prematurely," *McCall's* LX (October 1932): 102.

22. Advertisement cited in Garrett, "Birth Control's Business Baby," p. 271; "The Incompatible Marriage: Is it a Case for Doctor or Lawyer?" *McCall's* LX (May 1933): 107.

23. "The Incompatible Marriage: Is it a Case for Doctor or Lawyer?" *McCall's* LX (May 1933): 107.

24. "The Incompatible Marriage: Is it a Case for Doctor or Lawyer?" *McCall's* LX (May 1933): 107; Garrett, "Birth Control's Business Baby," p. 271; J. Rorty,

"What's Stopping Birth Control?" *New Republic* 65 (January 28, 1931): 292–94.

25. Mary P. Ryan, "Reproduction in American History," *Journal of Interdisciplinary History* X (Autumn 1979): 330; Ray and Gosling, "American Physicians and Birth Control," p. 405; Roland Marchand, *Advertising the American Dream: Making Way for Modernity, 1920–1940* (Berkeley, 1985), passim.

26. "The Accident of Birth," p. 112.

27. "The Serene Marriage . . . Should it be Jeopardized by Needless Fears?" *McCall's* LX (December 1932): 87.

28. "The Fear That 'Blights' Romance and Ages Women Prematurely," *McCall's* LX (October 1932): 102; "No Wonder Many Wives Fade Quickly With This Recurrent Fear," *McCall's* LX (August 1933): 64.

29. "Why Wasn't I Born a Man?" *McCall's* LX (May 1933): 93; "Marriage is No Gambling Matter: Better Find Out, Better Be Sure About It," *McCall's* LX (March 1933): 107.

30. Garrett, "Birth Control's Business Baby," p. 270; Reeves, "The Birth Control Industry," pp. 286–87; Bromley, "Birth Control and the Depression," p. 570; Anne Rapport, "The Legal Aspects of Marketing Feminine Hygiene Products," *The Drug and Cosmetic Industry* 38 (April 1936): 474; Himes, *Medical History of Contraception*, p. 202; "The Accident of Birth," p. 85.

31. "The Accident of Birth," p. 112.

32. "Feminine Hygiene in the Department Stores," *The Drug and Cosmetic Industry* 40 (April 1937): 482; "12 Ways to More Sales in Feminine Hygiene Products," *Chain Store Age* (June 1941): 54.

33. Garrett, "Birth Control's Business Baby," p. 269; Reeves, "The Birth Control Industry," p. 287; Kennedy, *Birth Control in America*, p. 212.

34. Ad quoted in Palmer and Greenberg, *Facts and Frauds in Woman's Hygiene*, p. 12.

35. "The Accident of Birth," p. 114.

36. "The Accident of Birth," p. 114; Bromley, *Birth Control: Its Use and Misuse*, p. 93; Dilex Institute to Mrs. M. Hoffman, 31 August 1931, reel 29, Margaret Sanger Papers, Liberty of Congress.

37. "Birth Control Industry," *The Drug and Cosmetic Industry* 46, no. 1 (January 1940): 58.

38. "The Accident of Birth," pp. 108–14; "Birth Control Industry," p. 58. According to Mary Ryan, before the Pill became widely available, only twenty percent of American women consulted physicians about birth control. See Ryan, "Reproduction in American History," p. 330.

39. Sanger to Harrison Reeves, June 16, 1936, reel 29, Margaret Sanger Papers, Library of Congress. Sanger's careful monitoring of the commercial side of birth control is evidenced in reels 29 and 30 of the Margaret Sanger Papers, Library of Congress.

40. Sanger to Reeves, June 16, 1936, reel 29, Margaret Sanger Papers, Library of Congress.

38   Testimony on Oral Contraceptives

John R. McCain and Washington Women's Liberation

In 1960 the Food and Drug Administration (FDA) approved the commercial distribution of oral contraceptives. Developed by Gregory Pincus of the Worcester Foundation for Experimental Biology and Harvard gynecologist Howard Rock in the mid-1950s, the so-called Pill revolutionized contraceptive practices in America. By 1966, with nearly six million women—one-fifth of all women of child-bearing age—taking oral contraceptives, the Pill had become the most popular contraceptive in the country. Its initial availability generated tremendous excitement in the scientific and medical communities.

Unfortunately, however, this encomium tended to draw attention away from the Pill's side effects, which included nausea, migraine headaches, depression, and, in a few instances, strokes. (It should be remembered that the first generation of oral contraceptives contained significantly higher concentrations of hormones than do today's pills.) As reports of Pill-related health problems increased, its safety and efficacy became the subject of extensive media attention, lawsuits, and congressional hearings. From among the latter, two 1970 commentaries on the Pill are presented here. In January, Dr. John McCain, an obstetrician and gynecologist in private practice in Atlanta and clinical professor at Emory University, spoke about oral contraceptives before Senator Gaylord Nelson's subcommittee on competition in the pharmaceuticals industry. Subsequently, in March, Washington (DC) Women's Liberation, dissatisfied with the conduct of the Nelson hearings, also addressed the Senate subcommittee.

From "Statement of Dr. John R. McCain, in the Private Practice of Obstetrics and Gynecology, Atlanta, Ga." and "Washington Women's Liberation Statement on Birth Control Pills," U.S. Congress, Senate, Subcommittee on Monopoly of the Select Committee on Small Business, *Competitive Problems in the Drug Industry: Present Status of Competition in the Pharmaceutical Industry; Oral Contraceptives*, 91st Cong., 2d sess. (Washington, DC: Government Printing Office, 1970), 3: pt. 16:6470–71; and 3: pt. 17:7283–84.

Statement of John R. McCain, M.D.

THE DEVELOPMENT OF THE ORAL CONTRACEPTIVE pills has been one of the major achievements of modern medicine. The availability of the contraceptive pills and the publicity associated with them have stimulated a concern for the worldwide population explosion. The pills have also provided a method by which this rapidly increasing problem can be controlled.

As one considers the use of the oral contraceptive pills in private practice, it is well to remind ourselves as physicians that our prescriptions of pharmaceuticals to patients are usually for the treatment of specific illnesses. Virtually all medications, even those as simple as aspirin, carry the possibility of danger to some individuals. Physicians are accustomed to evaluate the risk of the medication against the risk of the disease and then to decide whether or not the drug should be prescribed. The usual woman who does not desire children does not have any disease. If the contraceptive pills do carry some risk to the patient, the physician should prescribe them with caution to the individual woman. If the contraceptive pills do involve risks, the physician should be even more cautious in advising their use on a population-wide basis.

On the other hand, the risks of an unwanted, unplanned pregnancy must also be considered. Even though the patient herself may have no illness, she is exposed in such a pregnancy to all of the risks it involves. The infant, all too frequently, faces major socioeconomic problems which will seriously limit a child's development in our society. It is my opinion that the risks of such a pregnancy are definitely greater than the risks of the oral contraceptive pills. If the patient does not find other methods of contraception acceptable on the basis of economic, social, moral, or religious reasons, I believe that she should have the contraceptive pills prescribed for her protection, and I have done so. The theoretical ideal must be balanced against the practical reality.

Statement of Washington Women's Liberation

The furor and confusion about the pill which has erupted during the last two months has made one thing very clear. Over the past ten years women throughout the world have been taking a pill about which they knew little or nothing.

The idea for Women's Hearings on the Pill grew out of Senator Gaylord Nelson's hearings which were supposed to deal with the pill and informed consent, that is, whether or not doctors told women about the possible risks they were taking in choosing the pill as their form of contraception. . . .

During the first round of the Nelson hearings, members of Women's Liberation rose up to question the way in which the hearings were being conducted as well as the issues that were being covered. In spite of the fact that it is women who are taking the pill and taking the risks, it was the legislators, the doctors, and the drug company's representatives, all men of course, who were testifying and dissecting women as if they were no more important than the laboratory animals they work with every day.

As one of the doctors said: "In an age in which preventive medicine has high priority it is distressing to have women exploited as guinea pigs in order to establish the absolute certitude of the causal relationship of the pill to cancer and other complications. Though it must be admitted that women make superb guinea pigs—they don't cost anything, feed themselves, clean their own cages, pay for their own pills, and remunerate the clinical observer."

The pill has been falsely projected as the only effective safe means of birth control and the answer to the control of the population explosion. We think these projections are misleading. The media, the drug industry, and the medical profession have advanced the idea that the pill has led to the sexual liberation of women. But is this really true? Families, they maintain, will be smaller, but the women's place is still in the home. And it is still women who carry the primary burden of contraception and the full responsibility for child rearing.

The pill has not significantly lowered the birth rate and it has not become the panacea for population control. The lowest birth rate in this country occurred in the 1930s, long before the advent of the pill (implying the importance of social and economic factors). Most proponents of the pill, including the FDA's Advisory Committee, say that the benefits outweigh the risks, but the benefits they are talking about relate to the generalized social philosophy of population control and the risks are taken by us, specific individual women. The only countries that have succeeded in controlling their population growth are Japan and Bulgaria, and this through legalized abortion and not the pill.

If one takes the time to survey the literature in the field, one can see that most of the positive reports on the pill come from drug company-sponsored studies, and those adverse reports, which people like Dr. Guttmacher are doing so much to discredit, come from researchers unconnected in any way with the drug companies.

It is not our mission to have all women on the pill discard it and change to another form of contraception. Our mission, if such it can be called, is to rise up, as women, and demand our human rights. We will no longer let doctors treat us as objects to be manipulated at will. Together we will ask for and demand explanations and humane treatment by our doctors, and if they are too busy to give this to us we will insist that the medical profession must meet our needs. We will no longer tolerate intimidation by white-coated gods, antiseptically directing our lives.

We are trying to offer the facts so that women can exercise a truly free choice and make decisions for themselves. And we are trying to create a forum here for meaningful discussion of these facts.

We are not opposed to oral contraceptives for men or for women. We are opposed to unsafe contraceptives foisted on uninformed women for the profit of the drug and medical industries and for the convenience of men.

39   Testimony on the Intrauterine Device

John G. Madry, Jr., and Russel J. Thomsen

Alarmed by the Pill scare, many women in the first generation of Pill users switched to a new commercial contraceptive, the intrauterine device. IUDs had been around for centuries, but two post-1945 innovations—antibiotics for uterine infections and malleable, inert plastic—made the device significantly safer. The most popular IUD in the early 1970s was the Dalkon Shield, manufactured by the A. H. Robins Company and designed in 1968 by gynecologist Hugh Davis and inventor and electrical

From "Statement of John G. Madry, Jr., M.D., Melbourne, Fla." and "Statement of Maj. Russel J. Thomsen, M.D., Fort Polk, La.," U.S. Congress, House, Subcommittee of the Committee on Government Operations, *Regulation of Medical Devices (Intrauterine Contraceptive Devices)*, 93d Cong., 1st sess. (Washington, DC: Government Printing Office, 1973), 4–6, 11; and 49–52.

*engineer Irwin Lerner. Dalkon Shield ads promised women and
their physicians "trouble free" insertions and removals and a
1.1 percent pregnancy rate. As a result of design flaws and inadequate testing, however, many women became pregnant or
suffered from uterine perforations, painful insertions and removals, pelvic inflammatory disease, or even sterility.*

*In 1974, after considerable media attention, reported
deaths, a congressional investigation, and the complaints of
thousands of women and general practitioners, A. H. Robins
stopped domestic sales. A decade and 7,700 lawsuits later, the
company recalled the Dalkon Shield. In 1973, prior to the re-
call, Dr. John Madry of Melbourne, Florida, and Dr. Russel
Thomsen of Fort Polk, Louisiana, testified before Congressman Lawrence Fountain's subcommittee of the U.S. House of
Representatives concerning their negative impressions of the
IUD. Their statements convey an idea of the range and severity
of the problems experienced by users of the device.*

Statement of John G. Madry, Jr., M.D.

I AM IN THE PRIVATE PRACTICE of obstetrics and gynecology. In this
capacity I represent the lowest common denominator within the
medical profession; I provide primary medical care within my specialty to patients who pay me for my services and advice. These
individuals rightfully expect to obtain from me the safest care and
most reliable of medical advice. Their rights to this quality of medical care are reaffirmed almost daily in the various courts of our
country. . . .

Early in my medical career most methods of contraception were
simple and commonly available without prescription at any drug-
store. The amount of time required then to adequately provide care
and advice regarding contraception did not exceed 1 percent of my
practice time. With the availability of oral contraceptives—pills—
this time requirement increased. As practice experience with oral
contraceptives increased, so did physician and patient confidence.
Then reports of thrombophlebitis and other alleged complications
related to usage of oral contraceptives began to appear, physician
and patient confidence were eroded, and time required for contraceptive advice increased substantially.

Almost simultaneously with increasing adverse publicity
given the pill, intrauterine contraceptive devices (IUDs) became

available, and they too were used cautiously, as had been the pills. In part from the published literature on IUDs, but primarily from personal experience with their usage, it became unmistakably and abundantly clear by early 1969 that IUDs were causing problems. Whereas in seven years' experience with the pills we had seen no side effects or complications not immediately reversed by discontinuing the medication, and no patient had ever required hospitalization, patients using IUDs were constantly telephoning the office with complaints. Two IUDs were removed in the office after perforation of the cervix (one device also perforated into the left ischiorectal fossa), and two patients required hospitalization and D. & C. [dilation and curettage] for removal of the device.

Examinations of our office records revealed that we had removed more IUDs, all for cause, than we had cumulatively inserted. Accordingly, we discontinued the use of IUDs in early 1969. . . .

The philosophy of most IUD advocates is . . . impersonal and population-control oriented, and a high complication rate may be more readily acceptable if their primary goal of reducing pregnancy on a global basis is accomplished.

On the other hand, most providers of contraceptive advice on a personal and individual basis cannot long tolerate methods which are fraught with complications, and they are more apt to advocate the use of oral or other contraceptive methods. Most physicians engaged in the private practice of medicine are, perforce, in this latter group, carrying the moral and legal obligations of patient care totally on their individual backs.

Because of the prodigious flow or prominent distribution to physicians of reports by population planners, as well as occurrence of friendly news articles in lay publications, American physicians in private practice appear to have unwittingly become participants in a great experiment in population control, utilizing as experimental subjects patients for whom the IUD was not even the prime target for usage. Yet neither physicians nor patients have been provided sufficient facts by researchers or manufacturers to allow for any IUD to have been inserted on the basis of informed advice by the physician or informed consent by the patient. . . .

The IUD of today is reputed to date from some 2,000 years ago when stones were placed by camel drivers into the wombs of their beasts of burden. The camel driver knew not how the stone prevented pregnancy, but he knew that it did work sometimes. If the animal became sick or died, then the camel driver undoubtedly asked his gods the nature of the offense he committed; he certainly had no conception of rates of morbidity or mortality due to "camel stones." We might compare ourselves today with that camel driver of long ago, and, asking ourselves the same questions, arrive at virtually the same answers.

Statement of Maj. Russel J. Thomsen, M.D.

Like many physicians trained in the 1960s, I was introduced to the new generation of plastic IUDs without the inherent bias against intrauterine contraception which older practitioners held. Within the context of the raging furor over the oral contraceptive tablet, the IUD and its promotional claims made good sense. . . . I inserted hundreds of IUDs. I was enthusiastic enough about IUD contraception so as to encourage women to use them. Especially in welfare patients and Planned Parenthood clinic patients did I find a fertile group for IUD insertion. . . .

With the passage of time, encounters with serious IUD complications, and the delivery of a number of babies with the omnipresent IUD lodged in the placenta, I began to use IUDs with that respect which only a recognition of their complication-producing potential can produce.

Then, about a year ago, I faced a crisis. In my practice there were at one time six women pregnant while also using the Dalkon Shield IUD. . . .

It was then that I looked with renewed candor at the glossy advertising for the particular IUD. What I found at first intrigued, then revolted me. I extended my search through the advertising for the other IUDs. I reviewed the medical literature and pulled articles from popular women's magazines. I wrote and phoned drug companies, the FDA, the FTC [Federal Trade Commission]. I talked to other gynecologists.

What I found was the evidence that despite adequate proof that IUDs are capable of producing serious and even fatal complications in young women, they are in that lucrative arena of medical devices which—being beyond FDA regulation—breeds poor research, deceptive advertising, and actual medical hucksterism. . . .

The A. H. Robins Co.—in its information brochure for Dalkon Shield users, for the patients—condescendingly allows that "some women have cramps for a short time after insertion, but these are generally mild and usually pass in a few minutes."

The person who wrote that was probably a man and most certainly had never undergone the experience of receiving a Dalkon Shield.

A recognized complication of IUD insertion is pain. Certainly some patients are able to tolerate pain more than others. And it is also true that a woman whose cervix has been previously dilated by a pregnancy will generally undergo less IUD insertional pain than the woman who has never been pregnant. But the general dismissal of this side effect in company brochures like the one put out for the Dalkon Shield is definitely misleading and borders on falsehood.

I have seen a number of women faint following IUD insertion and particularly from Dalkon Shield insertion. This probably relates to the large diameter of the shield which, with its applicator, must be forced through the cervix.

I also find it interesting that many patients—especially those having undergone severe pain during insertion—look forward to its removal with such apprehension as to request to be "put to sleep" during that fateful event. This, of course, is rarely done, but many patients benefit by being given pain medication prior to the removal of the IUD. In fact, pain medication, a lead bullet to bite on, and a short memory are the requisites of some IUD removals, particularly with the Dalkon Shield and the Majzlin Spring.

Suggested Readings

Brodie, Janet Farrell. *Contraception and Abortion in Nineteenth-Century America*. Ithaca, NY: Cornell University Press, 1994.

Chesler, Ellen. *Woman of Valor: Margaret Sanger and the Birth Control Movement in America*. New York: Simon and Schuster, 1992.

Costa, Marie. *Abortion: A Reference Handbook*. Santa Barbara, CA: ABC-CLIO, 1991.

Davis, Angela. *Women, Race, and Class*. New York: Random House, 1981.

Degler, Carl N. *At Odds: Women and the Family in America from the Revolution to the Present*. New York: Oxford University Press, 1980.

Ehrenreich, Barbara, and Deirdre English. *For Her Own Good: 150 Years of the Experts' Advice to Women*. Garden City, NY: Anchor Press/Doubleday, 1978.

———. *Witches, Midwives, and Nurses: A History of Women Healers*. Old Westbury, NY: Feminist Press, 1973.

Gordon, Linda. *Woman's Body, Woman's Right: A Social History of Birth Control in America*. 1977. Revised ed. New York: Penguin Books, 1990.

Grossberg, Michael. *Governing the Hearth: Law and the Family in Nineteenth-Century America*. Chapel Hill: University of North Carolina Press, 1985.

Kennedy, David M. *Birth Control in America: The Career of Margaret Sanger*. New Haven, CT: Yale University Press, 1970.

Leavitt, Judith Walzer. *Brought to Bed: Childbearing in America, 1750–1950*. New York: Oxford University Press, 1986.

Luker, Kristin. *Abortion and the Politics of Motherhood*. Berkeley and Los Angeles: University of California Press, 1982.

McCann, Carole R. *Birth Control Politics in the United States, 1916–1945*. Ithaca, NY: Cornell University Press, 1994.

McMillen, Sally G. *Motherhood in the Old South: Pregnancy, Childbirth, and Infant Rearing*. Baton Rouge: Louisiana State University Press, 1990.

Mohr, James C. *Abortion in America: The Origins and Evolution of National Policy, 1800–1900*. New York: Oxford University Press, 1978.

Petchesky, Rosalind Pollack. *Abortion and Woman's Choice: The State, Sexuality, and Reproductive Freedom*. 1985. Revised ed. Boston: Northeastern University Press, 1990.

Ratcliff, Kathryn Strother, ed. *Healing Technology: Feminist Perspectives*. Ann Arbor: University of Michigan Press, 1989.

Reed, James. *From Private Vice to Public Virtue: The Birth Control Movement and American Society since 1830*. New York: Basic Books, 1978.

Rodrique, Jessie. "The Black Community and the Birth Control Movement." In *Unequal Sisters: A Multicultural Reader in U.S. Women's History*, ed. Carol DuBois and Vicki Ruiz. New York: Routledge, 1990.

Rothman, Barbara. *In Labor: Women and Power in the Birthplace*. New York: W. W. Norton and Company, 1982.

———. *Recreating Motherhood: Ideology and Technology in a Patriarchal Society*. New York: W. W. Norton and Company, 1989.

Sobol, Richard. *Bending the Law: The Story of the Dalkon Shield Bankruptcy*. Chicago: University of Chicago Press, 1991.

Solinger, Ricky. *The Abortionist: A Woman against the Law*. New York: Free Press, 1994.

———. *Wake Up, Little Susie: Single Pregnancy and Race before Roe v. Wade*. New York: Routledge, 1992.

Ulrich, Laurel Thatcher. *A Midwife's Tale: The Life of Martha Ballard, Based on Her Diary, 1785–1812*. New York: Alfred A. Knopf, 1990.

Weddington, Sarah. *A Question of Choice*. New York: Grossett/Putnam, 1992.

Wertz, Richard W., and Dorothy C. Wertz. *Lying-in: A History of Childbirth in America*. New York: Schocken Books, 1977.

Suggested Films

Contraception: The Stalled Revolution, 1992, color. Journalist Linda Ellerbee interviews congressional representatives to determine current political views on contraception. Distribution contact: The Cinema Guild.

From Danger to Dignity: The Fight for Safe Abortion, 1995, color. Historical documentary on efforts in the 1960s and 1970s to change abortion laws. Distribution contact: Concentric Media.

La Operación, 1982, black and white/color. Historical documentary on the problem of widespread sterilization among Puerto Rican women. Distribution contact: The Cinema Guild.

Leona's Sister Gerri, 1994, color. Relates the story of a young Ukrainian-American woman who died from a botched abortion in 1964 at the age of 27. Distribution contact: New Day Films.

Margaret Sanger: A Public Nuisance, 1992, color. Explores the life of the birth control pioneer through reenactments, vaudeville skits, actual films, and Sanger's own words. Distribution contact: Women Make Movies.

When Abortion Was Illegal: Untold Stories, 1992, color. Doctors, health care workers, and women speak openly about performing and having illegal abortions. Nominated for an Academy Award. Distribution contact: Concentric Media.